no place like home

WORLDS OF DESIRE
THE CHICAGO SERIES ON SEXUALITY, GENDER, AND CULTURE
A Series Edited by Gilbert Herdt

no place like

Relationships and Family Life among
Lesbians and Gay Men

christopher carrington

The University of Chicago Press   Chicago and London

The University of Chicago Press, Chicago 60637
The University of Chicago Press, Ltd., London
© 1999 by The University of Chicago
All rights reserved. Published 1999
Paperback edition 2002
Printed in the United States of America

08 07 06 05 04 03 02   2 3 4 5
ISBN: 0-226-09485-5 (cloth)
ISBN: 0-226-09486-3 (paperback)

Carrington, Christopher.
    No place like home : relationships and family life among lesbians and gay
men / Christopher Carrington.
        p.   cm. — (Worlds of desire)
    Includes bibliographical references.
    ISBN 0-226-09485-5 (cloth : alk. paper)
        1. Gay couples—California—San Francisco.   2. Gays—California—
San Francisco—Family relationships.   3. Households—California—San
Francisco.   4. Housekeeping—California—San Francisco.   I. Title.
II. Series.
HQ76.3.U53S253   1999
306.84'8 — DC21   99-19780
                                                                              CIP

To James Arthur Dibble and

To Lesbian and Gay Homemaking and Homemakers

contents

acknowledgments

This project took the better part of a decade to complete. So many people gave graciously of their time and energy to the project that the final product seems more like a collective rather than an individual achievement. I am forever indebted to many people for their contributions. Most critically, I wish to thank those who agreed to participate in this research and who opened their homes and family lives to observation and scrutiny. I hope that you will learn something about your lives from this project just as I have learned much about my own life from watching and listening to you.

I also wish to express thanks to the many fine academics who have taken me under their wing. These scholars have nurtured, guided, challenged, inspired me, and on several occasions fought off the predatory attacks of heterosexist and/or homophobic administrators and professors. I owe my very existence as a scholar, writer, and successful doctoral candidate to their interventions. I thank them for doing the right thing.

Bringing forth this book, and the lines of thought within it, happened not in solitude but under the overlapping influences of feminist research and scholarship, as well as those of lesbian and gay research and scholarship. I hope that this work will enhance the dialogue between these two intellectual and social movements and bring greater awareness of our joint concerns and recognition of the avenues for coalition building.

It is my pleasure to acknowledge a variety of individuals to whom I am personally and intellectually indebted. They did the work (some were paid, and some not) that created and continues to sustain me. My mother, who struggled through poverty and abuse to carve out a space for her children, deserves special recognition. I learned to persevere in the face of opposition and hardship from her. Thanks, Mom.

I owe a debt of gratitude to Naomi Gerstel, my dissertation chair at the University of Massachusetts at Amherst. She provided me with continuous and meaningful personal and intellectual support, and enabled me to see the real value of this work. Alongside Naomi, I am also indebted to a long line of feminist professors who awakened me to the pervasive and often under-estimated dynamics of gender inequality and the ways that homophobia and heterosexism buttress that inequality: Sheila Davaney, Barbara Hargrove, Martha Gimenez, Marcia Westkott, Janet Jacobs, Joyce Nielsen, Nancy Fol-bre, Ann Ferguson, and Arlie Hochschild.

I wish to thank the host of thinkers who provided me with thoughtful cri-tique and comments through the many revisions: Jack Hewitt, Nancy Fol-bre, Ann Ferguson, Naomi Gerstel, Barry Adam, Ellen Lewin, Gretchen Stiers, Stephen Murray, Alice Julier, Arlie Hochschild, Rachel Kahn-Hut, Patricia Guthrie, Diane Beeson, Joe Sadusky, Karen Loeb, Sally Gallagher, and Lee Badgett. I wish to thank Marj DeVault, Peter Nardi, and Gilbert Herdt, who provided extensive and efficacious reviews for the University of Chicago Press.

I also wish to acknowledge Patti Adler, at the University of Colorado, Boulder. Patti taught me the research skills and the tricks of the trade and en-couraged my passionate love of field methods.

Special thanks to Lisa Wormser and Gil Schamess, who suggested the book's title. I also extend thanks to Doug Mitchell, my editor, who made this process pleasant, smooth, and affirming. Thanks also to Erik Carlson at the University of Chicago Press for holding my hand and showing me the way.

During my research, I also received fellowship support from the Martin P. Levine Memorial Dissertation Fellowship Fund, administered by the Sex and Gender Section of the American Sociological Association. The fellowship fund is named after Martin P. Levine, one of the pioneers in the sociology of gay and lesbian life and culture. Dr. Levine died of AIDS in 1993.

Finally, I wish to thank my lover and companion of nine years, Jim Dibble. In his acts of kindness, his steadfast commitment to fairness, his keen intelligence, his careful editing, and his appreciation for all things domestic, he has contributed much to my happiness and to my success.

no place like home

Solidarity is not discovered by reflection but created. It is created by increasing our sensitivity to the particular details of the pain and humiliation of other, unfamiliar sorts of people. Such increased sensitivity makes it more difficult to marginalize people different from ourselves by thinking "They do not feel as we would," or "There must always be suffering, so why not let them suffer?" This process of coming to see other human beings as "one of us" rather than "them" is a matter of detailed description of what unfamiliar people are like and of redescription of what we ourselves are like.

RICHARD RORTY, *Irony, Contingency and Solidarity* (1989)

introduction

This was a law developed for the purpose of ensuring that people can care for their families. It's inappropriate for a senator to cheapen the meaning of family by saying family is a "fill in the blank."

KRISTI HAMRICK, SPOKESPERSON FOR THE FAMILY RESEARCH
COUNCIL, COMMENTING ON NEW JERSEY SEN. ROBERT
TORRICELLI'S DECISION TO VOLUNTARILY EXTEND SOME OF THE
PROVISIONS OF THE 1993 FAMILY AND MEDICAL LEAVE ACT TO
LESBIAN AND GAY MEMBERS OF HIS STAFF (www.glinn.com
March 13, 1997)

As I write these words, a cultural debate in the United
States rages over the status of lesbian and gay families,
most notably in the struggles over lesbian and gay marriage, as well as in the struggles to gain "domestic partnership" benefits. Much of the current debate about
lesbian and gay families stems from the threat that such
families are perceived to pose to the dominant organization of family practices in contemporary Western so-

cieties (Mohr 1994; Stacey 1996). However, a pervasive sense of crisis in the American family has existed throughout much of American history (Skolnick 1991; Coontz 1992), and the national debate concerning lesbian and gay families is but the latest grist for the mill. This sense of family crisis pervades the political efforts to block lesbian and gay people from attaining legal marriage and the benefits of domestic partnership. The sense of crisis, and the rhetorical overkill that accompanies it, not only makes it difficult for political debate to focus on the everyday realities of lesbian and gay families but insures that many people will both understand such families in stereotypical ways and impede efforts to improve the quality of lesbian and gay family life. The quotation at the beginning of this chapter from Ms. Hamrick denies the possibility that lesbian and gay families exist, much less acknowledges that they should enjoy any kind of cultural recognition.

The debate over the cultural place of lesbian and gay families rages not only among the predominantly heterosexual, mostly male, affluent European Americans in the centers of economic and political power but within the various lesbian, bisexual, and gay communities as well. It remains an open question in the minds of at least some lesbians, gays, and bisexuals whether "marriage" is worthy of the political capital it will take to achieve it, or even worthy at all (Eskridge 1996; Polikoff 1993; Ettelbrick 1989; Sullivan 1995). And the same rhetorical overkill that characterizes the national debate also permeates the lesbian, bisexual, and gay communities. William Eskridge, a gay-male proponent of same-sex marriage, in a rhetorical flourish conceives of same-sex marriages as a move from "sexual liberty to civilized commitment" (1996). This formulation implies the presence of some uncivilized menace in the present lives of lesbian and gay families. Don't believe it. For while many lesbian and gay families face difficulties in their family lives, difficulties often resulting from heterosexism and homophobia, the notion of some uncivilized phantom dwelling at the heart of such families is demonstrably false. Actual lesbigay families, like most other American families, face the struggles of balancing work and family commitments, of managing the stresses and strains of waxing and waning sexual desires, of maintaining open and honest communication, of fighting over household responsibilities, and, most frequently, of simply trying to make ends meet. The latter point deserves much more attention, for if any phantom lurks in the lives of lesbian and gay families, it is their inability to achieve financial security, the foundation of a happy, communicative, and stable relationship (Voydanoff 1992).

This is a study of "family life" among a group of fifty-two lesbian and gay families (twenty-six female and twenty-six male). This study provides an ethnographic and empirical account of how lesbians and gay men actually construct, sustain, enhance, or undermine a sense of family in their lives. Rather than an excursion into the frequently symbolic politics of gay marriage, or into the debates about the liberating possibilities of lesbian, bisexual, or gay-male sexuality, this work explores the seemingly ordinary terrain of everyday life within and among lesbigay families. I use the term *lesbigay*, which is coming into wider use, because it includes lesbians, bisexuals, and gay men, all of whom participate in the families I studied. Of the fifty-two adult women participants, two consider themselves bisexual, as does one of the fifty-three adult men.

In this study I reflect upon the *details* of everyday life in the households of lesbigay families, and explore the relationship of such detail to the actual experience of and creation of family in the lives of lesbigay people. The participants in this research, similar to many other citizens, use the term *family* in diverse and often contradictory ways. At one moment a participant will conceive of family as a legal and biological category, a category that they reject, and might even define themselves as over and against. In a different place and time that same participant will conceive of family as a way of behaving and will reject the formal understandings of family in favor of an understanding that emphasizes the labors involved and not the socially sanctioned roles. And at yet another place and time that same participant will embrace the legal and biological definitions of family with the hopes of achieving lesbigay inclusion into those categorizations (for example, advocating lesbigay legal marriage or attempting to secure custody of a child on the basis of biological linkage).

In my analysis the crucial element for defining what or who constitutes a family derives from whether the participants engage in a consistent and relatively reciprocal pattern of loving and caring activities and understand themselves to be bound to provide for, and entitled to partake of, the material and emotional needs and/or resources of other family members. I understand family as consisting of people who love and care for one another. This makes a couple a family. In other words, through their loving and caring activities, and their reflections upon them, people conceive of, construct, and maintain social relationships that they come to recognize and treat as family (Schneider 1984). In this sense a family, any family, is a social construction, or a set of relationships recognized, edified, and sustained through human initiative. People "do" family.

This research ponders the deceptively simple activities that constitute love and care, activities that frequently go unnoticed in most families, including most lesbigay families. These may entail trips to the store to pick up something special for dinner, phoning an order to a catalog company for someone's birthday, tallying the money owed to friends, sorting the daily mail, remembering a couple's anniversary, finishing up the laundry before one's spouse returns home, maintaining a photo album, remembering the vegetables that family members dislike, or attending to myriad other small, often hidden, seemingly insignificant matters. Decidedly not insignificant, these small matters form the fabric of our daily lives as participants in families. Moreover, the proliferation of these small matters produces a stronger and more pervasive sense of the relationship(s) as a family, both in the eyes of the participants and in the eyes of others.

Conceiving of them as labors of love, people customarily romanticize many of these domestic activities (Abel and Nelson 1990) and fail to recognize them as forms of work that consume the time and energy of those who do them (Jones 1985; Romero 1992). The reality that families consist of a multitude of often small, frequently unrecognized, laborious acts of caregiving, in addition to some set of codified roles (for example, mother, father, spouse, brother), tells us something else about why Kristi Hamrick's comments are so problematic. The notion that family cannot consist of a "fill in the blank"—that is, person(s) of one's choosing—contributes to concealing the labors that actually produce and sustain a family, any family. Emphasizing formal roles, a common tendency of family politics, family policy, and family law, detracts from the more basic reality that various forms of work dwell at the heart of family life.

Suggesting that various forms of work constitute the sum and substance of family life raises a number of questions about how to define work. While many citizens hold work in the highest regard in contemporary American society, viewing it as the answer to many of life's most fundamental questions, as well as the elixir to a host of life's problems, the question of what constitutes work eludes easy classification. Commonsensical notions of work often appeal to distinctions between productive and unproductive work, pleasant and unpleasant work, between producing and consuming, between the things we do for money and the things we do for love, or between activities we are willing to pay for and those we are not. Such categorical distinctions tell us much more about how we value particular forms of work, and who does them, than they tell us about the actual characteristics of that work. In contrast to these commonsensical notions, many sociologists make a convincing case that the idea that work consists of some quintessential meaning that transcends political and cultural context is untenable (Becker 1963; du Gay 1996; Hughes 1971; Urry 1990). For example, if I were to provide cleaning services twenty hours a week for an hourly wage, and over the course of subsequent revisits I begin a relationship with my wealthy employer, fall in love with him, begin a relationship with him, and eventually move into that very same house where I continued my cleaning work, nothing will have necessarily changed in the content of that cleaning work but it is highly unlikely that I would continue to receive a wage for my labors, and I would quite possibly conceive of my cleaning work in new ways. In mainstream economic accounts of work, as I made that transition from paid worker to unpaid lover, I also shifted from being productive (that is, contributing to the gross domestic product) to unproductive. Such a scenario makes it patently clear that we need a social and an interactional conception of work, one emphasizing its socially constructed character.

Vantage Points: Situating Myself

My preoccupation with work and family matters reflects the confluence of my personal biography with my intellectual pursuits. My own experiences with work and family life have left an indelible mark upon my understanding of domesticity. I am an openly gay, Euro-American, educated, and affluent male. In contrast to my adult life, I grew up in a working-poor, female-headed, single-parent family. Through much of my childhood, in order to make ends meet, my mother worked nights as a bartender. There were periods where she could not get enough hours and our family had to turn to food stamps and welfare. I remember fighting intensely with the older of my two younger sisters over who would pay at the checkout counter because we both wanted to avoid the stigma that came with using those food stamps. We also received free lunches at school, although these lunches were not quite as free as one might believe. Our school principal thought it important that we learn the value of earning our keep, so, in the fourth grade, several other poor kids and I had to clean the dining hall during the second half of our lunch hour. This included emptying the garbage cans into the dumpster. In order to do that, we had to drag the cans by all of the other kids on the playground over to the dumpster. One can well imagine the shame that I felt. Pile on top of these experiences the reality that I knew, and other kids seemed to know, that I was somehow "different" (gay) by the time I was ten years old, and one can appreciate the ferocity of my effort to escape such a life. I wanted to avoid stigma so badly that I would steal lunch money from my mother's inebriated customers at the bar. By the end of the fourth grade I had finagled and charmed my way into an illegal (in violation of child labor laws) after-school job at a flower shop where I could earn that lunch money. Such experiences fueled an intense desire within me to escape the working class and, for the most part, I have. None of this is to deny the importance of social-structural dynamics (job opportunities, educational opportunities, gender and racial privileges) that facilitated my escape, but it is to acknowledge the particular experiences that motivated me and subsequently influenced my perceptions of the world.

My childhood also taught me a great deal about domesticity. My mother's work as a bartender required her to work nights, which meant that she increasingly came to rely on me to keep the house going in her absence. We occasionally had baby-sitters, but they were frequently unreliable, and they rarely did any domestic work. By the time I was eleven years old, I knew how to do laundry, iron, clean, cook, baby-sit, and shop. Such experiences provided knowledge of things that most boys never come to know. It meant that much of the invisible work that women do became quite visible for me. My mother greatly appreciated these contributions, and I suspect that set the stage for me to question the widespread devaluation of domesticity. In some ways I was experiencing a nascent version of the second shift as an elementary-school kid. Each day I went to school until 3:00 P.M., to my paid job from 3:30 to 5:30 (which I held for three years), and then to my unpaid job at 6:00; my mother had to be to her shift starting at 6:00. In addition to my schoolwork each night, there was a meal to cook, cleaning activities, groceries to buy, and getting my sisters to take baths and get into bed. I would call my mother at work each night at around 9:00 to report that all was running smoothly and that my sisters were in bed.[1]

As I entered into my own adult family life, I brought a set of skills and an understanding of domesticity that most men do not have, including most gay men. I have spent much of the past fifteen years both participating in the everyday life of my own gay family, and those of others, and reflecting upon that participation as a budding sociologist. Over that period of time I came to realize just how problematic family life can actually become, especially for those gay men, bisexuals, and lesbians who wish simultaneously to pursue family, career, and community. I found myself increasingly identifying with and understanding the stresses and strategies heterosexual women use in their relationships to negotiate multiple commitments, to work, family, and community. I also found myself coming out of the domesticity closet. As the following pages reveal, gay or bisexual men who do domestic things, and lesbian or bisexual women who do not must carefully manage such information in order to avoid the stigma associated with violating widely held expectations about domesticity and its assumed links to gender. These expectations persist even if concealed by ideological commitments to egalitarianism among most straight, bisexual, lesbian, and gay people.

Vantage Points: Intellectual Traditions and the Study of Domesticity

My intellectual concern with domesticity appears at the intersection of three distinct lines of theory and research. First, my analysis is informed by a feminist-inspired literature exploring the paid and unpaid work of caring performed mostly by women but occasionally by men (Fowlkes 1980; Hertz 1986; Weskott 1986; Tronto 1987; Di Leonardo 1987; Abel and Nelson 1990; DeVault 1991; Diamond 1992; Glazer 1993; Gerstel and Gallagher 1994). Like the mid-August San Francisco tourist peering through the fog, attempting to discern the contours of the Golden Gate Bridge, this literature strives to discern the expansive structure of the work of caring. This caring work is often hidden by the fog of gender ideology, by "official" definitions of what constitutes work, and by the persistent devaluation of women, and the forms of work associated with them (Kessler-Harris 1990; Kemp 1994; Lorber 1994). This same fog envelops much of the work of loving and caring within and among lesbigay families. Even much of the newer literature exploring caregiving is restricted to care within traditional families.

The second line of thought relevant to this study emerges from the sociological literature exploring the relationship of paid work to family life. This literature investigates the division and organization of domestic labor within heterosexual families and includes the field-defining works of Komarovsky (1953; 1962), Lopata (1971), Oakley (1974), Stack (1974), Bernard (1982), Cowan (1983), Finch (1983), Gerstel and Gross (1984), Fenstermaker-Berk (1985), Rollins (1985), Hertz (1986), Smith (1987), Di Leonardo (1987), Daniels (1988), Coltrane (1989), Hochschild (1989), DeVault (1991), Romero (1992), and Glazer (1993). All of these scholars paid particular attention, either empirically and/or theoretically, to exploring the breadth and depth of domesticity, and to integrating domesticity into social analysis and theory. The work of these scholars provided me with the "sensitizing concepts" (Blumer 1954) that guided my fieldwork among lesbigay families and informed the kinds of questions asked of participants in the semistructured interviews (see appendix A).

Central among these sensitizing concepts are those that illuminate much of the *invisible* work of domesticity, including concepts like feeding work (DeVault 1991), kin work (Di Leonardo 1987), interaction work (Fishman 1982), consumption work (Weinbaum and Bridges 1976), emotion work (Hochschild 1983), and household status presentation (Collins 1992). These novel conceptualizations of work provide a wider and more inclusive understanding of what constitutes work encouraging us to recognize the political and economic factors that come into play in the process of defining what constitutes work worthy of wages and/or compensation (Zaretsky 1973; Tilly and Scott 1978; Collins and Gimenez 1990; Diamond 1992). Much of this kind of work remains invisible because individuals either are unaware of its presence or they lack a vocabulary for naming the activities that consume their time and energy. Some of this work is intentionally invisible for a variety of reasons. Sometimes making this work more visible might lead to conflict within the relationship. At other times the invisibility of such work contributes to the perception of its natural or normal status, or in other words, one didn't really need to work at it.

Moreover, many scholars have identified a persistent and vigorous effort to hide, and belie, the actual division of domestic labor and/or the extent of that labor (Hochschild 1989; Romero 1992; Glazer 1993). Hochschild discovered the use of "family myths" (1989, 19), which are myths intended to veil the actual unequal division of labor yet simultaneously affirm the basic equality of the relationship. Hochschild's discovery led me to wonder if such myths might exist within lesbigay families as well. They do. When I first began the exploration of domesticity among lesbigay families, I was perplexed by the public responses to my inquiry. My field notes capture dozens of social occasions where couples, upon learning about my research, began to smile, giggle, laugh, and/or tease one another. Most of those occasions also ended with a clear public affirmation of the basically equal division of domesticity among those couples. Something was very strange about this. Why, if a basically egalitarian division of labor prevails in these families, should raising the topic provoke smiles, nervous laughter, teasing, and public affirmations of equality? Because lesbigay families are neither as egalitarian as they would like to believe nor as we would prefer that others believe. This, of course, does not make lesbigay families pathological or dysfunctional or exceptional. It makes them rather ordinary.

Finally, a third line of research and theory influencing my work consists of the cross-disciplinary literature exploring lesbian, bisexual, and gay relationships and family life. A review of the research into the domestic lives of lesbigay families reveals the presence of a somewhat odd, historical pattern in the findings. Assuming the reliability of findings, lesbigay families before the mid-1970s lived rather different family lives than they did thereafter. The question of whether a behavioral change or an ideological change took place deserves closer attention, but let me describe the historical distinction that exists in the research.

Social-scientific research efforts in the 1950s and 1960s examined gay and lesbian couples and concluded that one of the members of a gay or lesbian couple took on the "masculine" role while the other member took on the "feminine" role (Bieber 1965; Ellis 1965; Haist and Hewitt 1974; Jensen 1974). Such a pattern conformed to the classical sociological distinction between "instrumental" and "expressive" roles within the family articulated by Parsons and Bales (1955), who argued that such a distinction of roles constituted an efficient division of labor within the family and provided for the well-being of all members. For Parsons and Bales, women in heterosexual families usually play the expressive gender roles, taking care of nurture, maintaining personal relationships, providing emotional solace to men who spend their days in the male sphere of competition and practical achievement. Within this model men play instrumental roles characterized by pragmatic concerns with sustaining the family economically. This Parsonian model also fits the stereotypical butch/femme hypothesis that many people used to assume characterized gay and lesbian relationships (Tripp 1975). In this model the butch partner plays the instrumental roles while the femme partner plays the expressive roles.

Into the 1970s the butch/femme model held sway. Haist and Hewitt (1974), using a multiple-choice questionnaire with two hundred gay men, found that most gay-male couples conformed to the butch/femme hypothesis. Jensen (1974), interviewing thirty-four Euro-American, coupled lesbians in three Western states, found a similar pattern among lesbians. Both studies investigated the division of domestic labor and included this division in the butch/femme conception with the performance of most forms of domestic labor conceived of as femme. Jensen included a relatively extensive list of household tasks (house repairs, dish washing, groceries, vacation planning, bill paying) and emotional tasks (who praises spouse, tells spouse about day at work, sees spouse's point of view), and asked respondents to indicate who routinely performed each task. Jensen concluded that "the results of this research lend support to the assertion that female homosexuals adopt differentiated sex roles when they set up quasi-marital relationships" (1974, 366).

While research from the 1950s to the early 1970s confirmed the instrumental/expressive distinction within gay and lesbian couples, empirical work in the subsequent decade fundamentally challenged such a model. Studies in the 1970s and 1980s discovered gay and lesbian couples often exhibit significantly more egalitarianism and less role-playing than heterosexual couples within intimate relationships (Saghir and Robins 1973; Harry and DeVall 1978; Bell and Weinberg 1978; Blumstein and Schwartz 1983; Harry 1984; McWhirter and Mattison 1984; Lynch and Reilly 1985; Kurdek 1993). These scholars found that the division of domestic labor within gay and lesbian couples reflects a basic egalitarian impulse. Harry (1984) asserts that this egalitarianism emerges from several social factors, including the rejection of the dominant heterosexual model of marriage, the fact that partners in gay and lesbian couples receive the same gender-role socialization, and the rather small income differences that exist between partners in gay and lesbian couples. Arguing in favor of an equality model, Blumstein and Schwartz (1983) suggest that because gender roles do not serve as the institutional basis for the division of household labor in gay and lesbian couples, unlike their heterosexual counterparts, gay and lesbian couples must negotiate household labor. They assert that this negotiation leads to relatively egalitarian relationships. If inequality exists in gay and lesbian families, Blumstein and Schwartz found that it emerges as a matter of *happenstance* or *as a result of modeling their relationship on marriage* (1983, 323–25; emphasis added).

In a similar fashion, Bell and Weinberg reported in their 1978 study that less than 10 percent of the gay-male couples in their sample divided household labor in a "sex-typed fashion." They base this finding on results from face-to-face interviews with approximately 1,000 lesbians and gay men of whom 334 currently were in relationships. The interviews consisted of a long survey with mostly closed-ended questions. Among the few questions pertaining to domestic labor, the researchers asked the following: "If coupled, who does the household shopping?" to which respondents could answer: "partner," "shared equally," or "respondent." The interview also asked: "If coupled, does your partner do all the 'feminine' tasks?" to which respondents could answer yes or no. Based on responses to several of these kinds of questions, the researchers concluded that couples usually share domestic work.

While much of this social science literature from the 1970s and 1980s affirmed the presence of a great deal of equality within lesbigay families, some of these same scholars detected partial evidence of inequality within some lesbian and gay-male couples, though usually only when significant income and/or age differences exist among family members (Harry and DeVall 1978; Blumstein and Schwartz 1983; Caldwell and Peplau 1984; Harry 1984, 1988). McWhirter and Mattison (1984) apparently found some evidence of a butch/femme pattern in older, gay-male couples who they suggest "have assumed the gender-related patterns as a consequence of their upbringing" (1984, 231). Faderman (1991), a social historian who conducted hundreds of in-depth interviews with lesbians, confirms the existence of butch/femme role-taking patterns among older lesbians but notes a decline of the pattern in the 1970s. However, over the past few years, Faderman detects the reappearance of the butch/femme model among younger lesbians, although the new butch/femme practitioners seem more versatile and reject the "naturalness" of such roles that many lesbians felt in earlier decades in the twentieth century (1992, 264).

While Faderman indicates a recent change among lesbians from the insistent egalitarianism of the 1970s, at least in ideology, most social science literature in recent decades leads to the conclusion that younger lesbigay families exhibit a relatively egalitarian ethic in their relationships, unlike the "older" couples who lived in a more homophobic world where sex-typed behavior emerged in gay and lesbian couples. Overall, this literature suggests the presence of a great deal of equality with only occasional glimmers of inequality, or as Peplau and Cochran assert in their review of recent empirical research, "the majority of relationships develop roles similar to friendship—

with expectations that partners should be similar in age and equal in power and should share responsibilities fairly equally" (1990, 344).

My research findings stand in bold contrast to this more recent literature. In fact, my empirical findings strangely—and depending on one's perspective, perhaps disturbingly—resemble the work of the earlier generation of scholars. A number of factors contribute to this marked discrepancy in findings. First, unlike much of the recent research, I base my analysis upon both in-depth interviewing and upon ethnographic observation of the everyday lives of multiple lesbigay families. This dual methodology reveals that a chasm exists between what many of my participants report during in-depth interviews and what they actually do in their day-to-day lives.

Moreover, unlike much of the recent research, I interviewed participants in lesbigay families separately yet consecutively. This prevented the development of "seamless" accounts so common among joint interviews with couples (Aquilino 1993). This interview strategy results in significant discrepancies between partners in their portrayals of domesticity. Given the depth of the interview schedule, I conducted the wide majority of these interviews on Saturdays spending the morning with one partner and the afternoon with the other. In the early evening I would meet with both to gather the remaining information, including the square footage of the house, photos of the grocery list, the living room, and of the inside of the refrigerator, a look at the calendars, the budget, and a list of financial transactions for the last week.

Separate interviews with partners resulted in contradictory accounts of many aspects of domesticity. There were also many contradictions between what the interviews elicited and what I observed in the field study. Such contradictions point to the importance of recognizing that powerful ideological pressures influence participants' answers to questions about domestic work. Other researchers have noted this phenomenon as well. The research of Hochschild (1989) among heterosexual families parallels my findings. She revealed a persistent tendency among heterosexual couples to assert equality through appeal to myths that hide unequal divisions of domestic labor (1989, 19–21, 43–49). Not only does a similar dynamic exist among lesbigay families, but it may even be stronger. Let me briefly review some of the possible reasons for this.

First, many gay men opt for quite traditional masculine images for themselves; these men often draw clear distinctions between themselves and highly effeminate gay men. How might this affect the portrayal of domesticity within the household? Joseph Harry found that in gay-male couples, most individuals held that they "dominated" decision making in the couple (1984, 67). Apparently, individuals resisted acknowledging that they may hold a subordinate position in the relationship. Clearly, gay liberation has fought extensively against notions of the effeminate man, and a hypermasculinity came into existence in the American gay-male community over the past few decades to combat this notion (Humphreys 1971; Kleinberg 1992). In a recent study in Australia, Connell found that most gay men embody quite traditional patterns of masculinity: "In this sense, most gays are 'very straight'" (1993, 746). Gay men in my study often deny that they hold more of the responsibility for domestic work than do their partners, even when it is not true, and they fiercely declare allegiance to egalitarianism.

In parallel fashion, the extensive impact of the feminist critique of the heterosexual family has taken root among many lesbian families. Many lesbians, familiar with the extensive inequalities that exist in heterosexual relationships, perceive of lesbian identity as a way of escaping the dynamics of inequality. Among some lesbians there also exists a significant ideological commitment to egalitarianism, especially among the baby boomers. As Faderman observed, beginning in the 1970s, an intense critique of butch/femme roles for lesbians developed within feminism, and it became politically incorrect for lesbians to affirm such roles (Faderman 1992). This dynamic prevents many lesbian families from even acknowledging that any kind of differentiation takes place within the family unit, much less that some inequality might exist. Yet I found both differentiation and inequality in the domestic lives of many lesbian families, including among the baby boomers.

Furthermore, partners in many lesbigay relationships work together to camouflage the actual divisions of domesticity and to prevent threats to the gender identities of their partners, particularly for women who do little domestic work and for men who do a lot. Countless examples of this dynamic appear in the pages that follow. Lesbigay people, particularly those exposed to higher education, are quite aware of the politics of social research, and I suspect this influences their responses to social researchers, including me. I recall my own experience as an undergraduate, when my first partner and I were asked to participate in research conducted by the psychologist, Lawrence Kurdek (1988b; 1993).[2] We each filled out long survey forms multiple times over the course of many years. As I reflect back on those occasions now and talk to my first partner about them, we both have come to realize that we shared an overwhelming concern about what the world was thinking about gay people. We were young gay men, in the midst of an epidemic, under attack from right-wing political forces, and craving our place at the table. We portrayed our relationship in the reigning ideals of the era—equal, compassionate, balanced, and stable. In fact, it probably wasn't quite as ideal as we portrayed it.

Perhaps we were unique. My subsequent research suggests otherwise. We were actually a lot like many families (both gay and straight), organizing our domestic life around our jobs with the resources (time, energy, money) available to us and strenuously avoiding the potential for stigma from others in how we portrayed and understood our family life. We also knew that we were tokens, meaning that others would draw conclusions not only about us as individuals but about other lesbigay people as well, based upon their appraisal of us. We harbored a deep-rooted concern about the public image of our community.

While a concern with the public images of the lesbigay community might well influence how lesbigay families portray themselves to the outside world, the possibility also exists that the social and historical context has shifted dramatically in the last two decades, and that this contributes to different empirical findings. Some of those researchers who found pervasive equality in the late 1970s among lesbigay families asserted that one of the primary reasons for this was the rejection of the model of heterosexual marriage for lesbigay relationships (Blumstein and Schwartz 1983, 323–25; Harry 1984). Lesbian and gay marriage is now all the rage. This suggests something has changed. Perhaps the more conservative cultural climate encourages the lesbigay families of today to organize their family lives in more traditional ways.

Finally, I suspect one of the central reasons for this discrepancy in findings results from distinct conceptualizations and measurements of domesticity. Unlike much of the previous research, I define domesticity broadly and avoid the reduction of the complex dimensions of domesticity into simple and narrow concepts. For instance, rather than reducing the processes of providing meals to a few questions about who cooks or who buys groceries, I instead observed and asked for details. In the next chapter, I explore *feeding work* (DeVault 1991) in lesbigay families, and as that chapter will show, reducing feeding work to who cooks actually conceals more than it reveals about meal preparation. Many participants "cook" meals—meals conceived of by their spouses during their morning break, meals consisting of grocery items bought by their spouses during their lunch hour on dishes bought and washed and put away by their spouses. And these conceptions of what to have for dinner often subsume within them extensive rosters of knowledge about what spouses like and don't like to eat, about nutritional and dietary concerns, about family finances, of inventories of the food products at home in the cupboards and on the shelves at the local grocery store. So while someone may spend forty minutes cooking a meal, someone else may have spent hours enabling the cooking of that meal. Much of this labor will be hidden from view by asking who cooks. Too many of the recent studies of lesbigay families ask too few questions about domesticity, conceptualize that domesticity too narrowly, and ask questions that invite participants to portray their relationships in normative terms. Many of these same studies blithely accept verbal portrayals of domesticity without giving consideration to the ways in which that portrayal reflects complex personal and political strategies for the participants. good point

Caring and Domesticity among Lesbigay Families

Many aspects of domesticity, from tending to the sick to planning an evening meal, involve care. Much of contemporary opinion about domesticity assumes that women, either by nature or by nurture, intrinsically care for others (Chodorow 1978; Gilligan 1982). Care, in this widely held view, becomes an aspect of one's personality, often a component of a woman's femininity. This expectation, or perhaps more accurately, this imperative (Westkott 1986), that women care creates innumerable problems for lesbigay families. It creates problems because the assumption that care intrinsically dwells within the personalities of women, and less so among men, transforms the men who do more caregiving in gay-male families, and the women who do less caregiving in lesbian families, into gender deviants. The violation of these gender expectations, a violation that must occur for lesbigay families to exist, creates the potential for stigma, and it creates the need to manage such stigma. reality behind rhetoric

Despite all the rhetoric of the modern era about the fluidity of gender expectations, and the praise of men who nurture or of women who pursue male-dominated careers, the stark reality remains that many if not most people are not comfortable with violating gender expectations. One will see this with great clarity when looking at the lives of lesbian women on male-oriented career ladders or looking at the lives of gay-male "homemakers."

These women and men, as well as their friends and families, construct elaborate accounts to explain their identities to themselves and to others. The men struggle with issues of self-esteem and self-worth. The high-powered career women struggle with feelings of guilt about their lack of involvement in domestic matters. In the pages that follow I investigate the work involved in managing such stigmas, including the management of the feelings and emotions that such stigma generates among lesbigay family members.

In contrast to the view that care or caregiving exists as an intrinsic aspect of personality, particularly of female personality, I will show that care is the product of caring behaviors, behaviors often structured by organizational and institutional needs and expectations. Those who engage in caregiving become known to others as caring personalities, and so I do not conceive of caregiving as some inherent aspect of womanhood. Male nurses and male flight attendants seem to me excellent examples of individuals who learn to care because the organizational context where they work expects them to do so. And even if heterosexual males in these professions seem to care in a more masculine way, in order to avoid the stigma associated with other people conceiving of them as gay (Williams 1989), the fact remains that they must engage in caring activities. There no doubt exists a strong cultural expectation that women should engage in caring activities—even women in high-powered careers must confront this expectation—but acknowledging that expectation is distinct from the assertion that caring dwells within women. Men care, and they sometimes develop nurturing, caregiving identities, depending on the expectations that others hold of them and the expectations they hold of themselves. Men in gay-male families serve as vivid reminders of this social fact because without their caring activities, their families would crumble. And even in those cases where their families are literally crumbling, as in the case of family members dying from HIV-related illnesses, the caring activities of gay men proliferate and flourish.

Even so, much of the caregiving that transpires in lesbigay families remains hidden and frequently devalued. In so many respects, we do not possess vocabularies or typologies that capture the experiences of those who engage in domesticity. Many lesbigay family members find it difficult to talk about domesticity, not only because of the potential for stigma among the men who do it and the women who don't but also because they are not sure where to start or how to say it. They know that these experiences eat up their time and energy, but how does one express these experiences? Dorothy Smith, in *The*

Everyday World as Problematic, explores the disjunction that prevails between the actual experiences of domesticity and the officially mediated accounts produced by legitimate authorities of those experiences. In my observations of lesbigay households, and in my own experiences with domesticity, much of the work eludes parsimonious description. There is no easy way to express the experience of simultaneously waiting at home for a refrigerator repair person, conceiving of a dinner plan, answering a phone call from a telemarketer, envisioning a recreational activity for the weekend, noticing a spot on the carpet in the hallway, dreading a visit with someone at the hospital, worrying about the cost of the refrigerator repair and coming up with a plan to pay for it, all while sitting in one's home office working on a project that is due in a few days. Many of these discrete experiences and innumerable others constitute domesticity. All of them can occur simultaneously. Yet in official conceptions these experiences become "housework." Conventional measures of housework might capture the waiting at home for the repair person, or the time spent actually cleaning the carpet, but not the mental process of monitoring the carpet, or the anxiety of figuring out how to pay, or the dread of visiting the hospital, or the mental effort of thinking about dinner options in light of schedules, expenses, supplies, and the desires of family members. A valid measurement of housework requires much more attention to detail, a more rigorous effort to make visible the often invisible dimensions of domesticity. *⋆ I agree*

The Work and Family Lives of Lesbigay People

In recent decades, social scientists established a substantial literature concerning the influence of one's paid employment upon the character and extent of domestic work in heterosexual families, much of it relevant to lesbigay families, but rarely applied to them. For instance, Janet Finch's *Married to the Job* (1983) explores the impact of particular occupations upon the organization of domestic life. Finch shows us the enormous variations in the extent and character of domesticity depending upon the character of one's paid employment, and she reveals the ways through which heterosexual women often become incorporated into their husband's occupation. To read the extant literature on lesbigay families one would barely receive any hint that the character of one's paid employment greatly influences how much and what kind of domestic work happens in lesbigay families.

When looking at the occupational identities of lesbigay family members, and the influence of those identities upon domesticity, some notable patterns do emerge. For instance, lesbigay professionals (physicians, attorneys, optometrists, therapists, ministers) who serve lesbigay clientele, in contrast to those who serve predominantly heterosexual populations, dwell in families thick in domesticity. This thickness results from greater resources and from the use of the private residence as a place to serve or entertain one's clients. This impacts the various forms of domesticity in different ways. For example, these professional households follow more rigorous standards of household cleanliness. They entertain more often than others do. They maintain more elaborate friend and family connections. While occupation influences the extent and character of domesticity, it also significantly influences the division of domesticity. Those individuals in higher-status, higher-paid occupations do less domestic work than do their partners. Those individuals with flexible work hours, who work at home, or who face shorter commutes do more domestic work than their partners do. In chapter 5 I explore the complex set of questions related to the division of domesticity. Some research asserts that lesbigay families organize domesticity on the basis of choice or on the basis of individual interests (McWhirter and Mattison 1984; Harry 1984). This research leaves unexplored the question of context, the ways in which choices reflect the available options, and the ways in which interests develop over ones' individual life course, and the life course of the relationship. The reflections of those individuals who have had multiple relationships, and who have witnessed the changed character of their own domestic responsibilities across those relationships, testify to the importance of context in matters of choice and interest.

Equality, Egalitarianism, and Fairness

The traumas of the sixties persuaded me that my generation's egalitarianism was a sentimental error. I now see the hierarchical as both beautiful and necessary. Efficiency liberates; egalitarianism tangles, delays, blocks, deadens. CAMILLE PAGLIA, *Sex, Art, and American Culture* (1992)

Equality, efficiency, and happiness do not necessarily coexist well with one another. Achieving equality certainly slows things down. In the pages that follow it will become clear that many lesbigay families have opted for efficiency, not for equality. However, to suggest that they have "opted" for this

belies the importance of considering the social and economic contexts that
frame their individual and familial choices. Emphasizing the "chosen" character of focusing on domestic matters or upon career must be tempered by
attention to context. As chapter 5 will show in detail, those family members
who gravitate toward domestic involvement often do so under circumstances
that constrain their choices. The fact that they have come to like or even to
love their circumstances does not detract from the reality that they have not
achieved equality. Even so, many of the individuals who might recognize the
inequalities within their relationships also consider their circumstances fair.
One can theoretically argue that *fair* can mean different things. It is con-
ceivable that a lesbigay family might consider the domestically involved
partner's contribution as the equivalent to the contribution of wages, wealth,
or prestige. But it is more often the case that these family members are trading in different currencies, for very few consider domestic contributions the
real equivalent of cash, assets, and prestige. And as I will suggest in the concluding chapter, the fact that individuals are trading in different currencies
becomes patently clear if lesbigay relationships end.

The foregoing comments should not be understood as suggesting that lesbigay families are unique in this respect. They are not. In ways strikingly similar to heterosexual families, the character, extent, and division of domestic labor reflects the impact of influences well beyond any given relationship or
household. The character of work-family relations in an industrial and consumer capitalist economy sets the stage for how households will be organized
and what labors will take place within those households and which ones will
take place outside. Any discussion of the equity and fairness of a given household arrangement must not lose sight of this broader context. For instance, a
few lesbigay families will achieve greater parity in their relationships through
relying on the poorly paid labor of undocumented workers who clean their
house, tend their garden, and do their laundry and other domestic tasks. Any
discussion of equality within such a family must make clear that it is an equality premised upon on a broader pattern of inequality.

The Organization and Method of the Study

The organization of this study reflects my interest in creating a pool of participants that would allow me to both capture the diversity of lesbigay fami-

lies and to make meaningful comparisons with much of the current literature investigating domesticity in American family life. To draw a sample for this study, I used four selection criteria: (1) participants identify themselves as gay, bisexual, lesbian or queer; (2) participants dwell together in the same residence; (3) participants identify themselves as a family or couple; and (4) participants have dwelled together for two years or more. I set a minimum of two years together because I wanted to focus on established patterns of domesticity. As McWhirter and Mattison (1984) found, in the early stages of a relationship, when romance intoxicates the partners, even cleaning the bathtub may be a time of joint activity and joyous celebration. I wanted to look at families after the initial romantic veneer fades.

Concerned with reflecting the class, race, occupational, and age diversity of lesbigay families, my approach to identifying participants took several years to carry out. I used a snowball sampling technique, asking individuals to provide the names of other potential participants. As Beirnacki and Waldorf (1981) assert, snowball sampling serves as an ideal method for locating individuals who tend to keep a low profile.

I carried out the snowball sample in two steps. First I located initial participants. I made these contacts through lesbigay organizations, clubs, religious communities, cafés, computer chat lines, bars, laundries, dance clubs, gyms, and other public sites. The second step of the snowball sample involved the initiation of referral chains. I established referral chains by asking the first participants to name other people who possessed the salient characteristics for participation in my research. Unfortunately, my initial referral chains produced a mostly middle- and upper-middle-class, predominantly Euro- and African-American sample with a strong presence of male Asian Americans. In order to gain access to working-class lesbigays, as well as to contact Latino/a- participants and Asian-American lesbians/bisexuals, I needed to make initial contacts and begin referral chains using strategies that would provide me better access to these populations.

I did this in two ways. First I became involved in a labor caucus of one of the lesbian and gay political clubs. For the most part, those involved came from unions affiliated either with city and/or state government, as well as those affiliated with hotels and restaurants. These union activists provided me with excellent leads to lesbigay people in the working/service class. I dealt with the initial dearth of Latino/as and Asian-American women by becoming a participant at two ethnically identified dance clubs, one predominantly

Asian and one Latino. After several months of regular participation in these
settings, I came to know and be known by a variety of mostly men. These
men became "gatekeepers" (Atkinson and Hammersley 1993, 74–79) for
me, and facilitated initial contacts to lesbigay families that I could not otherwise have contacted. The Asian men, mostly Chinese and Vietnamese, that
I came to know provided me with links to Asian lesbian families. Similarly,
the Latino men provided links to both male and female Latino/a lesbigay
families.

[handwritten: interesting but I think valuable to have such diversity]

The Participants

My analysis draws on in-depth interviews with fifty-two families[3] and upon
weeklong field observations of eight of the lesbigay households (four male
and four female). Much of the fieldwork took place during the weeklong time
periods when I would dwell with the families I was studying. If I could not
spend the nights (usually because of inadequate space), I would arrive at the
same time that the first morning alarm clocks went off and begin my observations at that time. I usually carried a small notepad and wrote down activities as they occurred. Whenever someone was home, I would try to be there.
I also asked participants to keep track of any domestic activities they conducted at work, like phone calls to friends and family or making arrangements for some sort of service for the house (picking up dry cleaning, house
painting, carpet cleaning, or tree trimming). I asked each family how they
might respond to my presence for a weeklong period, and I chose families on
the basis of their receptivity. There is nothing particularly representative
about these families other than they appeared the most receptive to such observation. I had to cajole and beg several of them. I paid each family for my
food expenses and took each family out to dinner. Clearly, the families that
were the most receptive were families with whom I shared similar demo-
graphic characteristics. I also participated in the lives of numerous other
families through accompanying them in their domestic activities. Instead of
living with them I would tag along while they conducted their domestic affairs.
For instance, I went grocery shopping with fifteen individuals and four couples. I went to the laundry with three individuals and one couple. I went
shopping for furniture and other consumer products with seven individuals
and two couples. I went shopping for holiday gifts with four couples and six

*[handwritten margin: *could be a rare issue]*

individuals. Throughout the research I attempted to observe families engaging in their domestic lives in whatever way I could. I was particularly interested in observing domesticity and listening to their reflections about their participation while they performed domestic tasks.

Characteristics of the Participants

One of the crucial distinctions that prevail among lesbigay families in terms of the character and extent of domesticity is the family's socioeconomic context.[4] As I will show, social class distinctions appear more significant to domesticity than are other distinctions like gender and ethnicity or race. However, because gender, race, and ethnicity are often conflated with class in American society, people often make the mistake of thinking of class-related differences as the product of gender or ethnic/racial differences (Steinberg 1989; Epstein 1988, 116). While few in number, the families of more affluent lesbians or more affluent African-, Latino-, Asian-American families, when compared with the family lives of poorer Euro-American males, reveal a great deal about the salience of class distinctions to family life.

There are three distinct class groupings of lesbigay families in this study: working/service, middle, and upper middle class (appendix B, table B1). Overall, household incomes range from $24,000 to $230,000 per year, with a median household income of $58,500. This income figure might seem high, but it must be understood in context. The San Francisco Bay Area is the most affluent metropolitan area in North America—a circumstance driven by the Sillicon Valley and its place in the new world economy. The cost of renting, and of owning property, in the Bay Area far exceeds that of any other metropolitan area. The San Francisco Tenants Union reports that in 1997 the average monthly rent for a one-bedroom apartment in the city was $1200, while two bedrooms rented for $1700 (*San Francisco Independent*, 15 Apr. 1997, 13). Median annual household income in the six counties of the Bay Area hovers just under $50,000. Over one million households in the Bay Area earn $50,000-$75,000 a year, and another one million earn over $75,000 (*San Francisco Examiner*, 16 Feb. 1997, W21). Put another way, those Bay Area households earning below the national median household income, as reported by the U.S. Census in 1990 ($29,943), number about 1.5 million. The roughly four million remaining households in the Bay Area earn more, and often substantially more, than the median national income. By national standards, Bay Area residents, including lesbigay residents, are quite affluent. However, comparing Bay Area lesbigay residents with heterosexual ones reveals something quite different.

In this context, the lesbigay families of the Bay Area appear to mostly fall into the middle class. However, one should not generalize from lesbigay families to the wider lesbian, gay, and bisexual communities of the Bay Area, many of whom are single, younger, living in multiple-adult households, and probably less affluent than those in relationships. According to the Census Bureau lesbigay families who live in San Francisco proper live for the most part in the working- and middle-class neighborhoods of Castro, Upper Market, Western Addition, Bernal Heights, Inner Mission, and Hayes Valley (*San Francisco Examiner*, 12 Sept. 1993, 10). Relatively few lesbigay families reside in the more affluent, and predominantly heterosexual, neighborhoods like the Marina, Russian/Nob Hill, Pacific Heights/Sea Cliff, Presidio Heights, Laurel Heights, Twin Peaks, Forest Hill/St. Francis Wood, and Ocean View. For instance, the Census Bureau reports that 15,008 households live in Pacific Heights, a wealthy, mostly Euro-American enclave in San Francisco. Of those 15008 households, 235 are same-sex households, or about 1.5 percent (ibid., 10). According to the same census data, the greatest number of lesbigay families actually live in the Western Addition, a densely populated, mixed-income neighborhood not known for its affluence. The census estimates that one in twenty-seven households, or 835 of the 22,815 households in the Western Addition, is a same-sex household (ibid., 10). One in four of the families I studied dwell in the Western Addition, including many of the less affluent Euro-American males, as well as many of the Asian- and African-American lesbigay families. Overall, most lesbigay families in this study dwell in relatively spartan apartments, live in more socially and economically "marginal" (that is, between more affluent and poor districts) city neighborhoods, or in distant suburbs, resolutely defy the stereotype of gay affluence, and seem to represent the average and range captured by the census data.

In terms of ethnic and racial identities, of the 108 participants in the research, 63 were predominantly Euro-American, 15 Latino/a-American, 15 Asian-American, 13 Black/African-American, and 2 Native American (see table B4 in appendix B for further sample characteristics, and table B9 for ethnic/racial identities of particular participants).[5] The wide majority of

Euro-American participants migrated to the Bay Area from somewhere else, while the great majority of Latino/a-, Asian-, and Black/African-Americans grew up in the San Francisco Bay Area. The influence of racial and ethnic identities upon domesticity eludes parsimonious analysis. Such identity influences some aspects of domesticity in some families but not in others. Understandings of who constitutes family are a case in point. Notions of extended or "chosen" kin, and the stereotype that some racial/cultural groups value family more because they maintain large, extended families, impact how some lesbigay-family members portray their family life, but not necessarily the kind of family life they lead. For example, I will show that many of the African-, Asian- and Latina/o-American lesbigay families maintain stronger connections to "biolegal"[6] relatives, but this may simply be a function of the fact that many of their biolegal relatives also live nearby. Chapter 4 considers these issues in greater detail.

Domestic Diversity

Lesbigay family life takes many forms. Within this study I capture some of the diversity that exists among such families, particularly in terms of class, ethnicity/race, and occupation. However, there are multiple expressions of lesbigay families that this study does not capture. For instance, this is a study of urban lesbigay family life, and so does not capture the experiences of lesbigay families dwelling in small towns, midsize cities, or in rural communities.[7] Furthermore, as previously noted, San Francisco is somewhat unique among North American cities in that the urban core is not in economic decline.[8] This limits some comparisons with other urban lesbigay populations. This also impacts the urban/suburban distinctions that exist among lesbigay families in the San Francisco Bay Area that I discuss later. For instance, many Bay Area suburban lesbigay residents would like to live in the central city but economic costs prevent it. Moreover, I did not study lesbigay families where members live separately, either in the same region or even in another city. Nor did I study lesbigay single-parent families. Most of the families in this study consist of two adults, although one gay-male family consists of three adults. Children dwell with five of the families, although not always on a full-time basis. For instance, one gay-male couple shares custody of a child with one of the partner's ex-wife. The ex-wife lives in a suburban community, and the child shifts from one household to the other.

While I did not and could not capture the full diversity of lesbigay families, the methods used resulted in class, ethnic, race, gender, and occupational variation. I do not claim to have a representative sample. I suspect, based on what I know about several of the lesbigay families that turned me down for interviews, that my sample is more economically affluent and economically independent. One family turned me down for fear that exposure might endanger the unemployment benefits that one of the members receive. Another, a Latina couple, turned me down because, as one of the women put it, "I can't risk my mother finding out right now, because I need her help to make ends meet, and I never know when she might stop by."

Overview

I have organized this work on the basis of the different kinds of domestic work that occur in lesbigay families (for example, feeding work, kin work, consumption work, and housework). This organizational strategy reflects my commitment to providing lesbigay families themselves, and those who study them, with a more accurate and extensive vocabulary for talking about those family experiences. In chapter 1 I explore the processes and labors involved in feeding the lesbigay family, utilizing DeVault's typologies to make sense of feeding lesbigay families, and reflects on some of the unique dimensions of feeding in the lesbigay context. In chapter 2 I pursue housework, articulating a narrower conception of what constitutes housework, yet exploring that narrower conception in much greater depth. In chapter 3 I explore kin work by pursuing the question of who constitutes legitimate family in the eyes of lesbigay people and what forms of domesticity come into play in the creation and maintenance of that family. I address questions recently brought to the fore by anthropologist Kath Weston's provocative work *Families We Choose: Lesbians, Gays, Kinship*. My work brings a sociological perspective to these questions, emphasizing the significance of socioeconomic context to how lesbigay families both think about and construct family life. In chapter 4 I examine consumption work. Often mistaken for leisure, frequently invisible, and always time consuming, consumerism eats up more and more of Americans' time (Schor 1992). I reflect on the character of consumption work, the ways in which it has become central to family life, the distinct forms of work involved in doing consumption, and the importance of socioeconomic context to understanding consumption activities among lesbigay families. In chapter 5 I examine the division of labor in lesbigay families, focusing on the different patterns that division of labor takes, as well as the factors that appear to influence the division of labor. There I will reflect on the myths lesbigay families use to make sense of and to portray the division of labor in their homes. It is true that some lesbigay families achieve a great deal of "equality" in their domestic lives, but that often does not occur in a vacuum; rather, it occurs under a set of unique social and economic conditions. And the achievement of that equality does not correspond with a general sense of satisfaction with family life; in fact, just the opposite can happen. In the concluding chapter I reflect on the significance of this study for public policy debates, including those pertaining to domestic partnership and to lesbian and gay marriage.

feeding lesbigay families

> To housekeep, one had to plan ahead and carry items of motley
> nature around in the mind and at the same time preside, as
> mother had, at the table, just as if everything, from the liver and
> bacon, to the succotash, to the French toast and strawberry jam,
> had not been matters of forethought and speculation.
> FANNIE HURST, *Imitation of Life*

> Life's riches other rooms adorn. But in a kitchen home is born.
> EPIGRAM HANGING IN THE KITCHEN OF A LESBIAN FAMILY

Preparing a meal occurs within an elaborate set of social, economic, and cultural frameworks that determine when and with whom we eat, what and how much
we eat, what we buy and where we go to buy it, and
when and with what tools and techniques we prepare a
meal. Many people associate the activities of preparing
and sharing meals together with family. As sociologist
Marjorie DeVault convincingly argues in *Feeding the
Family* (1991), the work of preparing and sharing meals

creates family. Many lesbigay families point to the continuous preparation of daily meals and/or the occasional preparation of elaborate meals as evidence of their status as families. The labor involved in planning and preparing meals enables family to happen in both heterosexual and in lesbigay households. However, both the extent and the character of feeding activities can vary dramatically from one household to the next and often reflects the influence of socioeconomic factors like social class, occupation, and gender, among others.

In this chapter I pursue two objectives in the investigation of feeding work in lesbigay families. First, I explore feeding work through analyzing its character and revealing its often hidden dimensions. This entails some discussion of how families conceive of and articulate the work of feeding. For instance, participants use a number of rhetorical strategies to portray the organization of feeding in their households. Many participants use two distinctions: cooking/cleaning and cooking/shopping. I will show how these distinctions function to create a sense of egalitarianism and to obfuscate rather than clarify the process of feeding. This inevitably leads to questions about the division of feeding work in lesbigay households. While an investigation of feeding work reveals that a less than egalitarian division often develops within many lesbigay households, I refrain from any explanation of why until chapter 5. Second, in this chapter I explore how socioeconomic differences among lesbigay households influence feeding activities, and vice-versa. Therein, just as feeding work can create family identity for participants, so too can feeding work create gender, ethnic, class, and sexual identities.

The Character of Feeding Work

As DeVault (1991) so aptly describes in her study of feeding work in heterosexual families, the people who do feeding work often find it difficult to describe the task. Commonly held definitions and most sociological investigations of domestic labor often reduce feeding work to cooking, shopping, and cleaning up the kitchen—the most apparent expressions of feeding. But when interviewing and engaging in participant observation with people who perform these functions, it becomes clear that cooking and shopping refer to a wide range of dispersed activities that punctuate the days of those who feed. It includes things like knowledge of what family members like to eat, nutritional concerns, a sense of work and recreation schedules, a mental list of stock ingredients in the cupboard, a mental time line of how long fruits and vegetables will last, etc. Frequently, these activities go unnoticed because they often happen residually and unreflectively. For instance, the way that one comes to know about the character and qualities of food stuffs—through experimentation, through conversations with colleagues, through browsing in a cookbook at a bookstore, through reading the food section in the newspaper—these activities often appear as recreation or as an expression of personal interest and not as forms of work. Yet, to successfully feed a family, such activities must occur and consume the energy and time of those who do them. In order to illuminate the full character of feeding work in lesbigay families, I want to look behind the tradition typologies of cooking, shopping, and cleaning and reveal the dynamic and invisible character of much of the work involved in feeding these families.

"invisible" work of feeding families

Planning Meals

Feeding actually consists of a number of distinct processes including planning, shopping, preparation, and management of meals. Planning presumes the possession of several forms of knowledge about food, about the household, about significant others, and about cultural rules and practices toward food. In most of the lesbigay families in this study, one person emerges as a fairly easily identified meal planner; hereafter I refer to such persons as planners. Planning for most families means thinking ahead, perhaps a day or two or even a week, but in many cases just a few hours before a meal. For those who decide what to eat on a day-to-day basis, they often decide and plan meals while at work. Matthew Corrigan, an office administrator, put it like this:

> Usually we decide something at the last minute. Or sometimes we go out with someone. We rarely go out with just us two, but with others as well. If Greg is home in time and has an inspiration, he will make something, but the general pattern is for me to throw something together when I get home. I usually decide at work what to make.

A retail clerk, Scott McKendrick, reports: "We decide right before we eat. We go out to the store and buy enough brown rice for several days or a pack-

age of chicken breasts or broccoli. We shop every three days." "We" actually
refers to Scott's partner, Gary Hosokawa, a thirty-six-year-old bookkeeper
who works for a small hotel. Earlier in the interview Scott reports that his
partner cooks 75 percent of the time, and later in the interview he indicates
that his partner stops at the store several days a week. In fact, Scott makes few
planning decisions. His partner Gary makes most of them. Beth Wilkerson,
who works as a nonprofit fundraiser, reports: "I think about it in the morning and stop and pick it up on my way home from work. But, sometimes, I
get ahead of myself and will cook on a weekend for the next week."

Many times the partner who pulls together meals on a daily basis does not
consider what they do as planning. One computer engineer, Brad O'Neil, explains: "I hardly ever plan. It just happens at the last minute." Further questioning reveals he often decides at work what to make and often stops at the
store to buy missing ingredients. Like the other planners, Brad knows the
foodstuffs available at home, he knows where to go to get what he needs, and
he knows how to prepare the food. Mentally, he draws the connections between things at home, the things he needs, and a potential meal. He plans,
though he fails to recognize his efforts as such.

In some instances, someone plans for a longer period of time, often a
week. Those partners who plan by the week more readily recognize the planning they do. While some planners find the effort enriching and pleasant,
many others express a certain amount of frustration with the process, particularly in deciding what to make. Randy Ambert, an airline flight attendant,
expresses the frustration this way:

> I find that he doesn't give me any input. I rarely make things he doesn't like, but
> he doesn't tell me what he wants to have, I have to do that every single week. I am
> constantly searching for clues as to what he likes and doesn't like. I don't think he
> truly appreciates how much effort it takes.

Sucheng Kyutaro, an office manager for a real estate agency, explains:

> I also find it hard to figure out what she likes to eat, I think. It's a pain to get her to
> tell me what she will eat and then she becomes annoyed when I forget it the next
> time. I think about her every time I try to come up with some dinner items.

These comments illustrate one of the hidden forms of work involved in
feeding: learning what others will and will not eat and learning to predict

their responses. Hochschild (1983) uses the terms *emotion work* or *emotion management* to refer to this kind of empathetic activity, quite often performed by women, but as my research suggests, by many gay men as well. When thinking about domestic work, most people conjure up images of cleaning bathrooms, buying groceries and cooking meals. Emotion management involves the process of establishing empathy with another, interpreting behavior and conducting yourself in a way that "produces the proper state of mind in others" (Hochschild 1983, 7). Emotion management involves the management of feelings, both of your own and those of others. For example, it involves efforts to soothe feelings of anger in another or to enhance feelings of self-worth when someone "feels down." Sucheng's effort to "think about her partner every time" she plans a meal, in order to avoid producing "annoyance" in her partner, constitutes emotion work. Sucheng hopes to create an emotional state of satisfaction and happiness in her partner through her feeding efforts.

Most lesbigay families, just like most heterosexual families, do not engage in the emotion work of feeding in an egalitarian way. For example, partners in lesbigay relationships do not share equal knowledge of the food tastes and preferences of each other. Queries about the food preferences of partners reveals a highly differentiated pattern, where the planners possess extensive and detailed knowledge of their partner's preferences and food concerns, while their partners know comparatively little about the planner's tastes. In response to a question about his partner's food preferences, Steven Beckett, a retired real estate agent, reports that "he will not eat 'undercooked' or what the rest of us call normally cooked chicken. If he finds any red near the bone he will throw it across the room. Milk has to be low fat. Pork has to be quite cooked. He likes things quite spiced. He doesn't like peas or Brussels sprouts." Steven's partner, Anthony Manlapit, answers, "I think he likes a lot of things, I know he likes to eat out a lot." In response to the same question, Robert Bachafen, a school librarian, responds, "Yes. I stay away from radishes, shellfish, and certain soups. It's basically trial and error. He won't touch barbecued meats. I have learned over the years what he will and will not eat." His partner, Greg Sandwater, an architect, says, "I can't think of anything. He is not too fussy." Emily Fortune, a homemaker and mother of infant twins, as well as an accountant who works at home replies, "She doesn't care for pork. She has a reaction to shrimp. She doesn't like fish that much. Used to be that she wouldn't eat chicken. She doesn't like bell pep-

Good example (handwritten note in margin)

pers. She doesn't like milk." Her partner, Alice Lauer, a rapid transit driver, says, "There aren't too many things she doesn't like." A finance manager for a savings and loan company, Joan Kelsey, replies, "Liver, brussels sprouts, she doesn't like things with white sauces. She is not as fond of junk food as I am." Her partner, Kathy Atwood, an accountant, responds, "I can't think of much of anything she doesn't like."

Steven, Robert, Alice, and Joan all plan meals and hold responsibility for the lion's share of feeding work. The partners of these meal planners confidently assert that their partners tend to like most things. Not true. In interviews I asked explicit questions about food likes and dislikes and found that planners indeed hold food preferences though their partners often do not readily know them. The ease with which planners cite detailed accounts of their partner's food like and dislikes suggests that they use such knowledge with some frequency. Coming to know a partner's food preferences takes work: questioning, listening, and remembering. Successful feeding depends on this effort.

Learning about Food and Food Preparation

While learning the food preferences of others constitutes one dimension of the planning process, learning about food and preparation techniques constitutes another. The planners turn to a number of sources to inspire and guide their decisions. About half of the planners turn to cookbooks every few weeks. A part-time real estate agent, Lawrence Sing, provides the following insight into his process:

> It depends on what I am reading lately. I read a lot of food magazines and cookbooks, and we have a garden, which produces a lot of fresh greens and vegetables, that will have some bearing on it. It depends on what is seasonal. I am currently enamored with Dean Ornish's book *(Eat More, Weigh Less)*, which focuses on high-carbohydrate, low-fat, low-protein diet with lots of fiber. And I think that this would be salubrious for all of us so I am directing our eating in that direction by making sure that more of those kinds of foods appear.

The nutritional comments in this passage deserve comment, and I will return to them shortly. In addition to cookbooks, many planners read the food section of the local paper or magazines about food. Margarita Lopez, a graduate student in the social sciences, tells me:

I read the food section of the *Chronicle* every week. I often pick up recipes from there. She complains if we have the same thing all the time, so I am always looking for more creative ways to cook things. When we go on vacation, I will buy a new cookbook, and I always look to the cooking section when we go into a bookstore, sort of searching for ideas, you know.

Lance Converse, a forty-year-old healthcare administrator, remarks:

I make up a menu. Most of it is in my head. I make things up. He voices things that he likes and dislikes. I especially note when he says he doesn't like something. We eat lots of chicken and fish and avoid red meats. I read *Gourmet* and *Better Homes and Gardens* quite often to come up with ideas.

Others learn about food in conversations with friends and family. Michael Herrera, an office administrator, speaks of the importance of his mother to learning about food:

We tend to make the same things over and over. I make enchiladas a lot. I make a lot of pasta, with a salad and bread. But I try to include new things. Karen [a third member of the household] doesn't do as much of the cooking. I tend to keep it all together. I turn to my mother for help often. She gives me ideas about different things to make and I will call her in the middle of preparing something if I get confused about how to do something.

Others let the marketplace guide their process. Mary Ann Callihan, an artist and craftsperson, speaks of weekly trips to the farmer's market:

I try to decide many of the week's meals based on what is available. I often get ideas from other people I see there each Saturday. I have some acquaintances there, who I really only ever see at the farmer's market. We talk to the farmers and to their wives mostly and to one another, and I come away with ideas of how to prepare things differently.

In Mary Ann's case, shopping becomes much more than purchasing food stuffs; it becomes an occasion for learning what to prepare and how to prepare it.

Nutritional Concerns as Feeding Work

While the planners need to learn the food preferences of family members and continuously learn about food and its preparation from a variety of sources, they must also take into consideration a whole set of concerns about nutrition. Such concerns seem omnipresent in our society, though my research indicates some significant variation by both gender and age regarding this issue. Many of the planners work within fairly stringent guidelines regarding the nutritional content of the meals they prepare. As we earlier saw with Lawrence's effort to promote a healthy diet for his family through "directing our eating in that direction by making sure that more of those kinds of foods appear," the planners regularly oversee the nutritional strategies and dietary regimes. Many lesbian and gay-male (in particular) families fight over the nutritional content of food. These concerns cast a long shadow over the entire feeding process for some of the male planners. Joe McFarland, an attorney, states:

> We constantly fight about it. I am more conscious of fat and calorie content and seem to have to remind Richard constantly about it. He prepares great meals, but I am trying desperately to stay in shape. He gets upset because sometimes I just won't eat what he made or very much of it. I don't see why it's so hard for him to make low-fat stuff.

His partner, Richard Neibuhr, who does the feeding work, perceives of it this way:

> Yes. Well, we try to cut fat. We eat a lot less red meat. We eat fish and poultry and we always skin the poultry because that's not too good for you. We eat a lot of rice and potatoes and avoid white cheese and butter. It all boils down to him trying to sustain his sexual attractiveness, I think. It would be easier for me to tell you things he will eat. He will not eat pork, no sausage. He eats one or two types of fish, he eats chicken and pasta. Anything other than that, it's a battle royal to get him to eat it, it's too fat! He won't eat Greek, Mexican, Chinese—forget it. He will eat Italian, but only with light marinara sauces, sea bass, sole, skinless chicken, and that's about it. He is very picky and it all comes down to his effort to look beautiful. It's a lot of work to come up with meals that meet his dietary standards and yet still taste good and don't bore you to death.

Note the extent of Richard's knowledge about his partner's food preferences. Also note that Richard carries the burden of making sure the meals remain nutritionally sound.

Lesbian households also report conflicts over the nutritional quality of meals. Deborah James, a daycare worker, shares the following thoughts:

Yeah, she doesn't want me to fry things because it makes such a mess and she has to clean it up. She would rather that I stir-fry and make more vegetables. She likes my cooking because it tastes good, but she would rather eat healthier than I would. I think my cooking sort of reminds her of her growing up. She partly likes that and she partly doesn't because it reminds her of being poor and I think the food I make sometimes, she thinks she's too good for it, that she should eat like rich people eat. I try to keep her happy, though.

Emily Fortune, a work-at-home accountant in her early thirties who recently became the mother of twins, maintains concern over both her partner's nutrition and her newborn children's nutrition. Emily, in response to a question about conflict over food, states:

Yes, I am still nursing, so I watch out for what the babies are going to get. We are no longer vegetarians. We both were at one time, but I eat a lot of protein for the babies. I think Alice would prefer a more vegetarian diet that was better for her. I try to think up meals that are healthy for all of them, both Alice and the babies. It's hard, though.

In most cases the meal planner becomes responsible for preparing meals that conform to dietary preferences and nutritional regimes.

In sum, planning meals, learning about foodstuffs and techniques, considering the preferences and emotions of significant others, and overseeing nutritional strategies frame the essential yet invisible precursor work to the actual daily process of preparing a meal. However, before the preparation begins, one must shop.

Provisioning Work

Shopping includes much more than the weekly trips to buy food products. DeVault (1991) recommends the use of the term *provisioning* to capture to character of the work involved in shopping. Provisioning assumes several forms of mental work that precede the actual purchase of food, including determining family members' food preferences, dietary concerns, as well as culturally specific concerns about food. Further, provisioning depends upon the following additional activities: developing a standard stock of food, learning where to buy the "appropriate" food, monitoring current supplies, scheduling grocery trips, making purchases within particular financial constraints and building flexibility into the process. Each of these components appears in lesbigay households and most often fall to the planner to orchestrate and perform.

Quite often these dimensions of provisioning go unrecognized and get subsumed in the rhetorical strategies participants use to describe the division of feeding work. More than half of the lesbigay family members use the distinction cooking/shopping to describe the division of tasks in meal preparation. This distinction creates an egalitarian impression, as in the phrase "She cooks and I shop." But the distinction conceals. In most cases the person with responsibility for cooking either did the actual shopping himself or herself or they prepared a list for the other person to use at the market. Responses to queries about who writes grocery lists illustrate this dynamic, as Carey Becker, a part-time radiologist, put it: "I write the list for major shopping for the most part, as well. She knows what brand to buy, so I don't tell her that. But I am the one who knows what we need and I make the list up for her." Daniel Sen Yung, a health educator, speaks of a similar pattern: "During the week when *we* are cooking, *we* write things on the list. He is more likely to do that, I guess, because he is cooking and will run out of stuff, so I get it at the store. He knows what we need." Note the recurrence of the phrase "knows what we need." In both instances the phrase refers to the possession of a stock knowledge of foodstuffs. Planners develop and possess an extensive mental list of standard ingredients used in their kitchens. In the research I asked to see the current grocery list, should one exist. I saw thirty-two such lists. In the wide majority of cases, just one person wrote the list or wrote more than three-quarters of the items on the list. In those relationships where participants make a distinction between shopping and cooking meals, lists become longer and more detailed. For instance, many planners specify brand names or write down terms like *ripe avocado* instead of just *avocado*. The cumulative effect of such detailed list writing greatly simplifies the work of shopping and undermines the seeming egalitarianism of the cooking/shopping distinction.

The Significance of Small Grocery Trips

In most households, shopping includes a number of smaller trips to supplement throughout the week. In the wide majority of lesbigay families, one person makes these supplemental trips. In most cases, the person who bears responsibility for meal preparation does this type of shopping. They often stop at the store at lunch or, more often, on their way home from work. While many families initially indicate that they split cooking from shopping, in reality the person who cooks often shops throughout the week while the other partner makes "major" shopping trips, usually on weekends and often using a shopping list prepared by the planner at home. At first glance the intermittent shopping trips during the week appear ad hoc and supplemental in character. Yet for many lesbigay households, particularly in the lesbian and gay enclaves of San Francisco, these little trips constitute the essential core of feeding. Many planners shop at corner markets near their homes or places of work, frequently purchasing the central ingredients for the meal that evening—fresh meats and vegetables, breads, and pastas. In many respects the weekend shopping actually looks more supplemental. Again, the grocery lists prove instructive. They contain many more entries for items like cereals, granola bars, sugar, mustard, yogurt, and soda than for the central elements in evening meals: vegetables, fresh pasta, fish, chicken, bread, potatoes, corn, prepared sauces, and often milk.

The intermittent shopper often operates with a great degree of foresight. Alma Duarte, a bookkeeper for a small business, belies the ad hoc characterization of daily grocery trips:

> Every couple of days, I go to the store. I do the in-between shopping. Every couple of days, I run down and pick up stuff we need or are running out of. I buy vegetables, fish, and bread. I buy the heavy items at Calla Market because she has a back problem, so I buy like soda and detergent and kitty litter, but she does the big shopping on weekends. I almost always go and buy fish on Monday afternoons at a fish market near where I work and then I stop at the produce market near home. And I have to go and get fresh vegetables every couple days over there.

Alma speaks of at least three destinations, and she obviously organizes her schedule to accommodate these different trips. One might think that this kind of shopping appears rather routine, after all, she describes it as "in-between." Note that she does not consider this effort major, rather her partner does "big" shopping. Yet each of Alma's little shopping trips consists of a rather large number of choices about feeding. She must decide on what kind of fish and conceive of other items to serve with it. She decides when to go for vegetables and chooses among myriad varieties, making sure not to buy the same ones over and over yet also measuring the quality of the produce. Interestingly, she identifies her partner as the shopper, though she actually makes most of the feeding and provisioning decisions for her family.

Deciding Where to Shop

Deciding where to shop often appears as a matter of routine, even to those who make such choices. Yet these choices mirror complex thought processes and a variety of social-structural considerations. When asking participants where they shop, most offered the name of a large grocery store nearby. Most participants indicate that they chose grocery stores based on two factors: proximity and selection. However, when asking about and going with planners to where they shop, a much more elaborate answer emerges. To begin with, planners, like Alma, often shop at more than one store. Lily Chin, an office manager, describes her shopping strategy:

> I shop at Food for Less, Trader Joe's, Costco, and a corner market. It depends on what I need and how much time I have. If I have a lot of time, I might go over to Trader Joe's, but there it's hit and miss. Sometimes they have what I need and sometimes not. Usually, to go there, you take a lot of time and you thoroughly check out their selection. You let their products decide what you buy. If I am picking up fish for that night, then I stop at Andronico's because they have such a nice fish selection. If I just need some fresh vegetables I will go home and park the car and walk down to the corner produce market. Sometimes I call Carol and ask her to stop. She stops at Food for Less because she can get in and out quickly. She doesn't like to go to places where you have to find a parking space.

Her partner, Carol Len, a social worker, says that they shop at Food for Less because of the convenience. She said little else. In contrast, planners report thinking about a wide array of factors in deciding where to shop. Lily makes decisions based on a constellation of factors: menu, parking, time availability, and quality. Lily traverses this constellation of factors on a routine basis. The weighing of these factors and the creation of a daily strategy to achieve a successful meal remains mostly invisible, yet essential. Lily's partner portrays the shopping effort as one consisting of mostly convenience, a central factor in her own experience of shopping, but just one concern among many in an effort to feed a lesbigay family.

Moreover, the decision of where to shop involves concerns about social class, ethnic identity, and the sexual identities of lesbigay family members. Delineating the significance of each of these social-structural factors poses great difficulties, yet their import appears clear. For instance, concerns about the healthfulness of food reflect class-related concerns, but it also reflects concerns for many gay men about physical appearance. DeVault points to the centrality of food style as a marker of class identity in contemporary society (1991, 203–26). She notes the middle- and upper-middle-class concern with producing interesting and entertaining meals, the preference for elaborate and exotic meals, the preoccupation with the healthfulness of meals—all symbolic indicators of class standing in our society. These matters of style appear in lesbigay households as well, with more affluent, more professional families emphasizing such concerns. Working/service-class lesbigay families report much more routine in meal preparation, and they go to fewer shops. Partly this occurs because such families do not own automobiles, relying instead on public transportation, which of course is far less convenient. They emphasize the closeness of stores as central to their shopping habits. But beyond this, such families report a standard stock of meals cooked quite frequently. For instance, a lesbian family where one women works as a retail clerk and the other as an accounting clerk, often eat a product called Chicken Tonight at least twice a week. Letty Feldmen, who does much of the provisioning, remembers in her weekly shopping to buy chicken and two jars of the product. Such families report engaging in less feeding work in terms of the variety and elaborateness of the meals, although, as I will show shortly, working/service-class lesbigay families eat more meals at home and spend more time managing the cost of meals. For affluent families, the meal planner takes into consideration the class-related concerns about style in deciding where to shop. John Chapman, a homemaker partnered with a successful attorney, implies these class-related concerns in his shopping routine:

> I buy most things out of my head. I go down the aisle and it's like a major deal to go. I like to look and find out what's new. I go over the grocery store with a fine-tooth comb. I am always looking for something new and interesting to make. I try to get away from routine and keep things constantly new. I will pick up prepared meals sometimes from a specialty deli. And whenever we have someone over, well, then I really make sure it's something that people will enjoy and enjoy talking about. That often means that I will have to shop somewhere much nicer, like Petrini's Market or Andronico's in the inner Sunset.

In addition to these class-related concerns, many lesbigay families also take ethnic identity concerns into account in their shopping routines. Henry, a Latino social worker for a Bay Area county, pointed to the importance of maintaining his and his partner's Latino identity in his decision of where to shop:

> I go on Mission Street to the open markets a lot. I like the markets because the fruit and vegetables are good, and I can speak Spanish if I don't understand things. I think it's important to support the merchants in the community. Food is a part of our heritage, and I don't want us to loose that. I try to keep us connected, in part, through serving meals that reflect our identity. I can buy tortillas and cheese for cheaper prices at Costco, but I don't because that undermines the Mission merchants. It's more of an effort sometimes to find what you are looking for, but you also find things you can't find in white stores.

Sandy Chao, a director of a daycare center, sounded a similar theme:

> I try to get over to Clement Street when I can. There are many Chinese grocers and produce markets over there. I also try to go out on Ocean Avenue, where there is a new Vietnamese store. I try to support the Asian businesses as much as I can. It's just a part of being who we are, and without those things, we lose some of our identity.

While class and ethnicity shape the provisioning choices of meal planners, concerns about lesbian and gay identity and community also influence provisioning work. Many participants spoke of the importance of shopping in lesbigay-owned businesses, or at least in lesbigay-friendly territory. Bill, an artist and painter, expresses this sentiment:

> I try to shop in the gay community. A lot of times that means paying more. The "gay tax," you know. But I feel a lot safer; not that most of the city isn't safe, it's just that I like to be with my own kind. It makes it less stressful. Sometimes it means waiting in longer lines. Like Market Street Safeway, for instance. I could shop elsewhere, I have a car, but I like to go there because that's where the lesbigay people are. I often stop at Harvest Market in Castro, too. They have great produce and a lot of healthy foods, even though it's expensive, it's gay and it's healthy—both of those things are pretty important to me a lot of the time.

As the above quotations make clear, deciding where to shop involves a vast array of considerations. Balancing the various concerns mostly falls onto the shoulders of the planners in lesbigay families.

Monitoring: Supplies, Schedules, and Finances

Another component of feeding work revolves around the efforts of planners to monitor the supply of foods and other household products. DeVault suggests the complexity of monitoring work:

> Routines for provisioning evolve gradually out of decisions that are linked to the resources and characteristics of particular households and to features of the market. . . . Monitoring also provides a continual testing of typical practices. This testing occurs as shoppers keep track of changes on both sides of the relation: household needs and products available. (1991, 71)

Lesbigay family members, both planners and others, attest to clear patterns of specialization when it comes to who keeps tabs on both food products and other household products like cleaning supplies, toiletries, and items like dinner candles. Very few families reported splitting this effort up equally, and even those that did, did so gingerly. Susan Posner, an employment recruiter in the computer industry, recounts: "Neither one of us keeps track. It just kind of surfaces that we need something. We don't have a list or anything. I guess whoever runs out of toilet paper first. And I guess I run out of toilet paper a lot. *[Laughter]* Okay, so maybe I do it." Susan's comments should give pause to students of domestic labor. Her comments reveal not only that she does the work of monitoring supplies, but also that she seems either unaware or perhaps to be attempting to deny that she does it. The planners, who do much of the monitoring, frequently speak of the dynamic character of the work. Tim Cisneros, a registered nurse, describes how he needed to change his routine in order to get the right deodorant for his partner:

> I mostly shop at Diamond Heights Safeway, though now I go over to Tower Market as well, at least once a month. I started doing that because Paul is hyperallergic to most deodorants, and he needs to use one special kind, and Safeway stopped carrying it. I tried to get it at the drugstore next to Safeway, but they don't carry it, either. So now, I go to Tower to get it. I buy other stuff while I'm there, so it's not really a big deal.

Tim captures the dynamic quality of provisioning. As demands change in the household or products change in the market, he comes up with new strategies to maintain equilibrium. Among roughly half of the families reporting a shopping/cooking division, more discussion of products occurs. Narvin Wong, a financial consultant in healthcare, comments:

> We sometimes get our wires crossed. I buy what he puts on the list, and that's al-most always what we usually buy. I mean, I know what we need, but sometimes he changes his mind about what he needs and I don't always remember him telling me. Like a few weeks ago, he put olive oil on the list, and I bought olive oil. He says he told me that he wanted to start using extra-virgin olive oil. Well, I didn't hear that, and he yelled and steamed about it when he unpacked the groceries.

Narvin's comments suggest that perhaps less of this kind of conflict takes place in households where one person performs both the actual shopping and the provisioning work behind the trips to the store. Further, Narvin's partner, Lawrence Shoong, says that he often tries to go with Narvin to the store. Why?

> Because it gives me a chance to see what's out there. Narvin doesn't look for new things. Even if he does, he doesn't tell me about them. I like to know what's in sea-son and just to see what's new. And inevitably, he forgets stuff. I know I should write it on the list, which is what he says, but when I go to the store, I can go up and down the rows and remember what we have and what we need.

Again, this points to the interdependent and dynamic character of feeding work. To do it successfully, given the way our society distributes foodstuffs and defines appropriate eating, the meal planner needs to stay in contact with the marketplace. Many planners do this through reading grocery flyers in the paper or in the mail, but many also try to stay in contact with the store itself. As Lawrence's comments suggest, much of provisioning work takes place in one's mind, the place where much of the hidden work of monitoring takes place.

Just as the work of monitoring the household and the marketplace come into view as highly dynamic processes, so too does the planner monitor the dynamic schedules of family members as a part of provisioning work. This means that many planners shop with the goal of providing a great deal of flex-ibility in meal options. For instance, many planners report selecting at least some dinner items that they can easily move to another night of the week should something come up. Sarah Lynch, a graphic artist who works in a studio at home, captures the dynamic circumstances under which she provisions meals:

> I never have any idea when Andrea will get here. She may stay at the bank until 11:00 at night. Sometimes, she doesn't know up until right before 5:00 whether she will be able to come home. So I still want us to eat together and I want her to get a decent meal, so I try to buy things that I can make quickly and that still taste good. She will call me from her car phone as soon as she is leaving the city. That gives me about an hour. I often will make something like a lasagna that I can then heat up when she calls, or I buy a lot of fresh pastas, in packages, you know the ones, and I will start that when she calls. I also try to buy a lot of snacklike items, healthy ones, but things like crackers and trail mix and dried fruit so that she can eat those things if she is really hungry and went without lunch or something, and so I can eat while I am waiting for her to get here.

Similarly, Matthew Corrigan, an office administrator, provisions meals to accommodate the schedule of his partner:

> I sometimes find it hard to keep a handle on things. Greg is active in a number of voluntary things—our church and a hospice for PWAs—and he serves on a City task force on housing issues. I am never completely sure he will be here for the meals I plan. So I try to have a lot of food around that we can make quickly and easily, like soups, veggie burgers, and pastas. If it gets too tight, and it often does, we will eat out, or just he will eat out and then I eat something at home, and hopefully I have something here to make.

Both Matthew and Sarah provision their households in light of the need to build in flexibility around the work and social schedules of their partners and themselves. The effort they put into this kind of dynamic provisioning frequently goes unnoticed and often appears routine, but they clearly think about these scheduling concerns in the work of provisioning for their families.

In addition to the efforts planners make in monitoring schedules, supplies, and markets, many also report concerns about monitoring finances. Participants refer to financial concerns in deciding what to eat and where to shop. The cutting of coupons both illustrates financial concerns and demonstrates the de facto division of provisioning work in many lesbigay families.

Rarely do all family members report cutting coupons. For the most part, one partner, the planner/provisioner, cuts coupons. Tim Reskin, a clerk in a law firm, describes his use of coupons:

> Over time I have developed a sense of the brands that I know that we prefer. Sometimes I have coupons that I use. It's not like I will use any coupon, but if there's something that seems interesting or we don't have an opinion about, I might use that to decide. I always go through the Sunday paper and cut out the usable coupons. Cost is a big criterion for us.

In addition to cutting coupons, the less affluent households more often report that they compare prices, watch for sales and buy large-portioned products at discount stores like Costco and Food for Less. Lower-income planners also report spending more time reading grocery advertisements and going to different stores to buy sale items with the purpose of saving money in mind.

The estimates provided by participants regarding food expenditures provide additional insight into the division and character of feeding work. Weekly grocery expenditures vary significantly for lesbigay families, ranging from thirty dollars a week in the less affluent households to over two hundred and fifty dollars a week in the wealthier ones. Not that family members always agree on the cost of groceries. Planners estimate spending roughly thirty dollars more per week on groceries than their partners estimate. The thirty-dollar figure functions both as the mean and the median among the one hundred and three adult participants.

This knowledge gap in food expenditures points to several interesting dynamics. First, it reflects planners knowledge of the cost of the many small trips to the store during the week. Second, it indicates planner's greater attentiveness to the cost of food items. Finally, it often points to the expectation of family members that planners should monitor and limit the cost of food. Consider the following examples. Tim Reskin and Phillip Norris live in a distant East Bay suburb in a modest apartment. While they both work in the city, they live in the suburbs to avoid the high cost of housing in the city. Phillip performs much of the work of feeding their family. He plans the meals and creates much of the grocery list. In explaining why Tim does the larger shopping on weekends, they both speak about financial concerns. Tim puts it this way: "Money, that's a major part of the reason why he doesn't go to the store. For him, he doesn't take price into consideration as much as he should. I use coupons and don't get distracted by advertising gimmicks at the store. I am more conscious of money." Phillip sees things somewhat differently, but points to the issue of cost as well:

> He shops. He feels he has more control at the store. He feels he's a smarter shopper. I tend to look for high quality, whereas he tends to look for the best price. He does seem sharper. Well, he thinks he has a better handle on excessive spending. I don't know, though. You know, he does limit things during the major shopping, but then I have to go out and get things during the week. I am very, very careful about watching the cost. But you know what? Partly I have to go out and get things because of his complaints. He says that I cook blandly, like an Englishman. But the fact is, I work with what he brings home, and if he won't buy spices or sauces or whatever, in order to save money, then the food will taste bland. He denies that's what happens, but it is.

Phillip actually bears a significant part of the responsibility for monitoring food costs. Note the phrase "I am very, very careful about watching the cost." Phillip's comments illustrate the interdependent character of monitoring costs and planning meals, but further, he also must consider his partner's satisfaction with the meals.

A strikingly similar example emerges within a lesbian household. Marilyn Kemp and Letty Bartky live in one of the lesbigay neighborhoods of San Francisco. They both work in lower-level administrative jobs and find themselves struggling financially. They talk about the high cost of housing and how to cut corners in order to stay living in San Francisco. Letty, who performs much of the feeding work in the family, comments on Marilyn's approach to weekend shopping:

> Marilyn likes to shop like a Mormon—you know, be prepared for six months. She buys these huge boxes of stuff. I think it's silly. I am more into going two or three times a week. Also, I like to take time to make up my mind, while she just wants to get through the store as fast as possible. She bitches that I don't make interesting things to eat, but what does she expect given our financial constraints and her shopping regimen.

Marilyn sees it differently: "We don't disagree much at all about shopping. I do it because I am more cost-conscious than she is."

Both of the above families suggest that it is one thing to manage the cost of groceries while shopping, but another matter entirely to manage the cost of groceries in the broader context of feeding the family.

Preparing Meals

The actual physical work of preparing meals each day requires thorough analysis. In some instances, the physical preparation of the meal occasionally begins in the morning when meal planners take items from the freezer to defrost for the evening meal. Some planners report other early morning efforts such as marinating meats, vegetables, or tofu. Most planners begin the meal preparation shortly after arriving home from work. Many report emptying the dishwasher or putting away dry dishes from the rack as one of the first steps in getting ready to prepare the evening meal. This points to the ambiguity of the cooking/cleaning distinction offered by many participants. The majority of meal planners arrive home from work earlier than their partners, more than an hour earlier in most cases. Depending on the menu items, which vary widely, participant's estimate that meal preparation takes approximately an hour. The preparation of the meal involves mastering a number of different tasks, including coordinating the completion time of different elements of the meal, managing unexpected exigencies like telephone calls or conversations with family members, coping with missing ingredients or short supplies, and engaging in all of the techniques of food preparation, from cutting vegetables to kneading pizza dough to deboning fish to barbecuing meats.

Many meal preparers find it difficult to capture the character of the process involved in creating meals. Even those who seem well versed in cooking find it difficult to characterize the process in its true fullness and complexity. Clyde Duesenberry, who prepares most of the meals in the house, comments:

> We make pesto quite a bit. We have that with fried chicken or some sausage or whatever. We like breaded foods. We like Wienerschnitzel. We will have bleu cheese on burgers. We roast chickens quite often. We watch cooking shows quite a bit. The story about Mike, he can do it if he wants to, he knows the basics of cooking. One time I got called out on a call on a Sunday evening and he took over and we never had chicken as good as he made it. He cooks the broccoli. He knows how to do that. It isn't the recipe that makes a cook, it's the mastery of techniques. I can't even begin to cover all the territory of cooking you are asking about.

The meal preparer realizes the complexity of the work involved and struggles to put it into words. Usually their words belie the full extent of their effort as they struggle to express what they do. Another participant, Daniel Sen Yung, says:

> I tend to steam things a lot. I use dressings. A lot of salads and stuff. I don't know *[said with exasperation]*, it's hard to describe, I just do it. Each time it seems like there are different things to do. I call someone and ask them, or I look at a cookbook, or I just experiment and hope for the best. I make some things over and over and each thing has its own routine.

The daily physical process of meal preparation takes on a highly dynamic and thoughtful quality. While some meals take on a routine quality in some households, for most the process appears much more vigorous and multifaceted. It requires the constant attention, the knowledge, and the physical labor of meal preparers.

Feeding and Cleaning

In contrast to meal preparation, the cleanup of the evening meal appears much more routine, requiring less mental effort, less time, less knowledge, and less work. As previously indicated, many lesbigay households use a cooking/cleaning distinction to explain the organization and division of feeding work. However, in close to one-third of the sample, the person who prepares the meal also cleans up after the meal. The cleaning component deserves closer analysis. Those who clean up the kitchen estimate a median time of thirty minutes. They talk about clearing the dishes, loading the dishwasher, putting away leftover food, and wiping the counters and the stovetop. Some include taking out trash or wiping floors, but not most. Among the less affluent families, participants include washing and drying the dishes. As I briefly noted earlier, meal preparers often empty the dishwasher or put away dry dishes when they begin preparing the evening meal. The work of cleaning up is highly routinized in most lesbigay households, requiring little decision making and little emotional work. Barbara Cho, a shift supervisor for a hotel, notes that the cleanup actually allows her time to think and unwind from her day: "It's not a big deal. I clean off the table. Sandy helps bring in the dishes. I load the dishwasher, wipe off the counter, and put stuff away. It's a great time for me to think about things, I often reflect on my day or decide what I'm going to do that night. It helps me unwind." Rarely do meal planners/preparers conceive of their feeding work in these terms. Most spoke of the importance of staying focused on meal preparation in order to avoid burning meats or overcooking vegetables, and of coordinating meal items so they reach completion at the same time.

Several meal preparers also note that they make some effort to limit the mess caused by meal preparation and actually do a lot of cleaning as they go. Sucheng Kyutaro, who prepares most meals eaten at home, notes:

> She complains a lot if I make too much of a mess during cooking. So I kind of watch it as I go. I try to clean the major things as I cook. I will rinse out pans, like if I make spaghetti sauce, I will run all the remains from the vegetables down the garbage disposal and rinse out the sauce pan and I always wipe off the stove. She really doesn't like cleaning that up at all.

Gary Hosokawa, a payroll supervisor who does much of the feeding work in his family, remarks: "Usually I cook and he cleans. Although I am really anal about keeping a clean kitchen, so I clean a lot while I am cooking. There is not that much for him to do."

The preceding comments demonstrate the limited character of cleaning up after meals in many lesbigay households, and they further undermine the salience of the cooking/cleaning distinction employed by many participants to indicate the egalitarianism of their household arrangements.

Feeding Work and the Creation of Gender, Class, Ethnic, and Family Identities

Feeding and the Production of Gender Identity

Recent empirical and theoretical work on the sociology of gender conceives of the production or achievement of gender identity as resulting from routine and continuous engagement in certain kinds of work and activities socially defined as gendered (Berk 1985; Coltrane 1989; West and Zimmerman 1987). This perspective emerges from a school of thought in sociology that understands gender as a dynamic and purposeful accomplishment: something people produce in social interaction (Cahill 1989; Goffman 1977; Kessler and McKenna 1978). West and Zimmerman point to the significance of action, interaction, and display in the process of "doing gender": "a person's gender is not simply an aspect of what one is, but, more fundamentally, it is something that one does, and does recurrently, in interaction with others" (1987, 140). Gender is not the product of socialized roles in which individuals continually recast themselves. Rather, gender requires continual effort to reproduce in everyday life. Since in this society and many others gender constitutes an essential component of the system of social classification, "doing gender" results in keeping social relationships orderly, comprehensible, and stratified. Frequently, individuals possess an awareness of doing gender while deciding how to conduct themselves in daily life. How masculine should one appear while observing a sports event? How feminine should one appear in a television interview? Berk demonstrates how household tasks function as occasions for creating and sustaining gender identity (1985, 204). Coltrane (1989), in his study of fathers who become extensively involved in the work of childcare, shows how such men must manage the threats to gender identity that such work poses to them. To violate the gendered expectations of others often leads to stigma and to challenges to the gender identity of the violator. Coltrane found that men who care for (feed, clean, teach, hold) infants often face stigma from coworkers and biological relatives, and that oftentimes the men hide their caring activities from these people to avoid conflict and challenges to their masculine identity. Men performing domestic labor—or women who fail to—produces the potential for stigma, a matter of great significance for gay and lesbian couples, where the reality of household life clashes with cultural gender expectations.

Accordingly, managing the gendered identity of members of lesbigay families becomes a central dynamic in the portrayal of feeding work both within the family and to outsiders. In general, feeding work in the household constitutes women's work, even when men engage in the work. That link of feeding with the production of womanly status persists and presents dilemmas for lesbigay families. Let me begin my analysis of this dynamic by pointing to a rather odd thing that happened in interviews with lesbigay family members. I interviewed family members separately to prevent participants from constructing seamless accounts of household activities. In so doing, inconsistencies occurred in the portrayal of domestic work, including feeding work. In six of the twenty-six male families, both claim that they last cooked dinner. In four of the twenty-six female couples, both claim that the other person last cooked dinner. How can one explain this? Were the participants simply confused? Why a persistent gendered pattern of confusion? Lesbian families do more often report sharing in the tasks of meal preparation than do gay-male families, so here the confusion may reflect the presence of both partners in the kitchen. Participant observation confirms such a pattern. For instance, in two of the four female households observed in depth, both women spent the majority of time during meal preparation together in the kitchen. I do not mean to imply that they share every task or divide meal preparation equally. Frequently, they engage in conversation and one person assists by getting things out the refrigerator, chopping celery, or pulling something out of the oven. Mostly, one person prepares and manages the meal while the other helps. The question remains, Why do men who did not prepare a meal claim to have done so, and why do women report that their partners who assisted actually prepared the meal?

The answer looks different for female and male households. In some lesbian couples the partner who performs much of the feeding work seems to also concern herself with preventing threats to the gender identity of her less domestically involved partner. This pattern seems most persistent among lesbian couples where one of the partners pursues a higher-paying, higher-status occupation. Consider the following examples. Cindy Pence and Ruth Cohen have been together for eleven years. Cindy works as a nurse, and she does much of the feeding work in the family. Ruth works as a healthcare executive. Ruth works extensive hours, and it often spills over into their family life, something Cindy dislikes. Ruth acknowledges that Cindy does much of the domestic work in their relationship, including the feeding work. Ruth says that she tries to help out when she can, and she tries to get home to help with dinner. They each claim that the other person cooked the last meal at home. During my interview with Ruth I asked about work and family conflicts, and how work might impinge on family life. Ruth comments:

RUTH: Cindy's great about my work. She does so much. I don't think I could handle it all without her. She sort of covers for me, I guess and I feel guilty about it, but I also know that she appreciates how hard I work for us.
CC: What do you mean, she covers up for you?
RUTH: I mean, she gives me credit for doing a lot of stuff at home that I don't really do. I mean, I help her, but it's not really my show. She does it and I really appreciate it. But I feel terrible about it.

The same kind of feelings emerged in an interview with Dolores Bettenson and Arlene Wentworth. Both women work as attorneys for public entities, though Dolores's job requires less overtime and allows for a more flexible schedule. Dolores reports working for wages forty hours per week, while Arlene reports working for wages around sixty hours per week, including frequent trips to the office on Saturdays and on Sunday evenings. Dolores handles much of the feeding work of the family, while the couple pays a housekeeper to do much of the house cleaning. Both Dolores and Arlene initially report that they split responsibility for cooking. Arlene, in response to a question about conflicts over meal preparation, says:

> I think things are pretty fifty-fifty, we are pretty equal. I guess she does things more thoroughly than I do, and she complains about that, but she always gives me a lot of credit for the stuff I do. Sometimes, I think she gives me too much credit, though, and I feel guilty about it, because, as I said, she takes that kind of stuff more seriously than I do, I just don't have as much time.

Both Ruth's and Arlene's comments reveal a pattern of the more domestically involved partner assigning credit for completing domestic work that the less domestically involved partner did not do. I suspect that this occurs in part to provide "cover" for women who spend less time doing domestic work, less time "doing gender."

In a similar vein, the pattern among gay males appears the opposite, and more intensely so, in some respects. Engaging in routine feeding work violates gendered expectations for men. I emphasize routine because men can and do participate in ceremonial public cooking such as the family barbecue. Yet the reality of household life requires that someone do feeding work. In heterosexual family life, men are usually capable of avoiding feeding work, but in gay-male families, someone must feed. Only in a very few, quite affluent households did feeding work seem particularly diminished and replaced by eating most meals in the marketplace. Most gay-male couples eat at home, and among many of them I detect a pattern of men colluding to protect the masculine status of the meal planner/preparer. The conflicted claims of who last prepared an evening meal illustrate this dynamic and also reveal the ambiguous feelings held by men who feed about their status and their work. Bill Fagan and Rich Chesebro have been together for three years. Rich works at a large software company and Bill works as an artist. Bill often works at home and carries much of the responsibility for domestic work, including feeding work. Both men claim that they last prepared the evening meal. Other questions in the interview reveal that, in fact, Bill prepared the last meal. When I

asked about the last time they invited people over for dinner, Bill replied that
it was two days before the interview, on Saturday night. When asking about
what he prepared, he responded: "Well, let me see, *last night I made lasagna.*
Oh, and that night, Saturday, I broiled tuna." It turns out that Bill made the
last meal, though Rich claims that he did. Why should Rich make such a
claim? Part of the answer lies in Rich's concern, expressed several times, that
Bill not become overly identified with domestic work. When asking Rich
about who last went to the grocery store, Rich replies: "I think that Bill might
have, but it's not that big of a deal really. He really likes his work as an artist
and that's where *his true interest lies*" (emphasis added). This response initially
confused me. I ask about a trip to the store, and I receive an answer emphasizing Bill's work as an artist. I let this response pass, but later in the interview, I ask Rich about who last invited someone over to dinner, and who typically does this. In a similar rhetorical move, Rich says: "Well, I suspect Bill
might be the one to do that, but I don't think it's that significant to him, really. *His real love* is his work as an artist, that's where he puts most of his energy" (emphasis added). At this point in the interview I decide to pursue
Rich's intent in moving us from matters of domesticity to Bill's status as an
artist. I ask Rich why he brought up Bill's work as an artist in the context of
who most likely invites people to dinner. "Well, because I worry that people
will get the wrong idea about Bill. I know that he does a lot of stuff around
here, but he really wants to become an artist, and I don't want people to think
of him as a housewife or something. He has other interests." As these comments disclose, Rich attempts here to manage the identity of his partner.
This interpretation receives further confirmation on the basis of Rich's answer to a question about how he would feel about his partner engaging in
homemaking full-time and working for wages only partly or not at all:

> Well, I wouldn't like it at all. I don't see how that could be fair, for one person to
> contribute everything and the other to give little or nothing to the relationship.
> Plus, what about one's self-respect? I don't see how one could live with oneself by
> not doing something for a living. I would not be comfortable at all telling people
> that Bill is just a housewife. If he wanted to do his artwork and do more of the
> housework, that would be okay, I guess, but that's kind of how we do it already.

While Rich attempts to shield Bill from identification with domestic work,
both in order to protect Bill from the status of "a housewife or something"
but also to confirm his own belief that domestic work holds little value, the

reality remains that Bill does much of the domestic work, including feeding work. Doing feeding work ties Bill to a more feminine identity. Bill put it like this in response to a question about whether the roles of heterosexual society influence the character of his relationship with Rich:

> I think that the functions all need to be handled. There is a certain amount of mothering that is required and whether that is done by a man or a woman does not matter. But mothering per se is an important function. And there is a certain amount of fathering having to do with setting goals and directions and creating focus. I guess people do think of me as more of the mother in our relationship, because I cook and invest a lot in our home, but that's their problem. Sometimes I feel strange about it, but I like to do it and I like the family life that we have together.

Bill's words capture the ambiguity of feelings about feeding work and other domestic work that I heard frequently in many lesbigay households. On the one hand, Bill recognizes the importance of such work (mothering) to creating a family life. On the other hand, he feels strange about his participation in domestic work. His partner worries about people identifying Bill with domestic work and emphasizes Bill's identity as artist.

Another gay-male household illustrates a similar set of dynamics. Nolan Ruether and Joe Mosse have been together just under two decades. They live in an affluent suburban community outside the city. They both work in healthcare, though in very different settings and with quite different responsibilities. Nolan is a registered nurse and reports working forty hours per week. Joe works in a medical research lab and reports working closer to fifty hours per week. He also has a part-time job on the weekends. Nolan handles much of the domestic life of the family, including much of the feeding work. Both partners claim that they last cooked an evening meal. They actually eat separately more often than not, with Nolan eating a meal at home in the early evening that he cooks for himself and Joe either eating something on the run or eating something late when he arrives home. Joe indicates that he does the major shopping on weekends, though Nolan makes frequent trips to the market during the week and says that "I often pick up things that will be easy for him to prepare when he gets home from work, and I frequently will make something that he can simply warm up when he gets in." Nolan actually cooked the last meal, while Joe warmed up the meal when he arrived home late. Throughout the interview Joe emphasizes the egalitarian character of their relationship and diminishes the amount and significance of domestic work in the household. When I ask about conflicts over meals or meal preparation, Joe responds, "Um, well, we hardly ever eat meals at all. There is no work to conflict about. I eat out and he tends after his own." Nolan reports that they eat at home half the week, while they go out the other half. Nolan reports that they do not plan meals, though he says that they do communicate on the subject: "We don't plan meals, really. We either are both at home and I ask him what he wants or I call him at work and then I just go to the store and buy it. We don't keep a lot of food here, because I tend to run out to the store most every day." Nolan does much of the feeding work. He engages in routine provisioning work for the family, and he plans many of the family's social occasions that involve food. He also does most of the emotional labor related to food. Now consider Nolan's responses to questions about his feelings toward traditional gender roles for men and women in American society:

> I certainly see the value in it, in ways I never did before I was in a relationship. There's a lot of work to be done to keep a house nice and to make life pleasant. I get pretty tired sometimes, I don't think Joe has any sense of it, really. He is off so much doing work, but he works so much by choice. You know, I think I said, we don't really need the money, but he couldn't imagine being around here doing this stuff.

Does he think that traditional gender roles influence the pattern of domestic life in your relationship?

> Well, in the sense that I do everything and he does very little, yes, I think it resembles the traditional pattern. He would of course deny it and get angry if I pushed the topic, so I don't bring it up, and I feel it's kind of difficult to talk to anyone about it because, well, because they might think of me as a complaining housewife or something, and I don't think most people can understand a man doing what I do. So when he says there isn't that much to do around here, I just sort of let him believe what he wants. It isn't worth the trouble.

Notice the ambiguity of feeling Nolan expresses about talking to others about his situation. Nolan's restraint (emotion work) actually enables Joe to diminish the importance of the work that Nolan does to maintain family life. Joe's approach to his household life closely resembles the pattern of need reduction detected by Hochschild (1989, 202) among some men in her study of heterosexual couples. Consider the following excerpts from our interview:

cc: Tell me about your feelings toward traditional roles for men and women in the family in American society.

joe: I think those roles have declined a lot. It's more diverse now. I am really glad that such roles have declined. I feel that there should be two people out earning incomes. I don't think that people should stay at home. I can't see the value in it. Everyone should have outside interests. And I especially don't think that a man should be stuck in the home, cooking and stuff like that. Nolan works full-time, and we mostly eat out.

cc: Do you feel like the prescriptions for such roles influence or shape your relationship? Why or why not?

joe: Definitely not. We are both men and we both work for a living, and so we don't really fit those images. We don't have much domestic work here, especially since I am not here that much.

cc: What would you think of your partner or yourself engaging in homemaking full-time and working for wages only partly or not at all?

joe: I would not be too pleased with it. There has to be a common goal that you both work toward. For one to contribute everything would not be fair. I don't make that much of a mess, and so I don't think that there would be anything for him to do.

Throughout this exchange Joe not only diminishes the presence of domestic work through emphasizing how often he is gone but also expresses his concern that his partner not become overly identified with domestic work. Nolan's own feelings of ambiguity about doing domestic work, and the threat it poses to his gender identity, actually keep him from talking about his circumstances.

One observes another example of the salience of gender to the portrayal of feeding work in dinner parties. Using Goffman's conceptions of "frontstage" and "backstage" work, sociologist Randall Collins suggests that cooking meals for dinner parties constitutes a frontstage activity that "generally culminates with the housewife calling the family or guests to the table and presiding there to receive compliments on the results of her stage (or rather table) setting" (1992, 220). The backstage work, much more arduous and time intensive, consists of a wide array of different kinds of invisible work: planning, provisioning, and monitoring. The work is often invisible in the sense that these forms of work receive little public recognition during dinner parties. In most lesbigay families the responsibility for both the elaborateness and the exoticness of foods for dinner parties becomes the responsibility of the meal planner/preparer, and often this person takes front stage at the dinner party.

However, in ten of the lesbigay households, and in contrast to the normative pattern in heterosexual families described by Collins, the person who cooks for dinner parties often only engages in the frontstage work while the other partner performs much of the backstage or more hidden forms of work. These ten households share a common pattern. In the male families the person who performs routine feeding work and performs the backstage work for dinner parties also work for wages in somewhat female-identified occupations: two nurses, a primary education teacher, a legal secretary, a social worker, and an administrative assistant. The frontstage males work in male-identified occupations: two accountants, an engineer, an attorney, a physician, and a midlevel manager. In the female families exhibiting a split between frontstage and backstage feeding, frontstage women work in male-identified occupations: two attorneys, a higher-level manager, and a college professor. The occupations of the backstage females include two retail sales workers, a nurse, and an artist. Taking the front stage in such dinner parties may well function as a strategy on the part of these lesbigay couples to manage threats to the gender identity of the domestically engaged men or the less domestically engaged women.

Confirming this pattern in the words of participants proves somewhat elusive. None of the women who do backstage feeding work for dinner parties expressed dissatisfaction about this. And while several of the men complain that they do not receive credit for the backstage work they do in preparation for such dinners, they also seem reluctant to make much of a fuss about it. Tim Cisneros, who works as a nurse and does much of the routine feeding work, responds to a question about who last prepared a meal for dinner guests, and why, by saying, "Well, I guess you would have to say he did. Though, I am the one who did most of the prep work for it. He gets a lot of pleasure out of cooking fancy stuff for others, and while I think I should get some credit, I don't make a big deal about it. I would feel kind of weird pointing it out, so I just let him take the credit. It's easier that way." Tim's observations convey his awareness of an inconsistency between frontstage and backstage, and his assertion of the ease of maintaining that inconsistency makes it plausible to think that there is little to gain, and there may even be a cost, in disclosing the inconsistency.

As evidenced by the above cases, gender operates as a continuous concern for lesbigay families, but in ways more complex than many accounts of lesbigay family life indicate. The gender strategies deployed by the different participants suggest an abiding concern about maintaining traditional gender categories, and particularly of avoiding the stigma that comes with either failing to engage in domestic work for lesbian families or through engaging in domestic work for gay-male families. The portrayal of feeding work by lesbigay households conforms to these gender-related concerns, and partners tend to manage the identity of their respective partners.

Feeding Work and the Production of Class Identity

Feeding work in lesbigay families both reflects and perpetuates social-class distinctions. Patterns of meal preparation and patterns of sociability forged through the sharing of meals across families reflect the presence of social-class distinctions among lesbigay families. These social-class distinctions seem quite apparent but, historically, sociologists have found it difficult to find such class differences among lesbigay people. Two decades ago, when sociologist Carol Warren conducted a study of gay life, she concluded:

> it is clear that members tend to think of themselves, no matter what the abstract criteria, as members of an elite class. . . . since an elegant upper-middle-class lifestyle is one of the status hallmarks of the gay community, it is quite difficult to tell, and especially in the context of secrecy, what socioeconomic status people actually have. (1974, 85)

The families in this study do not lead secret lives: only five of the 103 adults interviewed completely hid their identities from coworkers, and only six hid their identities from biological relatives. It seems that as the lesbigay community becomes more visible, so too do differences among lesbigay people become more visible. Gender and racial distinctions pervade lesbigay life. Social-class distinctions also pervade lesbigay life and patterns of feeding often reflect and reproduce such distinctions.

The organization, preparation, and hosting of dinner parties plays a significant role in the production of class distinctions among lesbians and gays.

Upper-middle-class lesbigay families report organizing and participating in dinner parties for friends and coworkers with much greater frequency than middle- and working/service-class families, except for some ethnically identified families, to whom I will return shortly. In terms of household income, the top 25 percent of families report either holding or attending a dinner party at least two times per month. In the bottom 25 percent, families rarely report any such occasion.

These meals function to reproduce social-class alliances and identities. For example, these meals become occasions for professionals to identify potential clients, learn of potential job opportunities, learn of new technologies, or stay abreast of organizational politics. During election cycles, these dinner parties among the affluent can take on political significance. Many lesbian and gay politicians in the city of San Francisco use such occasions as fundraisers. The lesbigay politician attends the gathering and the campaign charges between $50 and $500 per person. Among the wealthier participants living in San Francisco proper and earning household incomes of over $80,000, nearly every household reports either attending or hosting such a meal. These dinner parties provide access to power and influence on policy, and they play a crucial role in the political order of San Francisco lesbigay politics.

In a wider sense, dinner parties contribute to the creation of social-class identities. As DeVault comments on the function of hosting dinner parties, "it also has significance in the mobilization of these individuals as actors in their class: it brings together 'insiders' to a dominant class, and marks their common interests" (1991, 207). Given DeVault's observation, what does it mean to claim that these shared meals "mark their common interests"?

Beyond the more obvious career advantages and the sheer social enjoyment of such occasions, part of the answer lies in the symbolic meaning people attach to cuisine and the style in which hosts present it. Collins conceives of the symbolic meanings people attach to such occasions as an example of "household status presentation" (1992, 219). In other words, the choice of cuisine and the style of serving constructs social-class identity for the participants. Further, dinner parties function as occasions for the display and sharing of "cultural capital" (Bourdieu 1984). Bourdieu conceives of cultural capital as knowledge and familiarity with socially valued forms of music, art, literature, fashion, and cuisine, in other words, a sense of "class" or "good taste." Bourdieu distinguishes cultural capital from economic capital, therein arguing that some members of society may possess higher levels of cultural capital yet possess less wealth, and vice-versa. The household often functions as the site where cultural capital or good taste finds expression. Dinner parties often operate as a stage upon which the hosts display and call attention to various forms of cultural capital, including everything from works of art to home furnishings, from musical selections to displays of literature, from table settings to the food itself. The elaborate and the exotic quality of meals play a central role in the upper-middle-class lesbigay dinner party. The higher-status participants often speak of specializing in a particular cuisine. Joe Mosse speaks of his interest in Indian cuisine:

> We often have Indian food when guests come over. I started cooking Indian food as a hobby many years ago. We've collected lots of Indian cookbooks, and I do a lot of different dishes. People generally love it. It's unusual and people remember that. You can get Indian food when you go out, especially in San Francisco, but how many people actually serve it at home?

Such dinner parties become elaborate both through the featuring of exotic menus and through the serving of a succession of courses throughout the meal: appetizers, soups, salads, main courses, coffee and tea, desserts, and after-dinner drinks. These dinner parties often feature higher-quality wines, and the higher-status participants often know something about the wine; this becomes part of the conversation of the evening. In sum, the dinner party serves as an opportunity for the creation and maintenance of class distinction.

Class differences impact the character and extent of everyday meals as well. More affluent families spend less time in preparing meals for everyday consumption than do the less affluent. A number of factors contribute to this. First, the more affluent eat out quite frequently. One in five lesbigay families report eating four or more meals per week in restaurants. Those who eat out more often earn higher incomes. Second, the more affluent use labor-saving devices like microwaves and food processors more frequently. Third, they often purchase prepared meals from upscale delis and fresh pasta shops. All of this purchasing feeding work in the marketplace enables more affluent couples to achieve a greater degree of egalitarianism in their relationships. These couples resemble the dual-career heterosexual couples studied by Hertz (1986). To the outside observer, and to the participants, affluent lesbigay families are more egalitarian in terms of feeding work, and they purchase that equality in the marketplace. As Hertz so eloquently argues:

> On the surface, dual-career couples appear to be able to operate as a self-sufficient nuclear family. Nonetheless, they are dependent as a group and as individuals on a category of people external to the family. Couples view their ability to purchase this service as another indication of their self-sufficiency (or "making it"). Yet, appearances are deceptive. . . . What appears to be self-sufficiency for one category of workers relies on the existence of a category of less advantaged workers.

Accordingly, scanning the lesbian and particularly the gay-male enclaves of San Francisco one discovers a preponderance of food service establishments offering relatively cheap and convenient meals: taquerias, Thai restaurants, pasta shops, hamburger joints, Chinese restaurants, and delis. Most of these establishments employ women, ethnic and racial minorities, and less educated, less affluent gay men. The low wages earned by these workers enables more affluent lesbigay families to purchase meals in the marketplace and to avoid conflicts over feeding work. Many affluent lesbigay families report deciding to simply eat out rather than face the hassle of planning, preparing, and cleaning up after meals. Less affluent families may not make that choice, and thus they spend much more time and effort in the production of routine meals.

Feeding Work and the Production of Ethnic Identity

While one's social-class status influences whether one attends dinner parties with much frequency, those families with strong ethnic identifications do report more shared meals. Among these groups the sharing of food, and the ethnic character of that food, becomes an important expression of ethnic heritage and cultural identity. Gary Hosokawa, an Asian-American of Hawaiian descent, speaks of the centrality of his *hula* group to his social life and understands that group in familial terms. In response to a question about how he thinks about family, Gary replies:

> Its really strange, hard to explain. In Hawaiian culture, your *hula* group is family. In ancient times, the *hula* teacher would choose students to become *hula* dancers and they would live together and become family. They ate together, slept together. They were picked from their own family groups and became a part of another fam-

ily group. My *hula* group is my family, we eat together, we dance together. It is a very deep, spiritual thing for me.

For Gary, the sharing of meals functions to create and sustain ethnic identity.

In like manner, Michael Herrera and Federico Monterosa, a Latino couple together for three years who live with a young lesbian woman, Jenny Dumont, consider themselves a family. They also speak of a larger family, consisting of other Latino and non-Latino friends, as well as Federico's cousins. Michael and Federico report recurrent dinner and brunch gatherings, often featuring Mexican foods. Michael remarks:

> We like to make enchiladas a lot, and sometimes we have meat, like beef or something, but always with a Mexican soup for our family gatherings. We get together every couple of weeks. It's very important to me. It's one thing that I think a lot of my Anglo friends feel really envious about, we sort of have a family and many of them don't.

When comparing the appeal of ethnically identified foods to the upper strata of the lesbigay community (mostly Euro-Americans) with the appeal of such foods to the Asian and Latino participants it becomes clear that the food symbolizes very different things for each group. For the affluent lesbigay families the food represents creativity and contributes to the entertaining atmosphere of the dinner party. It carries status due to its exoticness and the difficulty of its preparation.

In contrast, among Asian and Latino lesbigay participants, food expresses ethnic heritage and symbolizes ethnic solidarity, and sometimes resistance to cultural assimilation. Many Asian and Latino participants pride themselves not on the variety of cuisine but on the consistent replication of the same cuisine and even the same meals.

Feeding Work and the Production of Family

Feeding work plays a pivotal role in the construction of lesbigay families. The comments of meal planners/preparers suggest a conscious effort to create a sense of family through their feeding work. For instance, Kathy Atwood and Joan Kelsey, a lesbian couple in their midthirties and living in a sort of lesbian enclave in the Oakland neighborhood of Rockridge, both speak of sharing meals as constitutive of family. Kathy, talking about why she consid-

ers some of her close friends as family, says, "Well, we eat with them and talk
to them frequently. I have known one of them for a very long time. They are
people we could turn to in need. They are people who invite us over for dinner and people with whom we spend our fun times and because of that, I
think of them as family."

Other participants point to sharing meals, as well as jointly preparing the
meals, as evidence of family. Fanny Gomez and Melinda Rodriguez have
been together for nine years. Fanny does much of the feeding work for the
family. Fanny tells of how she and a close friend, Jenny, whom she considers
a part of the family, actually get together to prepare meals for holidays and
birthdays:

> I certainly think of Jenny as family. She is the partner of the couple friend that I
> mentioned earlier. She and I get together to plan meals and celebrations. It feels
> like family to me when we talk, go shop together, and then cook the meals. I mean,
> it's like family when we eat the meal together, too, its just that preparing the meal,
> I guess, it reminds me of working with my mother in her kitchen.

For Fanny, the planning, provisioning, and preparation of the meal constitutes family. The feeding work of Fanny and Kathy links material and interpersonal needs together and results in the creation of family.

We have seen that feeding work within lesbigay families is neither incon-
sequential nor simple. Strangely, much conversation and academic analysis
concerning feeding work reduces the complexity of the enterprise, mini-
mizes its significance, and legitimates the view held by many participants that
they don't really do very much feeding work—a view held by those who do
it as well as by those who don't. In part we can explain this sentiment by remembering that those who feed often lack the vocabulary to articulate their
efforts to others. Few people will tell others that they spent part of their day
monitoring the contents of their refrigerator, but they do. Such work remains invisible. We must also understand that many participants diminish
feeding because they don't want to face the conflict that a thorough accounting, as I have just provided, might produce in their relationship. Moreover, given the potential for stigma that exists for the men who feed, and the
women who don't, it becomes even clearer why the work of feeding remains
particularly hidden in lesbigay households.

Finally, concealing the labors of feeding reflects the cultural tendency to
romanticize domestic activities as well as to romanticize the relationships

such activities create. Spotlighting the labor involved tarnishes the romantic luster that people attach to domesticity. I can't count how many times I have heard people who feed respond to compliments by saying, "Oh, it was nothing, really." Perhaps this is just a matter of self-deprecation, but it might also suggest a cultural cover-up of the laborious character of such efforts. The dinner guests don't really want to hear about the three different stores one went to in search of the ingredients, nor the process of planning and preparing the meal, nor the fight one had with one's spouse about whom to invite or what to serve. A thorough investigation of the labors involved in feeding the family reveals that feeding is work. Recognizing feeding as work raises the impertinent question of why the effort often goes uncompensated, a question that leads directly to issues of exploitation and inequality, issues ripe with the potential for social and family conflict.

Given the social precariousness of lesbian and gay relationships, mostly due to the lack of social, political, and economic resources, the tendency of the participants to avoid such conflicts is probably essential to their long-term survival. When some resources exist, as in the case of economic resources, assuaging such conflicts becomes easier. When ample economic resources exist, feeding becomes less arduous with affluent families turning to the marketplace for meals and preparing meals at home teeming with creativity, quality, symbolic meaning, and nutritional content. When lesbigay families lack economic resources, as is the case among many of the working/service-class families, feeding looks different: routine, fatiguing, nutritionally compromised, and symbolically arid (in the sense that the capacity of feeding to produce a sense of family is compromised). Participants rarely conceive of eating ramen noodle soup on the couch as constitutive of their claim to family status, but they frequently conceive of eating a nutritionally complete meal at a dining-room table as constitutive of such a claim.

housework in lesbigay families

The content and intent of housework seem obvious to many people. Yet as the following excerpt compiled by Abby Diaz in the late nineteenth century reveals, the character of housework is contingent upon a multitude of historical and social factors:

Setting tables; cleaning them off; keeping lamps or gas fixtures in order; polishing stoves, knives, silverware, tinware, faucets, knobs, etc.; wiping and washing dishes; taking care of food left at meals; sweeping including the grand Friday sweep, the limited daily sweep, and the oft-recurring dustpan sweep; cleaning paint; washing looking glasses, windows, window-curtains; canning and preserving fruit; making sauces and jellies, and catsups and pickles; making and baking bread, cake, pies, puddings; cooking meats and vegetables; keeping in nice order beds, bedding, and bed chambers; arranging furniture, dusting, and "picking up;" setting forth, at their due times and in due order, the three meals, washing the clothes; ironing, including doing up shirts and

other "starched things;" taking care of the baby, night and day; washing and dressing children, and regulating their behavior, and making or getting made, their
clothing, and seeing that the same is in good repair, in good taste, spotless from
dirt, and suited both to the weather and the occasion; doing for herself what her
personal needs require; "letting down" and "letting out" to suit the growing ones;
patching, darning, knitting, crocheting, braiding, quilting,—but let us remember
the warning of old saying ["If you count the stars, you'll drop down dead"], and
forebear in time. (Diaz 1875, 13)

Few contemporaries make much jelly or polish looking glasses. And even the
activities identified by Abby Diaz that we continue to do, like setting tables,
sweeping floors, and washing clothes, have changed significantly over time.
Further, the intentions of those who perform housework, the meanings people attach to such work, and the standards people use to judge housework reflect the influence of a multitude of diverse economic, historical, and sociological factors. Recognizing this historical and social diversity does not mean
that researchers cannot identify common patterns or common factors influencing the extent and content of housework in different households, though
it obviously complicates the task. In the lesbigay households in this study, the
extent, the character, and the intentions of housework reflect the influence
of a variety of sociological factors, including class, occupation, and length of
relationship. In order to demonstrate these influences, I've organized this
chapter around several concerns. I explore the meanings lesbigay families attach to housework and the significance of housework to the social construction of lesbigay family life. First, I address housework in lesbigay families
through exploring the character of housework, the management of housework, and the *envisionment* of housework. Second, I chronicle the variations
in housework among different kinds of lesbigay families by emphasizing the
importance of contextual factors like social class, occupation, children, and
the longevity of relationships. Finally, in this chapter, I do not pursue factors
affecting the division of housework (see chapter 5), though just as the analysis of feeding work suggests that a less than egalitarian division prevails in
many lesbigay homes, so too do I allude in this chapter to similar patterns for
housework. Further, one should not assume that all of the housework that I
identify in these households is done by one of the primary participants in the
household. Often times, especially among the prosperous, cleaning services
and cleaning persons do some or most of this work—a phenomenon I explore in greater depth in chapter 5.

The Character of Housework

From an empirical point of view, a wide range of activities fall under the rubric of housework. Housework can include everything from paying a bill, to polishing furniture, to mowing a lawn, to waxing a kitchen floor, to remembering when to put recyclables out for collection. Despite popular conceptions otherwise, housework remains fundamental to the reproduction of our society and to the subsistence needs of families and most individuals. While the development of industrial capitalism clearly facilitated a division between paid labor in the workplace and unpaid labor in the household, many of the activities enabling subsistence and exchange continue to take place in the household, although without the benefit of wages or compensation. And despite the perception that capitalism increasingly commodifies housework, therein turning it into paid labor, sociologists and social historians point out that the amount of unpaid housework that individuals, mostly women, perform remains constant (Tilly and Scott 1978; Vanek 1983; Cowan 1983). Cowan (1987) argues that even though the introduction of new technologies in the twentieth century reduces the arduousness of housework, the number of tasks and the need to plan and coordinate the completion of them continues to expand. Some recent research even suggests an increase in the amount of unpaid work, mostly done by women, taking place in the private sphere (Glazer 1993). Berk's (1985) metaphor of a household as a factory appropriately captures the repetitive and pervasive process of production that continues in most American households.

While housework remains essential to the smooth functioning of households, and of the broader society, the status of housework remains mostly abject. Certainly, people express admiration for a clean and well-ordered home. Most seem to understand that homes without housework are impossible. Yet conceiving of housework as worthy of paid compensation remains outside the parameters of popular debate. Many scholars argue that this widely felt objection to wages for housework reflects the influence of concurrent efforts to romanticize the work as a "labor of love" and to reap the benefits of unpaid and low-paid work (Gimenez 1990; Romero 1992). In recent decades, many thinkers have suggested a link exists between gender inequality and the unpaid labor of women in the household (Oakley 1974; Hartmann 1981; Glazer 1987). These thinkers make the case that the devaluation of housework behooves men in their collective efforts to sustain both a patriarchal

and/or a capitalistic social structure (Hartmann 1976). Men reap the benefits of the labor of women, women who toil behind the scenes for little or no
compensation, yet who perform tasks essential to the reproduction of the social order of contemporary capitalist societies.

Other thinkers point to other dynamics in the devaluation of housework.
Collins (1992), contesting the essentialness of domestic labor, makes the
case that a significant proportion of it appears as "surplus" in character, and
therein makes a significant contribution to the creation of social-status distinctions, distinctions that would apparently be undermined by the payment
of wages. Hochschild (1989, 247) identifies an effort to preserve a domestic
tradition that preceded the logic of industrial and consumer capitalism with
its attendant notions of wage labor and market determination of the value of
work, including domestic work. In this case, opposition to wages for housework constitutes an effort to preserve a less rationalized and economistic way
of life. While this may explain part of why people oppose compensation for
housework, the fact remains that many people in this society consider housework unworthy and of little value, including many who perform it. The
widespread conception of the woman who invests significant energies into
domestic labors, and fails to work for wages, as "just a housewife" (Matthews
1987) points to a persistent devaluation of domestic labor. This devaluation
of housework permeates the lesbian and gay families in this study, with a few
notable exceptions. Only rarely could lesbigay family members conceive of
housework as worthy of compensation or of equal value to paid labor.

In sum, despite some countervailing tendencies, housework garners little
status even if it might contribute much to the creation of social status as
Collins (1992) asserts. Thus, when thinking about housework within lesbigay families, one must maintain an awareness of the essential character of the
work for a smoothly functioning household, the widespread devaluation of
the work, and the importance of this kind of work to the creation and sustenance of social-status distinctions, as well as, the creation of a sense of home
and family. But what exactly is housework?

In recent years sociologists of family life have attempted to delineate different forms of domestic labor, introducing new typologies and concepts for
understanding the character and content of domestic work. In this research
I utilize some of these emergent concepts, concepts like DeVault's feeding
work (1991), Di Leonardo's kin work (1987), and Weinbaum and Bridges's
consumption work (1976). Using these typologies, housework refers to a

more tightly defined set of activities than its conventional usage implies. For our purposes, housework excludes meal preparation (feeding work) and maintenance of family/friendship networks (kin work). It also excludes the work of consuming products including the extensive work of soliciting, evaluating, and purchasing consumer goods and services for the household (consumption and/or status work). I will characterize housework as broadly referring to a process of caring for the physical maintenance of the household. Housework includes both the performance and the management of such maintenance, as well as the process of defining tasks as necessary and devising standards for the accomplishment of them. More narrowly, and partially reflecting the influence of Berk's (1985) typology on my research design, I define housework to consist of cleaning house, caring for clothing and linen, caring for pets and plants, household paperwork and financial work, interactions with nonkin, house repairs and maintenance, and household maintenance-related trips. Let me now turn to a more thorough accounting of each of these manifestations of housework. Many readers will find this accounting somewhat boorish and self-evident, but attention to such details fills the minds of many people in their everyday lives, particularly women, and the appraisal of such activities as dull and boorish contributes to effectively making such efforts invisible.

Cleaning House

A wide range of activities falls under the rubric of cleaning house. For this study I conceptualize cleaning house as including: vacuuming, sweeping, scrubbing, mopping and waxing floors; cleaning stove tops, ovens, refrigerators, microwaves, coffee pots, food processors, and other small appliances; cleaning kitchen sinks, cabinets, and counters; washing and drying dishes by hand, loading and unloading dishwashers; setting, clearing, and wiping tables; dusting, cleaning, and polishing furniture; cleaning windows, mirrors, and window coverings; straightening and arranging furniture, books, magazines, newspapers, and toys; dusting and cleaning walls, baseboards, and ceilings; cleaning bathroom sinks, tubs, showers, and toilets; changing linens and making beds; cleaning and organizing closets, cupboards, storage spaces, and garages; emptying garbage and taking it out for collection; separating recyclables and taking them out for collection; cleaning garbage cans and recycling bins; and cleaning out fireplaces. You may think of others.

All of these activities take different amounts of time and occur at different intervals depending upon a number of factors, including: the time and energy requirements of family member's employment; the size and layout of the residence; the location of the residence; the extent of its furnishings; the climatic conditions; the age of the housing; the number of residents and guests; and the standards of cleanliness and orderliness. Larger homes with more furnishings, in most cases, necessitate more housecleaning. Households with larger numbers of guests necessitate more housecleaning. Households with children necessitate more housecleaning. The availability of time, or of material resources, permits more housecleaning to happen. I discuss the most salient factors influencing the character and the extent of cleaning house in an upcoming section addressing the variations in housework among lesbigay families.

Caring for Clothing and Linen

Similar to housecleaning, caring for clothing and linen entails both task and time dimensions, although the range of activities is somewhat narrower. The care of clothing includes sorting, washing, drying, folding, and putting items away. Often it includes gathering up scattered clothing from bedrooms, baths, and living rooms, and making decisions about whether such items need laundering or simply to be put away. Caring for clothing resides upon a foundation of knowledge about the care of fabrics and colors, knowledge often less ubiquitous than many think. Knowledge about the removal of stains from certain fabrics or strategies for reducing shrinkage or preventing wrinkles takes time and energy to acquire and frames part of the process of caring for clothing and linen. Forty-two of the lesbigay households have a washer and dryer, either in their residence or in their building or complex. Eight lesbigay families take clothing and linen to a laundromat. For some mostly prosperous families, laundry involves constant trips to shops to pick up laundered shirts and dry-clean-only items, while for other less prosperous ones laundry includes a hefty load of shirts and pants to iron. The care of linen includes the laundering, folding, ironing, arranging, and changing of bed linens, bath and kitchen towels, and table linen, including tablecloths, napkins, placemats, and liners. The care of clothing and linen also includes efforts to repair and alter items, either through sewing at home or taking items for tailoring.

Caring for Pets and Plants

Multiple housework activities revolve around the care of pets and plants. Most animals require feeding more than once a day. In this study exactly half of the households own pets: five with dogs, four with dogs and cats, fourteen with cats, four with birds, and four with fish. Dogs, in an urban environment, appear to be the most labor intensive, with a constant cycle of feeding, walking, and bathing. Most of these animals require occasional visits to veterinarians in the case of sickness and/or to receive vaccinations. Pets enjoin someone to arrange for others to care for the animals when the family goes away over the weekend or for a vacation. Pets oblige cleanup of feces in backyards and on sidewalks, in cat litter boxes, bird cages, and fish tanks. Pets entail significant amounts of additional housecleaning. Many lesbigay families with pets speak of the need to vacuum or clean floors or clean furnishings due to the mess the animals make. Despite all of this work, or more likely, because of it, families with pets harbor a much stronger sense of family. In part they conceive of the animals as family members, yet in another sense they think of families as consisting of certain characteristics, including the owning of pets. Several respondents thought of the introduction of pets into their household life as a move toward stability and family. Jessica Thyme, a twenty-nine-year-old lesbian woman who has been with her partner for four years, remarks:

> I remember when we first got Lance [a golden retriever] that it seemed like so much work. I didn't really expect that much. But it really helped make us into a family. I mean spending all that time training him and playing with him. We fought a lot about some of it, like taking him for walks, but it did bring us together closer, and it made me feel more like a real family. I mean we didn't have kids, maybe someday we will, but it was almost like that.

Akin to the care of pets, the care of plants consumes the time and energy of many families. In this study, twenty of the fifty-two households include gardens and lawns. This contrasts with other major studies of domestic labor in heterosexual households where a much larger proportion of households come with lawns and gardens (Berk 1985; Hiller and Philliber 1986). Gardening entails all of the obvious forms of labor, like planting, weeding, watering, cutting, and feeding, as well as the more hidden work of planning, envisioning, scheduling, monitoring, and learning about the garden. Some will object to the conception of these activities as work, for such critics gardening is about leisure and hobbies. Yet, as many studies of heterosexual households indicate, heterosexual men consider caring for yards and gardens one of their primary contributions to domestic labor. Further, and in ways quite similar to the presence of pets in the household, the care of gardens and lawns both symbolizes—and, I argue, composes—family with those lesbigay households with gardens and lawns possessing a more developed sense of their relationships as family.

Household Paperwork and Financial Work

Like clockwork, the mail arrives in most American homes each day. Someone gathers that mail, sorts it, opens it, sorts it again, and directs items to the appropriate place. On occasion, those appropriate places require another sorting. Time after time, someone in the lesbigay family speaks of "going through the piles" of "stuff" that accumulates on counters and in drawers and baskets. Not particularly exciting, perhaps, but the routine gathering, sorting, and organizing of information constitutes an often inconspicuous activity that recurs with great frequency in many households. The advent of e-mail complicates and amplifies this process, adding an additional source of information requiring monitoring, sorting, and organizing. In addition to the management of mail, routine paperwork includes directing and organizing information pertaining to insurance, taxation, pet care, medical and dental care, investments, frequent-flier programs, music and book clubs, and civic, voluntary, political, arts, and religious organizations. The financial work of households includes paying the bills; managing and servicing checking, savings, and investment accounts; and creating and updating budgets, whether formal or informal. Financial work often includes planning for future expenditures (for example, home, auto, and furniture purchases) or coping with unexpected expenditures (auto repair, medical costs, house and appliance repair).

Interactions with Nonkin

Many individuals come to or into the homes of Americans to deliver or render a wide variety of services. In the week preceding the interview, lesbigay family members report visits from the following delivery or service workers:

ten housecleaning workers; five garden workers; four food delivery people; four United Parcel Service delivery people; four meter readers from the gas/electric company; three phone company workers; two carpet cleaning workers; two appliance repair personnel; two furniture delivery workers; two childcare workers; one auto insurance appraiser; one clarinet teacher; one dog walker; and one real estate appraiser. The interaction with such individuals entails the effort to contact them, to arrange for the visit, to meet the service providers at the house, and to communicate household needs and concerns to them. For many families, someone must take time off or away from paid work in order to let these people into the house. For instance, the service visits by phone company workers require someone to stay at home for a four-hour period of time, say, from 9:00 a.m. to 1:00 p.m. Sterling Graves, a thirty-four-year-old social worker, comments on arranging for the phone company to run a new line to his home computer: "It was sort of a hassle. I usually have clients in the morning and I had to reschedule them in order to be here to meet the phone company. They won't come on weekends, and Wayne's work will not let him get away to do this kind of stuff." Many times, as in the case of housekeepers, gardeners, and childcare workers, no one needs to be home to greet these persons. However, quite frequently someone in the lesbigay household contacts these individuals before their visit, either by phone or by leaving a note, with instructions and comments for the service provider expressing concerns about particular cleaning, gardening, or childcare needs. Such efforts constitute domestic labor.

Household Repair

Often sporadic and residual in character, much of the work of household repair for lesbigay families becomes the responsibility of their landlords because most of these families rent their residences. Of the fifty-two families in the study, thirty-two rent. Most of the renting families do not face the sometimes arduous tasks of exterior painting or plumbing repair, two of the more widely reported tasks done by homeowning families. Among other examples of household repair families report: interior painting; floor refinishing; fixing broken appliances; remodeling projects; window replacement; and repair/replacement of phone lines. In many cases, household repair work consists not of the actual fixing of an item, but rather the effort to contact, meet, and gather estimates for the costs of the repair. For most renters, except those who live in large complexes, repair work often involves arranging to meet the repair people sent by landlords. For those families who live in large complexes, the security services of the apartment complex often accompany the repair personnel.

Household Maintenance-Related Trips

A significant portion of the day of American housewives over the latter part of the twentieth century revolves around the automobile. As Ruth Cowan writes in her book *More Work for Mother*, "the automobile had become, to the American housewife of the middle classes, what the cast iron stove in the kitchen would have been to her counterpart of 1850—the vehicle through which she did much of her significant work, and the work locale where she could most often be found" (1983, 85). In comparison to their heterosexual counterparts, lesbigay families seem to do a lot less driving to procure services. Obviously, a clear distinction exists between those lesbigay families who dwell in the suburbs versus those who live in the urban center. Overall, most lesbigay families live in the lesbigay "ghetto." I am using the traditional sociological conception of a ghetto, as put forward by Louis Wirth (1928), as an area of a city housing a segregated cultural community with the following attributes: a concentration of cultural institutions; a culture area; social isolation; and residential concentration. Clearly, the Castro in San Francisco constitutes such a ghetto with the presence of lesbigay institutions like temples, churches, theaters, cafés, and bars. A distinct culture area exists consisting of a relatively safe space for same-gender affection and desire (for example, many visitors to the Castro comment about the sheer pleasure of being able to hold their lover's and friend's hands in public). And despite the relative tolerance of the San Francisco Bay Area toward lesbian and gay people, social isolation persists with many lesbigay families experiencing homophobia and heterosexism, and therefore choosing to socialize with other lesbigay people and limiting contacts with heterosexuals (see the chapter on kin work for distinctions among lesbigay people concerning this). Finally, the 1990 census data suggests that residential concentration perseveres in San Francisco with over half of lesbigay households living in five neighborhoods (Western Addition, Upper Market, Noe Valley, Twin Peaks, and Mission), neighborhoods all adjacent to the Castro (*San Francisco Examiner*, 12 Sept. 1993, 10). The census data estimates that in Upper Market, one in every eight households is a lesbigay household. In comparison, consider the ratios in communities where some of the suburban lesbigay families in this study live: Mill Valley (1 in 66), Berkeley (1 in 90), Oakland (1 in 110), and Concord (1 in 185).

The sociological reality of the lesbigay ghetto transforms the character of household-related trips for its residents. Instead of driving to a dry cleaners, a shoe repair store, a photo shop, a pet food store, a daycare center, or a hardware store, residents of the ghetto walk to these services in the village near their homes. Driving in search of items and services for the households occurs, but at only a fraction of the rate the suburban lesbigay families report. In this dimension of housework, the ghetto diminishes the time and transforms the character of the work.

Managing and Envisioning Housework

In addition to the performance of tasks, housework also entails the management of tasks and of the time involved in the task. Many scholars researching the heterosexual division of domestic labor make a distinction between the actual doing of the work and holding responsibility for it (Oakley 1974; Berk and Berk 1978; Berk 1985; Coltrane 1989; Mederer 1993). This research posits that only occasionally do men hold responsibility for household tasks and that this usually occurs for labor that Fenstermaker-Berk refers to as "rigidly sex-typed," such as responsibility for mowing the lawn or taking out garbage (1985, 69–70). The research indicates that women think through, plan, and supervise the completion of most household labor. Even in dual-career heterosexual households, women retain the responsibility to arrange for both domestic workers and childcare providers (Hertz 1986).

The work of household management often remains unexplored in studies of domestic labor, particularly among studies of gay and lesbian families. Consider the following two studies. Harry, using a survey to study approximately fifteen hundred gay-male couples, asks several questions about domestic labor: "Who does the cooking in your household? Who does the shopping? Who does the necessary repairs around the house? Who keeps the books or manages the budget? Who does the housework?" (1984, 34–35). Respondents could reply using three categories: partner, shared equally, and neither. Kurdek's (1993) study of three hundred lesbian, gay, and heterosexual persons in couples compares the allocation of household labor among these groups and operationalizes the following typology of domestic work: (1) doing housework; (2) doing the cooking; (3) cleaning the bathroom; (4) doing laundry; (5) writing down items on a grocery list; and (6) buying groceries. For Kurdek's study, respondents use a five-point Likert scale where answering with zero represents that they do the task themselves and five represents their partner doing the task. The typologies that Harry and Kurdek utilize fail to capture the management dimension of housework. Harry picks up some management dimensions in terms of financial matters, but none in terms of housework. Kurdek's conceptualization picks up some of the more elusive work of feeding by asking about writing on a grocery list, but provides little in terms of household management. We need a stronger sense of housework management in lesbigay families with more focus on the work involved in planning, monitoring and supervising housework.

For instance, we need a clearer sense of who bears responsibility to see to it that various housework tasks get done. While partner A might well have last completed a load of laundry, did she do so only after constant cajoling, complaining, and supervision from partner B? Did partner B sort the laundry prior to washing on the basis of fabric or color to prevent partner A from damaging the clothing? Did partner A fold the laundry upon its completion of her own initiative? Did partner A fold the laundry only to fail to put it away until partner B asked her to do so? These questions need answers in order to move us closer to a more empirical understanding of the dynamics of housework. Such questions point to the complex yet often subtle and hidden dimensions of housework. Asking who does the laundry rigidifies and over-simplifies a heterogeneous and dynamic process of caring for clothing and conceals from view the social interaction between family members that surrounds the doing of any household task.

Further, who decides and by what criteria that now is the time to do a particular household task? Mostly hidden from view, the monitoring of housework constitutes a central component of household management. In general, monitoring consists of a spatial dimension, where one monitors the household for occurrences of uncleanness and unkemptness. The person engaged in monitoring recognizes the disorder and often strategizes a plan to deal with it. Monitoring also consists of a temporal dimension where one knows when a particular task last occurred and when it needs to occur again. For example, the changing of bed linens, in most cases, follows a temporal pattern (few families wait until the sheets become obviously dirty). It may heed a formal pattern where someone changes the linen weekly, perhaps on the same day and time. More often, among the families in this study the temporal dimension is less formal with one partner possessing an informal sense that the linen needs changing.

This informal sense reflects the presence of a mental calendar/clock at work in the mind of the one who monitors. Monitors often abide by a kind of hidden cadence of household activities. They know when the linens on the bed need changing, or the towels in the bathroom, or when the house plants need water or fertilizer, or the pets need new flea collars. Often times, one person in a lesbigay family functions as the monitor. Watching, smelling, feeling, listening, the monitor keeps mental tabs on the state of the house. The monitor often brings to the attention of other family members that something needs to be done. And while making family members aware of these needs might seem rather straightforward, in fact, monitoring often involves strategizing ways to bring these matters to attention and to achieve their completion. Hence, often times the monitoring process involves knowing the opportune moment to bring the subject up, and effective strategies to get participation and compliance from other family members. This can entail emotional labor (Hochschild 1983) for the monitor, given the need to interpret the behavior/disposition of family members to determine if now is the "appropriate" time to mention that the shower needs scrubbing or the garden needs weeding. For instance, I ask partners, "Do you feel like you need to prod your partner to help you with or to do household tasks?" In over half of the households, a clearly identifiable prodder emerges, with all family members recognizing this person as such. The comments of prodders reveal the presence of emotional labor. Ruth Cohen, in her current relationship with Cindy Pence for nearly a decade, comments:

> *Nag* is the word I use. I can be and have been a real nag. I have given it up. It doesn't seem to work. The housecleaners help. But I am much more crafty about it now. I have learned how to read Cindy for moods and I know when I can get her to do stuff and when I can't. It's sort of a subtle negotiation. I don't know if she realizes that I am scanning the moments waiting to ask her to clean out the fireplace or hose out the garage, but that's what I do. I sort get in tune with the rhythm of her life now and it seems to work.

Don Moorman, together with his partner, Gill Sumner, for just over two years, divulges his "annoyance" with doing this emotional labor:

Yes, I have to prod him; "bitch at him" is what he would say. I have found it difficult to figure out ways to bring up the condition of the house without creating too much of a fight. I sort of have learned that there are certain times to bring it up. I especially try to avoid bringing things up when he just gets home from work. I find he is more willing to help, or at least to hear it, later at night. Of course, he doesn't see any of this, it's annoying, nor does he recognize what an effort it is to get him to help.

Don and Ruth both do much of the work of monitoring housework. Their comments reveal that monitoring includes much more than observing the house, it also includes monitoring the emotional states of their respective partners.

In addition to monitoring the physical household and the emotional state of family members, many of the respondents who monitor housework also monitor the work/leisure schedules of family members. They try to weave housework tasks into the flow of work and leisure activities of the family. For instance, caring for clothes often reflects the presence of monitoring schedules. If the family plans to go away for the weekend, the regular routine of laundry work often changes with the monitor making the effort to speed up the laundry before departure or to catch up with the laundry when they return home. This work of scheduling becomes particularly apparent concerning larger housework activities like cleaning floors or windows, cleaning out storage closets, or cleaning ovens. Sarah Lynch, living in an East Bay suburb in a traditional ranch-style home, reveals the effort she makes to schedule larger housework projects:

> I have to think about Andrea's schedule in order to get the big things done, like washing the car or yard work. She works a lot of weekends and we like to try to go camping if we can. So, I try to plan the big chores around her schedule and around things like camping. [For example,] we needed to steam clean the carpets in the bedrooms. I called ahead to secure a steam cleaner machine, but before I did that, I needed to make sure that she was going to be around to help me. I wrote it down on the calendar so she wouldn't forget.

Sarah's remarks reveal one of the ever-present yet hidden components of housework, namely, the monitoring of work and leisure schedules.

Beyond the everyday monitoring of housework resides the more shadowy process of determining what tasks one must do and in accordance with what standards. Setting these standards entails a vision of what to do and how often to do it. In this sense, housework entails envisioning what the household should look like. Not surprisingly, every household constructs a different set of tasks and a different schedule for the repetition of tasks. For instance, with regard to task, some lesbigay households include ironing clothes as a dimension of housework while others never iron, either because they take the clothing to a laundry service, they possess few clothes requiring ironing or they simply don't iron their clothes. With regard to the frequency of tasks, some lesbigay households clean the kitchen floor weekly, others, monthly, and others even less frequently. Yet the question remains, from where do the standards emerge? Why do some homes clean the kitchen floor weekly and others once a month?

To begin with, in most lesbigay families, one person plays the part of arbitrator of standards, or, in other words, they envision the housework regime. I discuss why this specialization occurs in chapter 5. For the moment, let me say that the accounts lesbians and gay men provide to explain this specialization quite frequently consist of psychological accounts. These accounts often involve pop psychology notions like the "anal-compulsive personality," "obsessive personalities," or the "result of a dominant mother," Such popular notions notwithstanding, observing the everyday life of those who envision and manage housework suggests an omnipresent yet often unrecognized process of on-the-job training, in the sense of a trained eye for what a household should look and feel like.

The sources of this training are multitudinous, but observation of lesbigay households makes some of these sources fairly clear and suggests some sociological patterns at work. I consider this training, and the work it entails, hidden, or at least unrecognized, in the sense that many observers view the activities associated with learning about housework as leisure. Reading magazines or talking to family or watching television do not constitute work in popular conceptions of work in our society. Yet learning about housekeeping often occurs in these very settings. Magazines, newspapers, television shows, observing the domestic practices of lesbigay family and friends, and conversations with people about housework all function as the sources of learning about housework, as well as the authorities on the standards of housework. A particularly apparent example of these sources were the presence of popular magazines like *Martha Stewart's Living*, *Better Homes and Gardens*, *Architectural Digest*, *Metropolitan Home*, *House Beautiful*, and *Sunset Magazine* in many lesbigay households. In eighteen of the fifty-two households in this study, at least one of the aforementioned magazines appears in the living or eating area of the home. For the most part they appear in the homes of the more affluent middle- and upper-middle-class families. Most often, the person who manages and envisions housework reads these magazines, although many family members refer to these magazines to explain their vision of what their home should look like. This reliance on magazines coheres well with traditional sociological thinking suggesting that affluent families rely on professional sources of support to guide domestic life (Parsons and Bales 1955; Whyte 1956; Lopata 1971), in this case, the professional editors and writers of home magazines.

In addition to magazines, a number of individuals mention local newspapers as sources of information about housekeeping. Five respondents make direct reference to a weekly column in the *San Francisco Examiner* that answers questions from readers about household cleaning and repair. Six other respondents mention books about housekeeping that they had read. Two people, in separate households, brought forth a copy of a book entitled *Power Housekeeping*. This book contains strategies and ideas for organizing housework to make it efficient and inexpensive as well as helpful hints for dealing with things like stains on laundry or upholstery. Alongside the textual sources of standards and knowledge about housework dwells the television. Of course, television advertising provides a constant drumbeat of images of clean and orderly households, as does the content of television shows. Some shows furnish in-depth knowledge about housework and other domestic labor. Three gay men in this study mention watching *Martha Stewart Living* on Sunday mornings at 9:30 (they all knew the exact time) as a source of information about housekeeping.

Adjacent to textual and television sources, many people report that much of their learning about housework, and the standards they follow, come from observations of lesbigay family and friends. In instance after instance, people speak of seeing friends and neighbors clean or order things in a certain way, and they follow suit. Strikingly, very few respondents report relying on biolegal relatives for advice and information about housework. When it does, it happens most frequently among those individuals who grew up in the region and have biolegal relatives living nearby. In comparison, especially among those respondents who conceive of lesbigay friends as family, many people indicate reliance on lesbigay family for both advice and as a source of standards. In fact, in this respect, lesbigay families function in ways quite

similar to traditional extended families. Clyde Duesenberry and Mike Weltner, together as a family for just over ten years, both speak of the importance
of lesbigay family for doing housework. Asked where he turns for information about housework, Clyde comments:

> To our lesbian and gay friends. Recently, I wanted to know how to remove floor
> wax. You think I would know that after ten years. Well, we lived in mostly carpeted
> apartments for most of those years and our old kitchen had a brick floor. We
> moved here six months ago and the place has linoleum. I couldn't figure out why
> I couldn't get the dirt up and why the floor looked so dingy. Finally, I asked Beth,
> a lesbian friend of ours, and she says, "Did you remove the old wax?" Well, I didn't
> know we had old wax and I didn't know how to remove it. She explained that you
> needed ammonia to do it. I did it and it now looks great.

Mike, Clyde's partner, provides a similar answer: "I guess we turn to our
friends. Every once in a long while I will call my mother and ask her. But
mostly, I call Joie and Beth or Stan and they have the answer." Regarding
housework standards, Mike asserts: "I think we compare ourselves to our lesbian and gay friends. I am always envious of how nice Stan and Jeff's house
looks. It encourages me to help Clyde out more and to do things more nicely."

In sum, conceptions of housework in lesbigay households must incorpo-
rate the diffuse forms of activity comprising that work including the work of
monitoring, adjudicating, and envisioning housework, as well as the actual
performance and repetition of particular tasks. Let me now turn to some discussion of the particularities in household performance and the patterns of
housework that exist in different kinds of lesbigay households.

Variations in Housework among Lesbigay Households

The contours and features of housework vary from one lesbigay household
to the next, although common patterns of housework appear among those
sharing similar social-class positions, occupations, family sizes, and years in
the relationship. First and foremost, the contours and features of housework
vary by class with more affluent households engaging in more housework.
Second, occupational identities influence the extent and character of housework, most apparently when the worker uses the home as a stage for the entertainment of and/or the cultivation of clients. Third, and inexorably linked

to class and occupation, gay-male families do more housework than lesbian families do. Fourth, the number of people living in a household, whether families with children or multiple-adult households, increases the amount of housework. Here we will see the confluence of class and ethnicity, with a majority of Asian-American and disproportionate numbers of Latino-American and African-American lesbigay families living in multiple-adult households. Finally, longer-term families tend to do more housework than do more nascent relationships. Obviously, none of these factors operates in isolation from the others, and other factors come into play at times, but less consistently. For instance, in a number of cases, the degree to which one is out of the closet influences the frequency of visits from colleagues and clients to one's home. This impacts the character and extent of housework.

Housework and the Significance of Class

The character of housework varies significantly by social class among lesbigay families. More affluent households do more housework. They do so because they live in larger homes, they own more material items in need of care, they own more clothing and linen in need of care, they cook more elaborate meals in need of clean up, they own more pets (and messier ones), they tend to more gardens and yards (the more affluent the family, the larger these become), they confront a larger flow of household paperwork and manage more complex household finances. Their larger homes entail more repair and maintenance work, as do their greater number of vehicles. Finally, more people come to the homes of the affluent to consult, remodel, repair, deliver, visit, and stay over.

These distinctions prevail among lesbigay families in large part due to differences in socioeconomic conditions. For example, the living space available to the ten most affluent families in the sample is roughly twice that of the ten least affluent households (1850 vs. 900 square feet). The additional square footage usually results in larger rooms and an additional bedroom and a dining room. The most affluent one-third (seventeen households) of the sample have at least two bedrooms for two adults while among the least affluent one-third, only five have two bedrooms for two adults (many of these are multiadult households where couples actually share one bedroom). The larger size of affluent homes carries with it additional house-cleaning activities. Among the more obvious examples, the wealthier homes have more of the following items to clean, maintain, and organize: windows and window covers; floors, constructed of a greater variety of floor materials requiring different kinds of care (wood floors, carpets, tiles); additional bathrooms; larger kitchens with a greater variety of appliances (microwaves, food processors, bread machines); fireplaces; garages and storage spaces; yards and gardens; and furniture, constructed with a greater variety of materials (glass, wood, fabric), and in need of a greater variety of care (dry cleaning, steam cleaning, polishing, wood soap, and attention to climatic conditions).

In like manner, the affluent engage in more care of clothing and linen. They own more clothing and linen and own articles made of a greater variety of materials in need of special attention. The affluent families do laundry more frequently and wash more clothing. Some of the less affluent families use laundromats, and this entails the effort to get laundry to the facility, but they almost always do less laundry than those who do it in a private household, and they do it more quickly with multiple loads washing and drying simultaneously. This eliminates much of the work of monitoring the washer and dryer to see if the load is done and then to put in another load. Reports of weekly loads of laundry increase as one moves up the socioeconomic scale with the least affluent one-third of the sample reporting three loads per week and the most affluent one-third reporting five loads per week. My field research suggests that the estimates respondents provide often underreport laundry. In the eight households observed up close, an average of six loads of laundry are done each week. Most families report doing laundry on weekends, often conceiving of a particular day as "laundry day." Many respondents forget occasional washings that occur during the course of the week.

The difference in the volume of clothing in need of care between the less and the more affluent seems also to emerge from the fact that the affluent change their clothes more frequently. They tend to own specialized clothing for particular activities, like clothes for working out at health clubs and gyms. Among more than one-third of the gay-male families, one or more persons belong to a gym. This adds gym clothes, and often towels, to the quantity of laundry. Typically, the affluent change clothes after arriving home from work, only to put on another set of clothes to go out again in the evening. As an upcoming chapter on kin work will demonstrate, the affluent spend much more time out of the house at meetings, dinners, and recreational and cultural events. Participation in these activities increases the flow of laundry.

The care of pets and plants also varies substantially by socioeconomic sta-

tus among lesbigay families. The more pets in the household, the more affluent the household, and vice versa. Dogs appear disproportionately in the
homes of the affluent. Eight of the nine households with dogs report incomes above the median of the sample. This probably occurs mostly because
many of these families own their own homes, and the landlords of the less affluent will not allow dogs. Moreover, the initial expense to acquire a dog, the
time and expense required for training, and the expense of feeding seems to
play a role. In any case, the work of pet care proliferates among the more affluent.

In addition, housework revolving around yards and gardens expands as
one moves up the socioeconomic ladder. Twenty households care for gardens
and/or lawns (fourteen with gardens, six with both lawns and gardens). The
average annual household income for these twenty households is $105,000
while the median income for them is $98,000. Obviously, gardens and yards
come with wealth in the San Francisco Bay Area. Housework emerging from
the presence of gardens and lawns becomes quite substantial among the affluent. Respondents with gardens report watering it most every day. They
also report spending significant time and effort at weeding, cutting, planting,
and fertilizing plants and lawns, often on weekends.

Household paperwork and financial management also noticeably increases among the more affluent. More money means more money management. In the research I ask to see the household budget. In many prosperous
homes that means turning on the personal computer and opening up a file of
household finances. For the less affluent it meant opening up the checkbook
and counting transactions. Not every household was willing to share all of
this information, but nearly 90 percent of the sample did. The most reticent
respondents also report the highest incomes. Among the households sharing this information, a number of interesting distinctions emerge between
the more and less prosperous. First, the creation and maintenance of a
household budget appears much more frequently among the more well-
to-do households. Eighteen households use formal budgets to manage their
money, all but one of these households earn above the median household income of the sample. Second, while the affluent have more money, they also
have more bills and more transactions to manage. The number of Visa, Mas-
terCard, or American Express accounts; department store credit accounts;
gasoline charge accounts; Internet service provider and cable TV accounts;
and student loan, automobile loan, and mortgage accounts proliferate

among the more affluent households. A review of the financial transactions for the week prior to the interviews shows that the affluent households do all of the following more often: pay bills, make automated teller machine (ATM) withdrawals, and use debit cards. All of these forms of transaction need management. Many of these families report conflict over the failure of someone to record and/or save ATM and debit receipts. All of this financial activity requires additional management in the form of monitoring bills to make sure payments arrive on time, monitoring checking account balances to avoid overdrafts, and monitoring the flow of funds into accounts to ensure the availability of funds to pay bills.

Other forms of paperwork that increase among more affluent families include insurance and tax-related paperwork. Many of the less affluent, who tend to rent their residences, go without any form of property insurance, while more affluent homeowners often have such insurance. The more affluent renters often purchase renter's insurance. Such coverage entails more housework, with additional bills, and annual reviews of policies. The home-owning families face additional tax-related work, including forms for local property taxes as well as more complicated federal and state taxation forms.

To illustrate the preceding distinctions I will describe in great detail two particular lesbigay families who manifest dramatically different housework regimens and who reside at opposite ends of the socioeconomic range of families in this study. The two families I describe exemplify the housework distinctions between the affluent and the less affluent lesbigay households I became familiar with in this study. Virginia Kirbo and Clarice Pendleton live in an Oakland Hills neighborhood. Stunningly beautiful, Virginia and Clarice's contemporary home clings to the hillside near the top of a hill. From their living room, dining room, and deck one gets a panoramic view of the San Francisco Bay, the San Francisco skyline, the Golden Gate Bridge, and the Bay Bridge. Together for fourteen years, they bought the home in 1993 for $560,000. Clarice works as a vice president of human resources for a large California bank. Virginia works part-time as a consultant for software company. The software company grew expansively throughout the 1980s and early 1990s, and the family reaped a significant financial gain when the company's stock went public in 1991. They reported a household income of $145,000 for 1994. The home is quite modern, with floor-to-ceiling windows in the dining, living, and kitchen areas. The home decor reflects an Asian theme, including a placid Japanese garden off of the kitchen and dining area.

They bought extensive new furnishings when they moved into the house. Virginia comments, "We've spent a lot of time on the house over the past couple of years. I felt like I lived at Nigel's for a number of weeks. It was great to cut back at work in order to do all of this. It's been a dream for a long time." (Nigel's is a furniture store featuring rosewood furniture imported from Asia.) In terms of rooms, the main floor of the house consists of a large, contiguous living room/dining room/kitchen, as well as a study, laundry room, bath room, solarium, entry hallway, and the two-car garage. The living room includes a fireplace. Down one floor are two bedrooms, a bath, a storage area, and an outdoor patio. Up one floor is the master bedroom, a bath, a small sitting room, and a small deck. The floors in the kitchen, living, and dining area are hardwood, the bath and laundry are tiled, the study is carpeted, and the solarium is brick. The bedrooms on the lower floor are carpeted, and the storage and bath have tile. The master bedroom floor is hardwood, the sitting room is carpeted, and the bath is tiled.

Troy Diablo and Jeffrey Richards, together for three years, live in a large modern apartment complex developed in the mid-1980s in San Francisco's Western Addition neighborhood as part of a redevelopment effort. Parsimoniously furnished, the couple rents the one-bedroom apartment for $910 per month. The living/eating/kitchen area looks out unto another apartment building through either of two windows. Troy works as a sales associate for the Gap and Jeffrey works for a dance club tending bar, checking coats, and working the door. They reported a household income of $34,000 for 1994. Roughly one-sixth the size of the Kirbo-Pendleton house, the Diablo-Richards apartment consist of basically three rooms: a bath, a bedroom, and a contiguous living/eating/kitchen area. The walls of their apartment are white drywall, decorated with framed prints. The unit is carpeted throughout, except for the bath and in the galley kitchen, both of which have white floor tile. The kitchen includes a dishwasher. There is a shared laundry room on the floor. In terms of furnishings, the family has a queen-size bed and an old painted dresser in the bedroom. In the living/dining area they have a futon functioning as a couch, a TV and stereo placed on a wall unit constructed of oak, and a small oak kitchen table with three chairs.

Given these features, housework takes substantially different forms for the two households and the extent of that housework varies as well. The affluence of the Kirbo-Pendleton house both reduces certain forms of cleaning house and significantly increases other forms. In terms of reduction, their house contains a self-cleaning oven, a trash compactor, a dishwasher, and the home is constructed with modern materials (stain-resistant carpets and countertops, newly grouted tile), making housework less arduous. For the most part these things reduce the amount of time and energy one must invest in the work. The Diablo-Richards apartment comes with similar features, except they do not have a trash compactor, and they must take laundry down the hall.

In contrast, the affluence of the Kirbo-Pendleton household leads to additional and distinct forms of housework. The additional work consists of caring for a larger and more complex residence. Examples abound. The house requires more vacuuming of more carpeting on multiple levels, and the same holds true of mopping, sweeping, and waxing. The abundance of furnishings entails more dusting, cleaning, and polishing. The quality of the furniture encourages the same. Having three bathrooms involves more cleaning. All of these dimensions of cleaning house require additional monitoring and coordination of housecleaning for multiple spaces.

In terms of distinct forms of cleaning house, the process of cleaning up the kitchen after an evening looks quite different for each household. For instance, Virginia Kirbo cooks with an expensive line of cookware called Calphalon. One of the interesting attributes of Virginia's Calphalon is that you cannot put it in the dishwasher:

> We were very excited to be able to buy Calphalon. Sort of fancy-schmancy, I guess, but what the heck. So we bought it. We used to have some RevereWare stuff. I thought, Well, great, I love to cook and why not cook with the best, and for cooking, it's great. But now I have to wash the pots and pans by hand every night. It's not that big of a deal, but I usually let it soak and then come back and do it later. But the old Revere Ware, I just put that in the dishwasher and that was that.

Calphalon can make cooking more efficient (through quick and even distribution of heat), although its care requirements add more effort and time than are saved in the cooking process. Obviously, Calphalon functions as a status symbol ("fancy-schmancy"). It creates the aura of professional cooking in the home. The cleaning of Calphalon serves as a great example of how housecleaning can actually proliferate as one moves up the socioeconomic scale. Further, the Kirbo-Pendletons drink wine with dinner every few days. Every time they do so, Virginia must wash the crystal wine glasses by hand. For the Diablo-Richards, all of the glasses, dishes, pots, and pans go directly into the dishwasher.

In a similar vein, the Kirbo-Pendletons entertain guests quite a bit, and this facilitates more housecleaning. They invite someone over for dinner at least two times per month. These dinner gatherings involve additional cleaning in several forms. First, both Virginia and Clarice feel obligated to make sure the house is clean before guests come over. Virginia tells me that they usually leave the bed unmade, but if guests are coming, then they make it. And making the bed is certainly not the same in every household. For Virginia, making the bed consists of pulling up the sheets, fluffing the down comforter, arranging the pillows so that those with shams are in front, taking throw pillows from the chair and putting them on the bed, and using a lint brush to clean up hair left by the family cats on the comforter. She also mentions that they always make sure the bathrooms are clean and that the floors are vacuumed or spot-dusted. Second, and a distinct form of housecleaning among the more affluent, they often use different accoutrements for guests, like crystal wine glasses, china, table linen, and the fireplace. These items entail additional work. Both the crystal and china must be washed by hand. The table linen, including napkins, placemats, table cloths, and table liner require ironing and arranging prior to the arrival of guests. On cool and foggy nights, the family often lights a fire in the fireplace for such occasions. The family must clean out the fireplace every few months. In contrast, the Diablo-Richards household rarely entertain at home. They report inviting someone over for dinner just once over the previous six months. They don't own any china or table linen. They don't have a fireplace.

If the process of cleaning house looks so different for these two families, the distinctions among some of the other forms of housework are even more pronounced. The apartment complex that Jeff Richards and Troy Diablo live in does not allow pets. Clarice and Virginia own a dog and two cats. Their home includes a spectacular Japanese garden. For Clarice and Virginia the presence of pets and garden means an enormous expansion of activities to care for both. The animals require consistent feeding and walking. The animals entail additional housecleaning. They require additional management. For instance, Virginia speaks of trying to remember when the pets need to go for their annual shots. She also mentions the hassle incumbent with trying to make arrangements for the animals when the family goes away for the weekend. Undoubtedly, the pets make the family happier and they both conceive of the pets as members of the family.

Similarly, the Japanese garden at the Kirbo-Pendleton home is labor intensive. Virginia reports spending time watering, cutting, and weeding during the week, as well as joint efforts with Clarice on weekends. Clarice comments: "Two weekends ago, we had to clean the ponds out. We should've hired someone to do it. But Virginia got started on it early and asked me to come help. What a mess. We put fish into buckets. You're not supposed to have to do this, they say the pumps will keep the water clean, but it doesn't seem to work."

In addition to the obvious, and visible, forms of work necessary to maintain such a garden, a host of covert forms loom in the background. Virginia spends time reading books about Japanese gardens and reading the gardening section of the local paper. She visits nurseries seeking information about plants and pests. She monitors the garden for water, for soil problems, for pests. She keeps an informal calendar in her head about when she last sprayed a fungicide or fertilized particular plants. She arranges for professional help to come and service the garden. Similar to the pets that dwell in this family, the presence of a garden creates a sense of spatial permanence, a sense that enhances the perception of their relationship as family, both in their own eyes and in the eyes of others. Virginia, talking about what it's like to be a lesbian couple living in an affluent, predominantly heterosexual community, observes: "I think our neighbors are quite cool about us. *We are just like all the other families, maintaining our yard and building.* Everyone is quite pleasant with us" (emphasis added). While one might hastily conclude that gardening is about leisure, it is about much more than that. It is about social status (a point I return to in an upcoming chapter about status work) and it is about family. As Virginia's comment reveals, families maintain yards. It appears that maintaining gardens and yards functions as one way through which we create families.

Another form of housework that changes substantially among lesbigay families as one traverses the socioeconomic terrain is the work of managing household paperwork and financial matters. Troy and Jeffrey each maintain separate checking accounts. They both pay their own bills and balance their own checkbooks. For Troy this entails paying six bills per month: a Visa, a student loan, a Macy's card, the gas/electric bill, a cable TV bill, and the rent. He pays each of these near the end of the month. Jeffrey faces a slightly larger number of bills than Troy, mostly due to his automobile. He needs to make a car payment and an insurance payment. Neither Troy nor Jeffrey maintain a written budget of expenses. Instead they each operate with an informal sense of how much money is in their account. A review of their financial transactions over the week prior to our interview reveals a few additional financial tasks: paying for a magazine subscription, a parking ticket, a newspaper subscription, and a pledge to an AIDS fundraiser, as well as four ATM withdrawals, four debits at the same grocery store, and one payroll deposit.

In contrast, the Kirbo-Pendleton finances are joint, and notably more elaborate and complicated. Currently, Virginia manages the household finances. The family uses a joint checking account as well as a joint savings account. Most of their credit and loan accounts are also joint accounts. Altogether the family pays close to thirty bills per month, mostly in two waves concentrated near the middle and the end of the month. In the middle of the month, Virginia pays two Visa bills, an auto loan, an American Express bill, a furniture store bill, a phone bill, a gas and electric bill, a water bill, a trash removal bill, an auto insurance bill, a homeowner's insurance bill, a health insurance bill, and a garden service bill. At the end of the month she pays the mortgage, another auto loan, an American Express bill, a cable bill, an Internet service provider bill, three department store bills (Macy's, Nordstrom's, the Emporium), a housecleaning service bill, a long-distance phone bill (separate from the local phone bill), a Triple-A bill (auto service), a newspaper subscription, and a health club bill. In addition, Virginia makes out a check each week for their contribution to their local church. Virginia manages all of these transactions using a budget she keeps on her home computer. Clarice balances the checkbook each month, an activity that takes the better part of an evening given the volume of transactions. A review of the couple's transactions over the week prior to the interview reveals these additional financial tasks: three ATM withdrawals, seven debits to three different grocery stores, payment for theater tickets, a contribution to a local political campaign, payment for a mail-order CD, a payment for stamps by mail, and a payment for a piece of furniture bought at an antique auction.

In addition to the routine management of weekly and monthly transactions, the Kirbo-Pendletons' affluence results in a continuous, albeit less routine, flow of expenses to manage. Among these are property taxes, expenses for home renovation and upkeep, home furnishings, garden/lawn, pets, entertaining (for example, fresh flowers), automobiles (repair, service, registration), and sports/leisure expenses. The Diablo-Richards family spends on some of these items (often separately), but the Kirbo-Pendletons do so to a much greater extent. Further, the Kirbo-Pendletons also have significant investments that require management. These include a variety of mutual funds as well as company stock. In sum, the extent of financial and paperwork work appears much more formidable for the more affluent Kirbo-Pendleton family than for the Diablo-Richards family.

Just as prosperity seems to amplify financial paperwork, it also amplifies other forms of housework, including interacting with service providers, household repair and upkeep, and running errands associated with all of the forms of housework. Interactions with goods and services providers illustrate this dynamic. Neither Jeffrey Richards nor Troy Diablo could recall a visit from any service provider or a delivery that required them to be home in the last six months. Clarice Pendleton remembers arranging for and meeting the gardening service once, a roofing company once to make an estimate for repair, a financial consultant, a computer repair technician, and a window replacement company. Virginia Kirbo recalls arranging for and meeting a gardening service on four separate occasions, two separate furniture deliveries, two roofing repair companies making estimates, a refrigerator repair, a hotwater heater repair, an upholstery cleaning service, and two painting companies making estimates to refinish the exterior of the house. She also recalls many deliveries from United Parcel Service, but she can't recall an exact number. An obvious pattern emerges here. Affluence, and its concomitant homeownership, bring more housework in the form of arranging, meeting, and interacting with goods and service providers.

Thinking about Gender

The comparison of the Kirbo-Pendleton household with the Diablo-Richards household points to the importance of socioeconomic factors in making sense of the extent, character, and even the division of domesticity. The Kirbo-Pendleton home is quite unique for few lesbian households possess such extensive resources. One would much more likely come across a gay-male household with these kinds of resources, but even gay-male households with such resources would be exceptional. However, the general finding of this research that gay-male households do more housework than do lesbian ones[1] is inexorably tied to these socioeconomic dynamics. The greater wages and wealth of the male households encourages the development of more elaborate and labor-intensive domestic regimens in their homes, regimens like the one that developed in the Kirbo-Pendleton family.

When considering the importance of gender to these dynamics, a very complicated picture emerges. First, the gaps in wages and wealth that prevail between men and women in this society find expression in the housework regimens of same-sex relationships. In general, more income and wealth equals more domesticity, and consequently more housework. Second, housework performed by men in gay-male households is probably more visible than housework performed by women in lesbian households. People notice when men do domestic things because it is exceptional. For women the work becomes less notable, more invisible. People often view the domestic activities of women as natural expressions of personality, altogether unremarkable. Third, the discrepant accounts that appeared between some partners in their recollections of feeding work also occurred in recollections of housework. Discrepant accounts among male relationships include five instances where both claimed that they were the last one to do laundry, four instances where both participants claimed that they were the last one to clean the oven, three instances where both claimed that they last one to dust or polish furniture, and two instances where both claimed they were the last to clean the bathroom sink and/or toilet. In contrast, discrepant accounts among female relationships include six instances where both claimed that their partner was the last one to do laundry, three instances where both women said that their partner was the last one to clean the refrigerator, two instances where they both asserted that their partner was the last one to vacuum or clean floors, and two instances where they both gave credit to their partner for cleaning the bathroom sink. Obviously, recollections about such matters are subject to error. However, as in the case of feeding, the error does not appear randomly distributed. During the housework-related questions of the interviews (see appendix A), only three instances occurred where both men assigned credit to their partner for last completing the same task, and four instances where both women claimed to have last completed the same task. The discrepant accounts provided by women are much more likely to be ones that give their spouses credit, and vice versa for men. As suggested in the previous chapter, these discrepant accounts often reflect efforts to manage the gender identities for those women and men whose domestic involvement, or lack thereof, creates the potential for stigma and devaluation.

Race and Ethnicity and the Multiadult Households

As in the case of gender, teasing out the influence of race and ethnicity from the influence of class is not easy. However, in ways quite similar to gender, it appears that the more limited access to income and wealth among Asian-American, Black/African American, Latino-American, and American Indian participants impacts the extent, character, and division of housework (see table B9). Having fewer economic resources means that these participants are much more likely to live in multiadult households, and this circumstance alone greatly influences housework. Eighteen of the forty-five Asian, Black, Latino, and Indian people in the study live in multiadult households compared with nine of the sixty-three Euro-Americans. The majority of these eighteen participants live in densely populated neighborhoods in mostly smaller and older apartments and flats. These participants often earn less than Euro-American research participants requiring one to share older and smaller housing with more people. Shared housing often entails less housework for several reasons. First, the homes are smaller. Second, many individuals living in multiadult households, particularly among younger participants, do not invest much meaning or labor into the shared rooms within the households. In other words, the shared rooms (kitchens and living rooms) of multiadult households often have a spartan and utilitarian quality to them. In general, the individuals do not decorate them or invest a great deal of money or energy in creating spaces thick in domesticity. Rather, greater investment is made in more private spaces like bedrooms. Third, many couples living in multiadult households expressed the hope of moving into a space of their own where they could invest more energy in the entire living space. Among these individuals hoping to change their living arrangements, the common spaces were particularly spartan. In some sense, the reluctance to conceive of these living arrangements as permanent discouraged the development of spaces requiring a great deal of housework. Fourth, several participants expressed a certain hesitancy about "taking over" public spaces like living rooms and kitchens for fear of having to take responsibility for maintaining them, as well as to avoid conflicts with others using the same space. Overall, this set of factors means that lesbigay persons of color are disproportionately living in smaller spaces with less elaborate domestic regimens and this in turn means there is less housework to do.

Further, the housework that does occur is often more equally distributed in multiadult households than in two-adult households, with different tasks often assigned on a rotating basis to all individuals. In some instances responsibility for cleaning particular rooms would shift from week to week or month to month. In other instances a particular task, like dusting or vacuuming, would shift on a similar rotating schedule. This means that a disproportionate share of people of color are also living in households with shifting schedules for completing housework tasks. The greater consciousness of schedules and shifting responsibility results in greater equity in the distribution of tasks in multiadult households than in two-adult ones where such schedules are less common and less enforced.

However, even within multiple-adult households, it is important to note that frequently other householders will treat the couple in their midst as one unit. For instance, consider the case of Tim Cisneros and Paul Leal. Tim and Paul are both Latino and have been together for five years. They share an old house with three other housemates in the Mission district of San Francisco, a neighborhood with a large Latino presence. All of their housemates are single. The household divides domestic chores into four parts: kitchen, bath, shared rooms, and outside/trash/recycling. One week a month, each housemate is responsible for one of the four chores. Tim and Paul share their responsibility as one unit. The household negotiated this arrangement. What is striking about this case is that Tim serves as a kind of household manager for the entire household. He calls house meetings, keeps track of the rent, gas/electric and phone bills, and interacts with the building owner. Because he does these additional tasks, everyone agreed that he and Paul should be considered one unit. However, Tim also carries a much greater burden of the work than does his partner. Listen to Tim's responses to the questions about bathroom cleaning:

cc: Who last cleaned the bathtub/shower?
TIM: I did.
cc: Typical?
TIM: No, we all share it like the other rooms on a rotating basis, so last week was our turn.

cc: You say "our turn." Do you and your partner remember who cleaned the bathroom last month when it was your joint turn?

TIM: I doubt it. *[Laughter]* I probably do it more. He is often so busy with work, and he grew up in family where his mother did practically everything—you know, that Mexican mom thing—so that he really doesn't know how to do it or at least how to do it right. So I fill in for him I guess. Sometimes, he will do it.

Tim's account identifies Paul's work and his "Mexican mom" as the reasons Paul infrequently cleans the bathroom. In some sense, ethnic identity in this instance functions as a rationale for explaining Paul's behavior. Oddly, Tim also grew up in a Mexican household with a mother who stayed at home during his childhood, but this did not prevent Tim from knowing how or actually cleaning the bathroom in his present circumstances. Hence, determining the actual impact of ethnic identity upon housework is very difficult and in this particular case, a more plausible account would emphasize the impact of Paul's demanding paid-work situation.

In sum, the influence of race/ethnicity on housework appears significant in the following way. One's racial/ethnic identity influences the educational and employment opportunity structures available to individuals. In general, African-American, Latino-American, Asian-American, and American Indian participants operate within more limited opportunity structures and this limits their respective incomes and assets. This limits the amount of material surplus, in terms of money, time, and energy, that is available for the development of homes thick in domesticity. Paradoxically, the limited incomes of such participants results in living in multiadult households where the division of domestic labor is more equitable. The equality stems from the fact that there is less domestic work to do and more people to do it.

Housework and Occupation

The influence of occupational identities upon the extent and character of housework becomes most apparent in those households where a family utilizes the household as a location for business and/or career-related entertainment. First, let me offer two examples of the influence of operating a business out of the home upon housework, and then I will address career-related entertaining. Clyde Duesenberry works part-time as a real estate broker and maintains an office in his home. He and his partner, Mike Weltner, who works as an office manager for a nonprofit organization, earn an annual household income of around $80,000. Their home, a restored San Francisco Victorian they bought in the early 1970s, is furnished throughout in Victorian decor. Clyde puts in a great deal of effort keeping the house immaculately clean, "pleasant," and in order:

> I put quite a bit of time into this place, keeping it pleasant, partly because I like it that way, but I also want to leave a good impression with clients and potential clients. People walk right by the living room and Mike's study on their way to my office. People use the front bath quite a bit as well. And all that means that I spend a little bit of extra time keeping that up. I always check the front bathroom and encourage Henry to keep his study clean. The house is a kind of showcase, and I tend to specialize in selling Victorian homes, so many people want to see the place, and so we generally keep it quite clean.

Clyde's comments suggest an intensification of housework directly related to his occupational pursuit.

In similar fashion, Brent Navan and Christopher Saylor also live in a restored Victorian house, in the Alamo Square neighborhood of San Francisco. They earn more than half of their annual family income of $70,000 by operating their home as a bed and breakfast. Brent mostly maintains the bed and breakfast while Christopher works as a chef in a local restaurant. Christopher prepares breakfast each day for the bed and breakfast. Running a bed and breakfast carries with it a substantial amount of housework. In fact, to a great extent, a bed and breakfast constitutes a commercial replacement for domestic labor with someone receiving compensation for preparing meals and keeping a home clean, attractive, and well ordered. Questions about housework with the couple inevitably revolve around the bed and breakfast. The routine of daily chores turns around the presence of guests and the number of guests, and it is highly regimented with Brent using a daily, weekly, and monthly calendar, either written or in his head, to govern domestic work. The house can accommodate six guests, although most of the time they have only one or two. The standard of household cleanliness is quite high, as Brent suggests: "We spend a lot of time keeping the place neat and inviting. We depend on repeat customers, and so I want them to feel the place is always spick-and-span and very comforting, like a home away from home." Brent spends a substantial portion of his day managing, cleaning, and provisioning the bed and breakfast. Not surprisingly, and in contrast to much of what I hear about housework from lesbians and gay men, both Brent and Christopher offer spirited testimonies to the value of housework. Brent comments on the standards of housework:

> We follow pretty rigorous standards around here. It is very important in order for people to have a pleasant experience. One thing this business has taught me is that people may not be all that conscious of how the house looks and feels, but it is crucial to how they feel about the stay here. I guess what I am saying is that they don't readily believe that housework is that important and they often express amazement that we can make a living providing these services, but deep down inside these people they really appreciate a pleasant and helpful setting, and they come back again to have that experience again.

They both perceive of housework as essential and as worthy of compensation. This comes as little surprise given that they receive compensation for doing it and doing it well.

Beyond these examples of home businesses where occupation can augment housework are the cases of occupations where workers use the home to entertain and cultivate clients. This pattern surfaces among professionals, particularly among attorneys, physicians, clergy, and councilors. However, this matter is complicated, for occupation alone does not necessarily lead to this dynamic. Rather, it appears that occupation in conjunction with serving a particular client base facilitates increases in housework. So, for example, when comparing the various attorneys to one another in the sample, housework becomes more important among those who are in private practice and who serve a predominantly lesbigay clientele. A similar pattern exists among physicians and counselors. I did not interview clergy who were not openly lesbian or gay, but I suspect a similar pattern prevails. These families with openly lesbian and gay professionals invite people over more often and invest more energy and time into housework. Among those attorneys who work for a large firm and/or who serve a predominantly heterosexual client base, the use of the home for entertaining diminishes. This is partly a question about sexual identity and how open individuals and families are about sharing their lesbian or gay identities. For many lesbigay professionals a clear distinction operates between their private lives and the public occupations (Woods 1993).

For those professionals who are out of the closet and who serve lesbigay clients, the private/public distinction fades. Under such circumstances, lesbigay families frequently entertain. Glenna O'Conner and Beth Wilkerson have been together for four years. They live in an Arts and Crafts style bungalow in an East Bay suburb. Glenna works as an attorney. She and another lesbian women run a law practice together, providing legal services for the lesbigay community. Much of their legal work involves wills and living trusts, powers of attorney, child custody, adoptions, personal bankruptcy, and services for small businesses and nonprofit organizations. Beth, who works as a director for a small nonprofit organization, reflecting on who in their relationship invites people to come over for dinner, makes the following observation:

> You know, I think she invites many of the people who come over. She is always very careful to let me know about it, so that I can take care of the things I need to, to prepare for people coming over. She seems to know a lot more people than me, but I think it's about her work mostly. She is trying to cultivate her and Diane's law practice, and so we have a lot of people over to parties and brunches in order make connections, in order to solidify the practice. I mean, I really love it, too, so don't get me wrong, I am not complaining about it. It's just what we do.

Entertaining these guests leads to additional and more extensive domestic labor. Both Glenna and Beth comment on the need to make sure the house is clean and presentable for such occasions, and Beth spends extra effort on the production of meals for these events. They both report a more intense schedule of household cleaning than do most lesbigay households.

In a similar vein, Scott Hale and Carl Maynard, together for nine years, also seem to do more housework due to occupational expectations. Scott works as a minister in a progressive church in San Francisco, a church consisting of both straight and gay congregants. Carl works independently as an artist. He works out of a studio attached to their San Francisco home. Scott's ministerial work obscures the private/public distinction in many ways. Through his work in counseling relationships, engaging the spiritual lives of individuals, building community, and working with individuals confronting the process of death and dying, his work often entails a complete submersion into the private lives of parishioners. The Hale-Maynard household mirrors this blurred line between public and private worlds with parishioners gathering there often for dinners and social occasions. Scott reports entertaining guests four times in the last month while Carl reports seven such occasions. In either case, the frequency of such visits keeps them both aware of the state of the house and its "presentability." Relative to other lesbigay families, they clean with much greater frequency and adhere to more rigorous standards. Carl invests a great deal of energy in keeping the house clean and inviting people over for gatherings. He takes a great deal of pride in their home, and I suspect derives a great deal of self-esteem from the opportunity for guests to view his artwork.

Children and Housework

The presence of children expands both the range and the extent of housework for lesbigay families. Although much of the increased load of housework involves cleaning up after the children through putting away toys, or cleaning up after their meals, there is more to it than meeting the subsistence needs of kids. These families intentionally do more domestic activities with the goal of creating a stronger sense of family. Three of the families in my study have children under the age of eighteen living in their homes. Among these families I can see some fairly clear patterns of increased housework. Due to the children, these families spend more time and effort cleaning house, doing laundry, and managing expenses related to the children. They also interact more frequently with nonkin, including babysitters, daycare providers, teachers, and their children's friends and parents. Beyond these efforts, families with kids intentionally create more housework for themselves. They do this to create and maintain a stronger sense of family. For instance, two of the families with kids could easily afford to eat out much more often than they do. However, they choose to eat at home. Joan Kelsey and Kathy Atwood, the parents of eleven-year-old Erica, both speak of the importance of sharing meals together at home as symbolic of their family bonds to one another. Joan comments: "We rarely eat out. Sometimes I miss that but, it's important for Erica to have a sense of stability and family, and we do that through sharing our meals together." Here we see how the symbolic commitment to creating a sense of family leads to an increased load of feeding work, and the related housework activities of cleaning up after such meals. Another family, Emily Fortune, Alice Lauer, and their two-year-old daughter, Kelly, recently moved into a new suburban house. The house comes with a large backyard. Alice, talking about yardwork, reflects: "The yard is a lot of work, but its great to have because it makes life with Kelly much better. She has a place to play safely outside. Plus, I think it's given us a stronger sense of ourselves as a family, and I think we needed that. Emily and I work out there together, with Kelly playing nearby, and it's just really nice." Alice's observations show us how the additional work of maintaining a yard actually produces family. The presence of children enhances the desire to create and sustain the symbolic edifices that our culture associates with family, notably single-family houses and yards, edifices that increase housework.

Housework and Relationship Longevity

The longer a family has been together, the more extensive and varied housework becomes. Much of this increased load of housework among those in longer, more established households correlates strongly with other factors, particularly economic stability. Longer-term relationships appear much more affluent than do shorter-term ones. The ten longest-term relationships in the sample have been together an average of twenty years (with a median of seventeen), and these same ten families earn on average $110,000 a year (median $86,000). In contrast, the ten shortest-term relationships have been together an average of three years (median three) and earn $40,000 a year on average (median $36,000). No family together longer than ten years earns less than the median, with most long-term families concentrated at the top of the socioeconomic ladder. Given the paucity of longer-term, lower-income families, the crux of the argument that longevity contributes to increases in housework rests upon comparisons of longer-term prosperous families with shorter-term prosperous families. Several distinctions exist between these two groups. First, shorter-term prosperous families live in smaller homes, partially reflecting the ever-increasing costs of the Bay Area housing market over the past several decades, and the ability of more established families to afford larger spaces. Second, longer-term families eat more meals in the home. Third, longer-term families entertain more often. Finally, the longer-term families care for more pets, lawns, and gardens.

Each of these factors deserves some elaboration. In earlier sections I made clear the importance of the size of the residence to the type and breadth of housework. Not surprisingly, longer-term families more often own their own homes. Among the ten families together fifteen years or more, nine own their residence. Seven of these families bought homes in the 1970s, many in the Castro district in San Francisco. At that time the Castro district held great appeal to many gay homesteaders because of the affordability of housing in the former working-class neighborhood. Gay men and lesbians functioned as agents of gentrification in the neighborhood. They bought up many properties, often restoring the buildings, and diminished the population density of many residences. Victorian houses that had been carved up into multiple apartments were restored to larger residences. One couple in the study moved into a large Victorian residence in 1972. When they first bought the unit they bought it with three housemates. Over time they bought out their housemates and took over larger and larger parts of the space. Today they occupy approximately twenty-four hundred square feet. The cost of buying such a space today far exceeds the capacity of most younger lesbigay families. Many of the younger, more affluent families buy homes in newly gentrifying areas, and they buy much smaller spaces. Among the shorter-term prosperous families, several live in much smaller loft spaces or condominiums in the South of Market district, a former warehouse district in San Francisco. This contributes to significant differentials in the size of homes, and consequently to differences in the amount of housework. The larger homes of the more established families require more housework.

Along with the larger homes, the longer-term families eat more meals at home. Steven Beckett has been together with his partner, Anthony Manlapit, for twenty-seven years. When I ask Steven about going out for meals, he comments: "Don't do much of that anymore. Too tired to get gussied up and go out. Plus, I can cook better at home. We're not as adventuresome in our eating as we used to be. I can't eat all that spicy, fatty food. So we eat at home most of the time." Similarly, Amy Gilfoyle and her partner, Wendy Harper, have been together for twenty-three years. Amy comments: "We just don't go out like we used too. I think we have changed some. We like to be together, and just have our meals here. It's less hectic, and we really enjoy it. I am a little pickier than I used to be, and I would rather make food the way I know we like it." Both Amy's and Steven's comments suggest a pattern of increasing domesticity over the course of a relationship. Some might view this as the product of individual aging as opposed to a dynamic of the relationship itself. I tend to view it as a product of the relationship because I can point to several families together for only a few years yet consisting of older individuals who tend to eat out a great deal. In the case of Amy (age forty-three), and Steven (sixty-seven), almost twenty-five years separate the two, yet both share similar views about eating at home. Both speak of eating out much more frequently when they were first together. For Steven that means back when he was Amy's age. More established couples report eating at home more often, and they tend to view this activity as indicative of their stability. When asking Steven Beckett about how his family life compares to that of heterosexuals, he elaborates:

> We're just an old married couple, really. We're just as stable as most of those families are. We eat together like they do, pay our taxes—actually we pay more than they do—and we have homes like they do. Maybe we have a little more fun that most heteros do, but it seems pretty comparable to me. I have this woman friend I work with. I have known her for two decades. She's married and she bitches about her husband all the time. But let me tell you, it all sounds a lot like what I have to say about mine—my husband, that is. *[Laughter]*

Steven's comments point to the importance of doing feeding in order to conceive of a relationship as stable. Such feeding entails additional housework, particularly in terms of cleaning up and maintaining kitchen and dining spaces.

Longer-term families also maintain larger kin groups, a point illustrated in an upcoming chapter about kin work. These larger kin groups engender more housework. The increase in housework results from a larger number of kin participating in the ebb and flow of dinners, brunches, parties, holiday gatherings, and visits to the homes of longer-term families. Again, the economic affluence of longer-term families accounts for much of this dynamic with the affluent entertaining with much greater frequency. Yet those families together less than ten years and possessing similar if not greater economic resources report fewer of these activities. The longer-term families tend to know more people, they are more established within their respective communities, and they seem to feel more comfortable in their role as host to such occasions. In response to a question about how he felt about the last time they invited someone over to dinner in their home, Lawrence Sing, together with his partner, Henry Goode, for twenty-two years, remarks:

> I felt great. We love to entertain. We are sort of the epicenter of our friendship network. A lot of people know of one another through us, and the gatherings we have at our house. We have been together a long time, and that means that we know a lot of people. I sometimes feel like we are the grandparents of a large gay family.

They come to our house because there is room for everyone, and because I have the time to organize and arrange for those kinds of events.

A part of that organizing and arranging consists of additional housework. Lawrence feels obligated to make sure the house is clean before guests arrive. He describes a mental process of checking each room, particularly the bathrooms, and the floors in the living and kitchen areas in the days and hours before visitors come. He makes a special effort to pull the bed together: "Most days, I let the bed go. It's a pain to pull it all together—the shams, and the throw pillows, and the comforter. It takes a while to make it look good. I don't do it, or ask Henry to do it, unless I know someone is coming over. I always do it then."

The affluent families together less than ten years know fewer people, are less established within their communities, are less comfortable in the role of host, and they do less housework. Their circumstances seem to flow from the occupational opportunity structures of the affluent young. These families move more often to begin new careers, and therein they are less connected and rooted into communities and kin groups. They comment often on their efforts to establish themselves professionally. They focus more energy on meeting new people, rather than cultivating established relationships, and their modes of entertaining reflect this. For instance, the shorter-term affluent families go out to dinner more often than do either the less affluent or the longer-term affluent. Narvin Wong and Lawrence Shoong have been together five years. They both talk about the importance of meeting new friends and of establishing themselves in the community. Together they earn close to $120,000 a year. Despite their affluence, they both feel less than established and spend more of their social time out of the house. Narvin, in response to a question about how often they invite people over to dinner, replies:

> Maybe once in the last couple of months. We don't really have a firm friendship network yet, so we don't do that too often, really. We have moved a couple of times to accommodate each other's careers, and that has been hard on building a friendship network. We go out a lot, trying to meet people, but we don't invite people over too much. I think we also don't because our jobs don't leave much time. I think we are both working really hard to get our careers established, and it just doesn't leave much time for having people over. It's so much easier to just go out to dinner, especially if I am working until 6:30 or 7:00, even on Fridays.

For the most part, the Wong-Shoong household does less entertainment-related housework than do their longer-term affluent counterparts because they are less connected and established in their communities and kin groups, and because they are attempting to establish themselves occupationally.

Similar to housework-related entertaining, the care of pets, gardens, and lawns appears more abundantly among the longer-term families. Again, I think a combination of economic resources, and less concern about establishing careers, contributes to more time spent on pets and gardens. Both pet ownership and gardening appear strongly related to home ownership, something most common among the longer-term families. In any case, longer-term families do a lot more of these activities with both pets and gardening contributing to an increased load of housework. With pets, the housework includes both the actual care of the pet (feeding, bathing, trips to vet, and so on), and the additional housecleaning resulting from the mess created by the pet (more vacuuming, more cleaning of floors and walls, more frequent changing of bed linens).

Housework and the Social Production of Lesbigay Family

I began this chapter by describing the various dimensions of housework, including its performance, management, and envisionment. Often taken for granted, and frequently obfuscated, housework looms as a central character in family life. Like all of the forms of domestic labor, the envisionment, performance, and management of housework provides another opportunity for the production of family. The consistent and continuous performance of housework creates and sustains a set of material and social relationships that many lesbigay family members interpret as family. The willingness of people to do these kinds of work often reflects their conception that their lesbigay family is a legitimate family. The claim to legitimacy paradoxically rests on the presence of domestic labor. I am reminded of Virginia Kirbo's claim: "We are just like all the other families, maintaining our yard and building." Engaging in housework substantiates the ideological claim to family. And if Virginia is correct, other families, presumably heterosexual ones, view Virginia and her partner as family because they do housework, among other forms of domestic labor. For me this raises a fundamental question about the capacity to "do family." What I find striking is how differentiated the ability to do family is among lesbigay families and how the claim to family status for lesbigay relationships seems fundamentally shaped by the material conditions that enable its production. Families with fewer resources use family metaphors and analogies to refer to their household lives less frequently, and far more tenuously, than those with abundant resources. Not surprisingly, much less housework happens among those households with humble resources. Their socioeconomic circumstances hinder the development of complex housework regimes, and simultaneously attenuate the perception of their household life in familial terms. Obviously, housework exists in every household, and to some extent, people in relationships associate housework with family, but it seems that the claim to family status is associated more strongly with what Collins (1992) would describe as the surplus forms of housework represented here by the care for gardens and yards, the care of pets, the upkeep of privately owned residences, and the care of fine furnishings and utensils. It is in reference to these forms of housework that lesbigay respondents speak of family. Rarely do people speak of family in the context of the other forms of housework. For instance, no one speaks of doing dishes as evidence of their status as a family, but many mention yard work, pet care, and household maintenance as such evidence.

In a similar vein, housework possesses an open-ended quality, a built-in capacity to continuously expand. Many respondents who envision and manage housework live with a constant sense that the housework is never finished. They live with a sneaking suspicion that things could be cleaner or more elaborate or better organized. Prosperity, in terms of resources and/or time, enables certain families to respond to this concern through expanding the housework regime. As they do so, these families become more familial and their claim to family status appears more legitimate in their own eyes and in the eyes of society. These prosperous families can move to larger, single-family residences, take on the care of animals, plant gardens, entertain guests, and buy high-maintenance products from cookware to furniture. All of these activities expand housework, and all are understood as constitutive of family life. The households that plant gardens or entertain guests or maintain single-family homes conceive of themselves as family because they do these things.

These observations can lead to several different conclusions about the character of lesbigay family life. On the one hand, I am not arguing that less affluent lesbigay families are not familial. After all, I refer to them as families, even in some cases where they would not readily identify themselves as such. Clearly, given my perception that family is something that we produce socially through engaging in different forms of labor, in as much as one can identify such labor in a particular household, I would consider that evidence of the presence of family. On the other hand, my interaction with many of the less affluent lesbigay households left me with a distinct impression of disappointment about family life. Many aspired to something more in terms of family. I would characterize many of these families as "minimal families" (Dizard and Gadlin 1990). These families simply could not afford the accoutrements of family life. They possess neither the time nor the resources to invest in the social production of an extensive domestic life. Workdays that run well into the evening, inflexible work hours, and exorbitant housing costs, in combination with pervasive heterosexism in terms of American family life, all lead to many lesbigay families making minimal effort at enhancing the quality of family life. The ability to achieve familyhood is differentially distributed, and the stark reality is that the affluent more easily, and more frequently, achieve that status for themselves.

kin work among lesbigay families

In recent years, scholars of family life have begun to document the forms of work that heterosexual women do in order to establish and sustain family relations. Some of this research reveals the forms of hidden and frequently unrecognized labor involved in maintaining kin relations (Rosenthal 1985; Di Leonardo 1987; Gerstel and Gallagher 1993 1994). Di Leonardo refers to these kinds of activities as "kin work":

the conception, maintenance, and ritual celebration of cross-household kin ties, including visits, letters, telephone calls, presents and cards to kin; the organization of holiday gatherings; the creation and maintenance of quasi-kin relations; decisions to neglect or to intensify particular ties; the mental work of reflection about all of these activities; and the creation and communication of altering images of family and kin vis-à-vis the images of others, both folk and mass media. (1987, 442–43)

The forms of kin work Di Leonardo delineates appear in lesbigay families as well, although much of the aforementioned empirical research fails to include such families. In writing letters, making phone calls, organizing holiday and social occasions, selecting and purchasing gifts, as well as the forethought and decisions about how to do these things, how much to do, and for whom to do them, lesbigay families engage in a great deal of kin work. In fact, engaging in kin work is essential to creating lesbigay family life.

Kith as Family

In most respects, lesbigay families engage in forms of kin work quite similar to heterosexual families, though many do so among intimate friends rather than among biolegally defined relatives (Weston 1991; Nardi 1992; Nardi and Sherrod 1994). In contrast to the traditional Anglo-Saxon distinction made between kith (friends and acquaintances) and kin (relatives), many lesbigay families operate with a different set of distinctions where kith become kin and, sometimes, kin become kith. For example, Mary Ann Callihan, a thirty-eight-year-old artist now living in Oakland, reflects:

> I do consider my close friends as my family. They are my real family, I mean, my other family lives back East, and I don't have much to do with them and they don't have much to do with me. They really aren't a family, not at least in how I think a family should be. The people who care for me, listen to me, and love me are right here. They are my kin.

And while Mary Ann's comments diminishing the importance of biolegally defined kin reflect the views of roughly a third of the sample, her sentiments regarding the definition of family capture a common theme found in many lesbigay households: a normative sense of family as a voluntary association, as *chosen*. Sociologist Judith Stacey identifies this pattern of chosen kin and voluntary family ties as the "postmodern family" (Stacey 1990 17, 270). Many lesbigay households operate with this postmodern conception of kin. Many respondents use the phrase "gay family" to designate their chosen family.

This conception of friends as family notwithstanding, lesbigay families make clear distinctions among friends. Anthropologist Kath Weston notes, "Although many gay families included friends, not just any friend would do"

(1991 109). Weston argues that "gay families differed from networks to the extent that they quite consciously incorporated symbolic demonstrations of love, shared history, material and emotional assistance and other signs of enduring solidarity" (109). Bringing the perspectives and findings of the literature on kin work to bear on Weston's findings raises a number of questions: What activities constitute symbolic demonstrations of love? What kind of work does material and emotional assistance involve and who performs that work? What activities/behaviors serve as signs of enduring solidarity and what forms of work come to play in those activities? Peter Nardi, describing the role of friendships in lives of gay people, points out that

> in addition to providing opportunities for expressions of intimacy and identity, friendships for gay men and lesbians serve as sources for various kinds of social support (ranging from the monetary to health care) and provide them with a network of people with whom they can share celebrations, holidays, and other transitional rituals. (1992 112)

Nardi's delineation of activities crucial to friendship suggests the presence of kin work: planning, provisioning, and coordinating visits, celebrations, holidays, and transitional rituals; making phone calls and sending e-mail on a consistent basis; sending notes, cards, and flowers at the appropriate times; selecting, purchasing, and wrapping gifts; providing or arranging for the provision of healthcare (not a minor matter given the HIV/AIDS epidemic); and reflecting upon and strategizing about relationships. All of these activities constitute kin work, and performing these activities *creates* and sustains family.

When laying claim to the term *family* to describe lesbigay relationships, most respondents point to particular phenomena as evidence of family: sharing meals, sharing leisure, sharing holidays, sharing religious community, sharing resources, relying on someone for emotional or medical care, turning to someone in an emergency, and/or sharing a common history. For example, many lesbians and gay men point to the sharing of holiday meals as indicative of the presence of family in their lives. Susan Posner, reflecting on those people with whom she and her partner, Camille, spend their holidays, comments:

> Well, we have them over to eat or they have us over. We have been together through thick and thin for so long from when we first came out of the closet, through our commitment ceremony, and through buying this house. That makes

us family. I have known one of them for a very long time, that's a lot of eating and sharing and crying and stuff.

Susan began to cry as she reflected on these events in her life. She then recounted several holiday gatherings where the joy that she experienced with her lesbigay family was so overwhelming that she began to cry during the events. Many lesbigay people can recount similar stories. In part, these are tears of exile from biolegal kin, but they are more than that. They are also tears of joy—joy in the discovery of a new home and a new family.

In addition to sharing holiday meals, other participants pointed to other kinds of kin work as evidence of family. Daniel Sen Yung, a twenty-eight-year-old accountant for a small nonprofit agency, offers another instance of kith becoming kin via various forms of kin work. Daniel, responding to my question about whether he considers his close friends as family, replies:

> Oh, yes, I know that I can depend on them for certain things that you would get from a family. If I were to get really ill, they would take care of me, house me, provide for me. We eat together, just like families should. I consider friends as family, especially as a gay person, I think that way. I definitely have a gay family. They look out for me and check in on me. They are the people who pay my bills when I go overseas for work, or who were with me when I had to take my cat to the veterinary hospital. They are the ones who came and visited me in the hospital, for God's sake.

Another participant, Raquel Rhodes, a thirty-one-year-old woman working as an assistant manager for a rental car agency, identified those who had loaned her money as central to her conception of family:

> I think you know who your real family is when you fall on hard times. My friends Rebecca and Sue, they came through for me when I lost my job. They lent me the money I needed to keep going. My own mother wouldn't because of all of her homophobic bullshit. That tells you who really counts and for me—Rebecca and Sue really count.

Loaning people money involves kin work. Managing and negotiating the feelings incumbent in such lending, particularly when a couple is doing the lending, as well as managing the money itself are both forms of kin work. Other forms of lesbigay kin work include all the efforts that people put into recognizing and celebrating their own and other people's relationships. The recent work by anthropologist Ellen Lewin (1998) exploring the commitment ceremonies of lesbian and gay couples reveals the extensive work entailed in creating these ceremonies. Lewin chronicles the efforts these couples put into selecting invitations, attire, and locations for the ceremony, as well as making arrangements for out-of-town guests. She also reveals the extensive emotional labor that goes into deciding who to invite—a sometimes gut-wrenching and potentially combative enterprise. When we do these things, we create family.

The Lesbigay Family Kin Keepers

Quite frequently, lesbigay relationships function as a center for extended kinship structures. To use an astronomical metaphor, these relationships become planets around whom a series of moons (frequently, single individuals) revolve. The planning, organization, and facilitation of social occasions (picnics, holiday gatherings, vacations, commitment ceremonies/holy unions, birthday parties, gay-pride celebrations, hiking trips) bring these individuals into an orbit around lesbigay relationships. These occasions often take place in the homes of couples, as contrasted with individuals, and one member of the couple often performs the work involved. In answering questions about holiday gatherings, lesbigay families frequently recount stories of shared Thanksgiving meals, Jewish Sedarim, gay-pride celebrations, and Christmas Eve gatherings. Many speak of the importance of making sure that everyone "has a place to go" on such occasions.

For example, Matthew Corrigan and his partner, Greg Fuss, have been together for thirteen years and live in San Francisco's Castro district. Matthew works as an administrator in a nearby hospital and Greg works as a salesperson for a large pharmaceutical company. Matthew responds to my question about how he decides whom to invite for holiday occasions by saying:

> We have a lot of single friends. Many of them would like to be in couples, but they just haven't found Mr. or Mrs. Right yet. So, we are kind of their family. I mean, we will still be family after they find someone, but right now, they come here for

holidays. I try to make sure that no one spends their Christmas alone. When we talk about who to invite, we always think about who doesn't have a place to go.

Matthew's comments capture a common dynamic where lesbigay families function as the center of kin relations for many single individuals. The lesbigay families can also function as a place where single individuals come into contact with one another and begin new relationships (Harry 1984 143). These families become the center due to a number of socioeconomic factors. First, the formation of lesbigay families leads to pooling of resources. The shared resources of family groupings allow for larger residences, larger meal expenditures, and, interestingly, more time for kin work. Family status brings with it the possibility of at least one member in a family reducing the number of hours they work at paid labor and spending more time on family/household matters. Second, as lesbigay couples and threesomes come to perceive of their relationship in familial terms, they begin to act in familial ways: inviting others over for dinner, and creating holiday occasions, among other things. Third, it seems that unpartnered individuals view couples in familial ways and hold expectations that these individuals will act in familial terms. Angela DiVincenzo, a thirty-three-year-old elementary school teacher, felt this expectation from her lesbigay family:

> I think that our friends have a stake in our relationship. A lot of them are single and they kind of view us as the ideal family. I mean, partly, I think, it's about their hopes of having their own relationship, but also, it's about the fact that we are their family. They look to us to act like a family. We all do things together, go on little trips or hiking or whatever. We are kind of a stabilizing influence in their lives. They know we are here and are interested in their lives, unlike many of their real families, that is, *supposedly* real families. We are the real family.

Moreover, in a number of the longer-term and more affluent lesbigay families, there emerges a person who becomes a family "kinkeeper" (Rosenthal 1985). This person functions as a sort of center for an extended lesbigay family. This individual actually coordinates some of the kin work across families. For example, Randy Ambert, a forty-two-year-old flight attendant, plans and coordinates many joint occasions for an extended kin group whom he and his partner, Russ Pena, both consider their extended family. They include in this extended family a lesbian couple, another gay-male couple, a single lesbian, and two single gay men. In talking with Randy about these activities, he observes:

I am sort of the family mom, if you get my drift. I tend to be the first person who thinks about what is coming up. I get everyone thinking about what we're going to do for summer travel, and I like to make sure that we don't forget anyone's birthday. With the other couples, that's not too much of an issue because they keep on top of each other's birthdays. But sometimes, the couples seem pretty busy and too worn out to make plans for things, you know, so I try to keep us all together. I plan a big celebration for Gay Pride each year that brings us all together.

In addition to planning these joint occasions, Randy reports making calls to gay family members who now live out of town and keeping them abreast of the news of the various people in the extended kin group. Randy's work sustains kinship; it makes real the claim of many lesbigay people, the claim to chosen family. Yet the work and the claim to family status occurs under a particular set of social conditions. Randy's relatively flexible work schedule and the relative affluence of his household allow Randy to invest more time in kin work, and to become a kinkeeper.

Arranging for such gatherings takes a great deal of kin work. In addition to the actual planning, provisioning and preparation of the food—all examples of feeding work—a number of other less observed labors make such family meals possible. Someone must envision such occasions and make decisions about whom to invite and when. Some people tend to think of the envisioning of such meals as a form of leisure, but in fact, this envisioning entails various hidden forms of labor. The envisioning of shared meals requires one to think and act in response to a number of different factors: individual, corporate, and societal calendars; whom to invite and how frequently; who gets along with whom and what mix of people would work; making phone calls or sending invitations; knowledge of social etiquette; and learning what foods guests like or dislike. Rich Niebuhr, a forty-one-year-old attorney working part-time, reveals the mental effort involved in deciding which people to invite to dinner:

> Well, it can be kind of awkward sometimes deciding whom to invite. Usually, I handle it because Joe doesn't like dealing with that kind of stuff. But, sometimes, I find myself torn because I know that we owe someone dinner, either we haven't seen them in a while and we run into them in Castro or at a movie, but I don't really feel like inviting them. Usually, I break down and invite them because I feel like a worm if I don't. I will think about whom to invite over at the same time— sort of to take the edge off, to make it a little less intense. It's okay. But, I kind of get mad that Joe just sort of expects me to negotiate all this stuff. Sometimes, I put

my foot down, and make him call them. It can be real draining trying to stay on top of all of this stuff.

Rich exemplifies the kinds of considerations that constitute kin work. Note how Rich bears responsibility for managing the interpersonal conflict and for strategizing the occasion because "Joe doesn't like dealing with that kind of stuff." Participant observation in Joe and Rich's home reveals that Rich performs much of the kin work, both in its visible forms (making calls and planning events), as well as in its invisible forms (thinking about whom they should call and planning when to make the calls).

Variations in Kin Work Patterns

Not surprisingly the character and extent of kin work varies dramatically depending on a number of different social factors. Class identities, the kind of community in which one lives, the presence or absence of children, gender identities, occupational identities, the length of relationship, and ethnic and racial identities all influence the context in which kin work happens and the character of that kin work.

Social Class and Lesbigay Kin Work

While most lesbigay families in this study fall into the middle and upper middle class, clear distinctions emerge between these groups in terms of kin work. More affluent, upper-middle-class lesbigay households engage in significantly more kin work and much more frequently conceive of friends as family than their middle-class counterparts. Those families earning more than the median annual household income ($61,500) report twice as many close friends (twelve per household) as those households earning below the median (five). This pattern conforms to other empirical research revealing that patterns of informal association become more extensive as one moves up the socioeconomic hierarchy (Hodges 1964; Curtis and Jackson 1977). Among the ten most affluent households, all family members conceive of friends as family. In contrast, among the ten least affluent, only within four households does even one family member conceive of friends as family. In part this pattern may reflect the relatively younger age of the less affluent families. It also appears that among the more affluent, friendship/family networks become more strongly lesbigay. Less affluent respondents' friendship/family networks, while smaller, consist of a greater proportion of straight people. Overall, more affluent households maintain larger family structures and they do family with other lesbigay people.

This means that the work of creating and sustaining such relationships becomes more extensive and requires more labor for more affluent lesbigay families. For instance, they invite others over for shared meals more often, entertain larger numbers of people at dinner parties and other occasions, and go out to dinner with others more consistently. These activities require extensive kin work in the form of planning for such occasions, deciding whom to invite, extending invitations, deciding where to go out to eat, and maintaining a record (mental or written) of previous engagements.

Lawrence Sing and Henry Goode, together as a family for over two decades, live in a restored Edwardian flat in a rapidly gentrifying neighborhood in San Francisco. Lawrence works part-time as a real estate agent, and Henry works as a physician. They both possess postgraduate degrees. Lawrence, who performs much of the kin-related work in the family, makes the following comments about some of that work:

> I'm the keeper of the social calendar. I decide whom to invite over and when. I keep a mental record of who came last and whom we would like to see. I ask Henry if there is anyone he would like to see, but generally, I know how he feels about certain people. I keep up our obligations. Some people we see once a year, but there is a core of twenty-five to thirty people who I maintain contact with and whom we see with some frequency.

Lawrence, speaking with great enthusiasm and affection for his family of gay friends, denotes other forms of kin work in the effort to maintain those family relationships:

> I write letters to our closest friends who live farther away, and we always send them birthday presents and cards and, of course, presents at Christmastime. We try to plan holiday travel and our vacations with some of them. I often call them on Sundays; that's the day I make many of the long-distance calls to everybody. It's a lot of effort to keep it all together, but I think it's worth it. They're our family.

Lawrence's observations reflect common forms of kin work among more affluent lesbigay households. In contrast to less affluent lesbigay families, the affluent ones engage in some forms of kin work much more frequently: writing letters; buying and mailing gifts for birthdays and holidays; sending flowers; sending birthday, anniversary, and get-well cards; and sending a larger number of holiday greeting cards. When dividing up the sample into thirds, the most affluent one-third sent an average of seventy-five greeting cards for major holidays; the middle one-third, forty-five cards; and the lower one-third, fifteen cards per household. The more affluent families keep in contact with out-of-town friends and biolegal relatives much more frequently than less affluent families. The affluent make more long-distance calls and spend more time talking. All of these efforts constitute kin work: deciding upon and purchasing gifts and cards, writing and mailing the gifts and cards, remembering to call and write and deciding for whom to do these things.

In like manner, the more affluent households report more extensive holiday celebrations, and they often point to the sharing of holidays together as evidence of the family status of their intimate friends. Kathy Atwood and Joan Kelsey live in the Oakland hills in an Arts and Crafts style cottage in a neighborhood with many other lesbian families. Kathy works as an accountant for a prominent bank headquartered in downtown San Francisco. Joan works part-time as a finance manager for a local savings and loan. Together they earn slightly over $100,000 per year. Joan has a master's degree in accounting from a prestigious college in the East and Kathy has a bachelor's degree from the University of California. Kathy expresses her conception of friends as constituting family:

> I consider my friends as family. I see them as often as I see my biolegal family. I discuss our relationship with them. They come here for holidays or we go to their house. Our shared holidays are symbolic of our familiness. We share personal experiences. I would want them here for significant events, like Christmas or our Holy Union or whatever.

Joan, who does much of the kin work in the family, engages in a great deal of effort to make the holidays pleasant and meaningful for her chosen family:

> I put quite a bit of effort into getting the house together for Christmas. We had a lot of people over at different times, and our chosen family over on Christmas Eve,

and we went to their house on Christmas day. I mean, I planned out the meals, a very special one for Christmas Eve. I bought and mailed invitations for a Sunday afternoon holiday party. I went to the Flowermart in the city and bought greens and stuff like that. I bought a new tablecloth with a holiday theme. We chose presents for them together, but I had the time to wrap them and stuff like that.

Nearly a dozen individuals from more affluent families conceive of shared holidays as constitutive of family, while only two individuals from families earning below the median speak in these terms.

Conversely, in most cases, less affluent households more often conceive of family in biolegally defined terms, they engage in less kin work and to some extent they do different kinds of kin work. In terms of household income, most respondents perceiving of family as uniquely consisting of biolegal relatives fall below the median. I would characterize many of them as "minimal families" (Dizard and Gadlin 1990). They do not create and sustain large kin structures, either biolegally defined or lesbigay defined, and their conceptions of family emphasize biolegal links. Although these families afford less time and energy to maintaining kin relations, the efforts they do make often focus on biolegal relatives. These families often feel isolated and spend more time alone. Social researchers made the discovery long ago that the wealthy and the poor maintain stronger ties to kin for economic reasons than do middle-class Americans (Schneider and Smith 1973; Stack 1974). Most of those lesbigay families falling below the median income in this sample clearly fall into the middle or the lower middle class, as opposed to the working class or the poor. For instance, Amy Gilfoyle and Wendy Harper, a lesbian family living in a distant suburb north of San Francisco, a place where they could afford to buy a home, spend much of their time alone. They spend major holidays "alone together," without the presence of others. They both conceive of family as consisting of their own relationship and possibly Amy's biolegal parents. They report one close friend between the two of them, and both express disappointment about this. They would like more friends, but they seem conflicted. Wendy, a student and landscape gardener, feels somewhat threatened by new friends:

> I would worry about getting too close to a lot of other lesbians. There are always issues about falling in love with friends and that ruining your relationship. And, we live so far away from the places where we might meet friends. I suppose we could

become friends with some gay men, but they don't live out here, or at least we don't have any way of finding those who do.

Wendy's comments point to issues partly beyond social class, to concerns about gender and sexuality. But the fact that Wendy and Amy live so far away from San Francisco speaks clearly of social class and the ability of more affluent families to buy and rent homes in the city. Interview questions focusing on the reasons for living in suburban communities almost always point to the cost of housing in the city as a factor in deciding where to live. Wendy and Amy bring in a household income of $35,000 per year. This places them somewhat below the Bay Area median household income of $41,459 (U.S. Census 1991). Like many other middle- and lower middle-class lesbigay families, they exert less effort in the maintenance of kinship structures than do more affluent families. They infrequently call friends or biolegal relatives. They rarely send cards of any sort. Together they sent eight holiday greeting cards in 1993. They rarely invite people over, though they actually have the space to entertain. Only once every few months do they go out to dinner, and then usually just the two of them go. They lead relatively isolated lives and feel ambiguous about changing this.

Leading a similar life, but more desirous of change, Tim Reskin and Phillip Norris, together for three years, live in a modest apartment in a distant suburb east of Oakland. Tim commutes thirty miles to downtown San Francisco, where he works as a clerk for a law firm. Phillip commutes twenty miles to downtown Oakland, where he works in a large retailer as an assistant buyer. Together they earn around $40,000 a year and pay $700 a month for a two-bedroom apartment. They would like to live in San Francisco but feel they cannot afford it. Together they have two close friends, a couple who moved back East several months ago, although neither Tim nor Phillip conceive of these friends as family. They spent the last three Christmas holidays separately. Tim stays at home, working the holiday shift and earning overtime wages. Phillip visits his biolegal family, though he says he really hates to go. They both speak expectantly of making more friends, and both perceive of this happening as soon as they can afford to move to the city. In terms of the various forms of kin work, Tim and Phillip actually do very little. They report that they do not really keep in touch with friends or biolegal relatives out of town. Tim's biolegal relatives refuse to speak to him because of his gay identity. Neither Tim nor Phillip write letters or send cards or presents to anyone. They rarely invite anyone to come over, but Phillip does some kin work in trying to establish new friends. Phillip comments:

> I try to organize stuff for the weekend. We do know some people in the city, and so I try to set up a movie or going out to the bars; the dance clubs are usually too expensive. Tim seems too tired to do it, and I know it's the only way we are going to make friends. I feel very isolated out here, but it's all we can afford. I keep saying that we should move to a poorer neighborhood in San Francisco, but Tim feels it would be too dangerous. But I really think we need a gay family, especially Tim whose biolegal family is so screwed up. He deserves it.

Overall, Tim and Phillip lead a socially isolated life, mostly due to their lack of material resources, but also due to their gay identity. They find it difficult if not impossible to meet other lesbigay people in the place where they live. They do not conceive of their neighbors as hostile, but they do not think of them as community, either. Their socioeconomic circumstances actually diminish the presence of many forms of kin work, with the exception of the effort to establish a kin structure, something they urgently desire.

In sum, social class appears to play a central role in the extent and the character of kin work among lesbigay families. As one ascends the social-class hierarchy of lesbigay families in this sample from lower middle class to upper middle class, the intensity of kin work increases. The character of kin work shifts from concerns about establishing kin relationships to managing and sustaining kin relationships. The flow of material exchange intensifies with affluent lesbigay families buying more gifts, throwing more parties, hosting more dinners, making more phone calls, and sending more cards. Explaining why more affluent households do more kin work than less affluent ones involves several interrelated influences. First, more affluent families live closer to the lesbigay enclaves due to the higher cost of living in the city. Proximity to other lesbigay people leads to larger kin networks. Yet, some lower middle-class lesbigay families live in the center of lesbigay enclaves and engage in significantly less kin work than their more affluent neighbors. Second, more affluent lesbigay families turn to the marketplace for other forms of domestic labor (for example, laundry and housekeeping) thus freeing these families to invest more energy in kin work. Finally, these class distinctions with occupational identities and concerns to which I will now turn.

Occupational Attributes and Lesbigay Kin Work

The character of one's employment greatly influences both the content and the quantity of kin work lesbigay families perform. Several dimensions of the work/family relationship seem relevant here. First, the wide majority of both lesbians and gay men in this study work full-time for wages. Second, the more affluent lesbians and gay men mostly work in more professional jobs, many allowing the individual some flexibility in terms of schedule, higher levels of job satisfaction, and more material resources to invest in kin work. Finally, the distinction between work-related contacts and family contacts diminishes among both lesbians and gay men in the professions.

The participation of lesbians and gay men in full-time paid work contributes to abatement in the extent of biolegal kin relations among lesbigay families. In this study, 80 percent of the respondents work year round, at least forty hours per week. This is not too surprising given the cost of living in the Bay Area, and that full-time employment enables one to maintain economic independence from biolegal kin, an independence that historically and currently enables lesbian and gay people to reveal and sustain their sexual identity (Faderman 1991, 94–96; D'Emilio 1983). Kin work patterns among lesbians and gay men probably prefigure patterns currently emerging among heterosexual dual-earners, given the long standing patterns of full-time employment for lesbigay people. Recent research on the changing character of kin work among heterosexual families, changes resulting from the influx of heterosexual women into the paid labor force, suggests a concomitant decline in the amount of kin work performed for biolegal kin (Gerstel and Gallagher 1994, 534). Simultaneously, these women begin to increase the level of kin work for friends. For example, Gerstel and Gallagher indicate that employed women provide more advice to others than do homemaking women (ibid.). This pattern directly parallels kin work patterns among lesbigay families: a decline in care for biolegal relations, and an increase in care for coworkers and friends, partly the result of participating in full-time, paid labor.

However, I do not want to suggest an equivalence in the extent of kin work among those families with two full-time workers with those families where one person works for wages part time or not at all. In fact, when looking at those lesbigay families who engage in the most extensive kin work, in addition to their affluence, I am struck by the number of families with one full-time and one part-time worker. These are families where one worker earns a significantly large salary, a salary that enables her or his partner to invest much greater time and energy in family life and to work fewer hours for wages. This kind of pattern appears much more frequently among gay-male families than among lesbians, for the most part due to the fact that few individual lesbians earn salaries large enough to support such an arrangement.

Nevertheless, returning to the predominant pattern among lesbigay families where primary partners work full-time for wages, a number of kin work differences emerge due to the character of paid employment. For example, those respondents working at less prestigious jobs report significantly less flexibility in their schedules and much more frequently feel exhaustion at the end of the day. This impacts kin work. Marilyn Kemp and Letty Bartky, a lesbian couple living in the Castro district in San Francisco and together for five years, illustrate this dynamic. Marilyn works as a legal secretary in a law firm while Letty works as a retail clerk in a bookstore. Together they earn roughly $42,000 per year. They pay $950 a month for a small one-bedroom apartment. Both work at least 40 hours per week, with Marilyn often working closer to 50 hours. Neither of their jobs offers much flexibility. Marilyn comments:

> I gotta be there when attorneys come looking for me. I often have to stay late because a filing needs to get done. I find it hard to get away. I mean, they come looking for me during my lunch hour, even. It bugs me that the attorneys can just go out for two hours at lunch but that would never be allowed for me. I really don't like working there, but you do what you gotta do. We are barely making it now.

Letty comments on Marilyn's arrival home each night: "I always try to have something cooking when she gets home. She's usually tired and emotionally twisted when she gets home. I mean, we are both tired, but she needs more of a cooling down." When asking Letty about friends, she reports that they find it hard to make friends and wish they knew more, but that it's hard to find the energy:

> I think we are just both too exhausted to go out and link up with people after work. I mean, years ago, I was active in lesbian politics, but I just don't seem to have the energy to do it. My work makes me tired and I just don't feel like going out of the house. So we stay home and watch TV and read fiction novels—I guess to escape.

Marilyn and Letty report few incidents of inviting someone over for a meal or of going out to dinner with people. They don't invite people over, because, as Marilyn says, "There is no room in this house to do that sort of thing, and we're usually too tired anyway." They report having few close friends, other than each other, and rarely spend much time with other lesbians or gay men, even though they live in the middle of a lesbigay ghetto. They conceive of family as consisting of their biolegal relatives and attempt to keep in touch with those relatives; Letty calls her mother every Saturday, but keeps it short to keep the phone bill from getting too large. The diminution of kin work in this family is partly the result of limited material resources, but it's more than that. Both Marilyn and Letty feel exhausted at the end of the day resulting from stressful and often unfulfilling paid work. The character of their paid work prevents flexibility in work schedules and hinders any integration of family life into their work lives. For instance, neither of them report calling friends and family from work. Marilyn indicates that attorneys would find this "unprofessional," and Letty says she spends much of her day on the sales floor, where both customers and her employer would object to her making calls. The reduction in lesbigay kin relations in the lives of Letty and Marilyn results from a number of factors, but the fatiguing character of their work, an intractable work schedule, and a hostility to family life seeping into the world of work all play their part.

If the lives of Letty Bartky and Marilyn Kemp illustrate the impact of constraining employment on diminishing kin work in lesbigay family life, the lives of Dolores Bettenson and Arlene Wentworth illustrate the opposite dynamic. Dolores and Arlene live in a Mediterranean-style home in the more affluent part of San Francisco's Mission district. Together as a family for three years, they met in law school and both work as attorneys. Arlene works for a large, prestigious downtown firm and Dolores works for a public agency. In 1993 Arlene earned just over $100,000 and Dolores just under $50,000. Together they report thirteen close friends, about half of whom they both consider as family. They often go out to dinner with friends and frequently attend functions at the homes of friends and acquaintances. Dolores, who performs a disproportionate share of kin work for the family, comments on why she does so and describes some of her effort:

> Well, I think I do quite a bit more of that sort of thing, and I know I do, we have
> talked about it and its fine, and I do more of it because my schedule is more flex-

ible and predictable. If I need to, I can take time in the afternoon and pick up stuff for a dinner or something. It's easier for me to call people from work. Arlene's work schedule is more intense, less predictable. Her clients and the partners at her firm expect a lot. She gets home quite late sometimes. I mean, she can get away, but I think she knows that right now, until she becomes a partner, that she needs to keep her nose to the grindstone. So I tend to handle things. She earns a lot and that actually makes some of it a bit easier. Sometimes, I will just have a catering service drop off something for a meal, especially if it's lots of acquaintances. We hired a bartender for a holiday party at our house. It took the pressure off of me and made things a lot easier. For close friends, well, then I cook. And actually, Arlene will, too. She makes certain special things that everyone likes.

Dolores's comments suggest the advantages that flexible work hours and ample resources bring to the effort to do kin work. Job flexibility often appears among those with more prestigious employment and higher compensation.

Overall, such flexibility enables some lesbigay families to engage in greater levels of kin work. Sometimes family members keep in touch with lesbigay kin via e-mail accounts set up at work. Many of those with higher salaries and higher-status jobs work for progressive companies that offer flextime in work schedules. Similarly, they often work for companies that offer paid leave for caring for sick partners or biolegal relatives, or for children in the first few months of life. Those with prestigious employment more frequently work for companies or institutions that provide substantive domestic partnership benefits to their employees including medical, dental, vision, and mental-health care. A number of lesbigay families indicate that domestic-partner benefits allow at least one partner to spend more time on family matters. Rich Chesebro, who works for a large Bay Area software company, commenting on landing a job at the firm, reflects:

We are very lucky I work for Silicon Graphics. I mean, lucky in the sense that, as gay people, we get what straight people, of course, feel they have coming to them. They completely cover Bill's [his partner's] medical and dental. It means that he can spend more time on his artwork and it allows him to spend more time taking care of stuff at home, which he actually likes to do anyway. If we didn't have it, he would probably have to work full-time at a bummer job. This way he doesn't have to worry about that as much.

Hence, the accoutrements of higher-status occupations make kin work more possible for generally more affluent lesbigay families. Individuals who work for

these firms and institutions speak much more glowingly about work and satisfaction with work, for obvious reasons. Even when tired, many of these more
affluent respondents spend their evenings not at home recovering from exhaustion but rather involved in community and civic affairs. Among the ten
most affluent lesbigay families, eighteen individuals report spending at least one
night a week in some voluntary organization ranging from church choirs to
AIDS hospices to affordable housing groups. Among the ten least affluent lesbigay families, the rate of participation in such endeavors shrinks dramatically
with only three individuals reporting a weekly commitment to such a pursuit.

Finally, in the case of the lesbigay professional families where at least one
individual pursues a professional career, two countervailing influences seem
to collide, producing discrepant patterns in the work/family lives of professionals. One pattern produces a clear distinction between work and family,
while the other blends the two dimensions together. The key distinction in
the lives of lesbigay professionals turns on the question of whether they provide services to the lesbigay community or to a broader, more heterosexually
defined public. But before describing these differences, a few comments
about professional and semiprofessional careers are in order. In accordance
with traditional sociological thinking about professions, the following characteristics distinguish the professions from other careers: the claim of au-
tonomy from outside regulation; postgraduate training; an ideology of service; abidance to a professional code of ethics; self-directed or autonomous
work; and generally higher income (Wilensky 1960; Etzioni 1969; England
1992). The semiprofessions, where most lesbigay professionals in this study
work, along with most women professionals in general, are characterized by
similar attributes though with lesser incomes and, in some cases, with less
stringent educational credentials. More than half of the lesbigay families include at least one professional or semiprofessional. Most of lesbigay professionals in the study, both male and female, work in the semiprofessional, female-dominated fields of health assessment and treating occupations
(nursing, occupational therapy), librarian and curator work, social work, and
elementary and secondary education.

Even among the more prestigious professional careers (attorneys, archi-
tects, physicians, professors), most lesbigay professionals work at the lower
rungs of those occupational structures. For instance, most of the professors
teach in community colleges instead of four-year institutions, most of the attorneys work as associates as opposed to partners or private practice, and

most of the physicians work for managed-care organizations instead of in private practice. This finding coheres well with recent research indicating the presence of a significant pay gap between people on the basis of sexual orientation (Badgett 1995). For gay males, Badgett finds that the differential in pay prevails between gay men and similarly situated heterosexual men, and concludes that "the income penalty for gay or bisexual men could be as much as 24.4%" (1995, 736). Not surprisingly, those lesbigay professionals who achieve the higher rungs of their career ladders provide services directly to the lesbigay community. Here one finds physicians, optometrists, dentists, lawyers, and counselors serving lesbigay clientele. This distinction between serving a lesbigay clientele as opposed to serving a broader clientele results in different patterns of kin work among the lesbigay professionals.

Accordingly, among those professionals serving the lesbigay community, the distinction between work and family life lessens and the attendant kin work intensifies. Greg Strathern and Robert Bachafen live in the Upper Market area of San Francisco, just above the Castro neighborhood. They live in a contemporary cliff-side home with a spectacular view of the city. Greg works as an architect for a gay-owned construction and architectural firm. Robert works for a public library in an East Bay community south of Oakland. Greg notes that his professional life and friendship network seem to overlap extensively. He emphasizes the importance of a lesbigay network to his firm's success: "While we do a lot of work outside of the gay community, the fact is most of our referrals come by word of mouth within the gay and lesbian community. Strangely, some of my clients actually have become some of our best friends. I try to stay connected and do the networking thing, it's important to developing the company." According to Robert, who performs much of the family kin work, Greg's occupational connections served as the source of friends and family. Robert, in response to a question about who in their family originally met many of their friends, responds:

> I think the answer to that is that Greg did, through his work, mostly. I have some friends through work, mostly straight women, though, and they tend to live in the East Bay. So Greg tends to be here in the city and working with gay people, so he meets them more than I do. I mean, I'm not unhappy about that. We have great friends.

In contrast to the Strathern-Bachafen kin work pattern, another pattern among professionals also exists. These professionals tend to serve a broader, heterosexual client base, and many of them are more discreet about their sexual orientation. In this pattern of kin work, a clear line of demarcation exists between work and family life, with little overlap, and, when overlap occurs, it can become the site of conflict and stress. Linda Yee works as an attorney for a prominent firm in Oakland. She has worked for the firm for six years. She remains "in the closet" at work and explains that she doesn't think the firm will promote her if they discover she is a lesbian. Her partner, Sucheng Kyutara, manages a small real estate office in San Francisco's Richmond district. Sucheng lives an openly lesbian life: out at work and involved in lesbigay politics. Sucheng feels angry about Linda's discreetness, and comments: "It annoys me that she is not out at work. I mean, I understand, but its a drag to sit at home while she goes to firm functions where all the heteros bring their spouses. I mean, I don't even want to go, really, but I should be able to go." Linda views her work/family life in starkly polarizing terms. She considers her work and family life completely separate and wants no interaction between the two. She comments: "I think everything is working. If I want my career to go where I want it to go, we have to live with it for now. I don't really think it's that big of deal. I don't want people at the firm involved in my private life, anyway. I don't poke into their business, and they shouldn't into mine." Linda Yee conceives of work happening on one side of the San Francisco Bay and family on the other side. This pattern actually resembles a pattern found among some heterosexual professional men. Sociologist Robert Zussman describes a pattern of work/family interaction among middle-class professional engineers where a pronounced distinction appears between work and family life (1987, 342). These engineers live in suburban bedroom communities and are not known to others in these communities on the basis of their occupational identities. These heterosexual men safely compartmentalize their work and family lives, attempting to limit the influence of either terrain upon the other. Zussman contrasts this new pattern with an older middle-class pattern among shopkeepers and fee-for-service professionals where the distinction between work and family life blurred, with professionals known to local communities in terms of occupation and involved in community life in part to benefit occupational success. Occupational success for some lesbigay professionals like Linda Yee closely resembles the newer middle-class model Zussman finds. For the Yee-Kyutara family, San Francisco becomes a bedroom community, with a clear and rigid distinction between work and family life. That rigid distinction conceals sexual orientation, while it simultaneously attenuates the extensiveness of kin, and the attendant kin work.

This set of social circumstances means several things for the character and extent of kin work in such families. Not surprisingly, in the Yee-Kyutara family, the substantial majority of family and friends come to the family through Sucheng. This carries direct consequences for the division of kin work, with Sucheng bearing much of the responsibility for creating and maintaining kin relations. Unlike the blurring of work/family activities among openly lesbigay professionals, particularly those serving the lesbigay community, where kin work happens at work (phone calls to family and friends, social gatherings at work, lunches together with lesbigay family and friends, quick trips to buy gifts), kin work for the discreet professional must take place at home. This actually shifts the work to the less closeted partner. The creation of an intense work/family split also leads to an attenuation of kin work with open lesbigay professionals engaging in more extensive kin work in comparison to their closeted peers.

Urban/Suburban Distinctions and Lesbigay Kin Work

Suburban residents invest more time in maintaining relationships with bi-olegally defined family than with lesbian and gay family. Eleven of the 52 families in this study live in suburban settings. Among those in this study who do not conceive of friends as family (24 of the 105 respondents), 17 live in suburban settings. This finding parallels other studies of lesbians and gay men that find that living in suburbs diminishes social involvement with other lesbigay people (Weinberg and Williams 1974; Lynch 1992) and impedes the development of a gay identity among individuals (Troiden and Goode 1980). In this study, suburban lesbians and gays report fewer close friends and rarely conceive of intimate friends as family (4 of the 22 suburban residents). Suburban residents invest more energy in relationships with biolegal relatives than with friends. In contrast to urban dwellers, the majority of suburban residents report making more phone calls to biolegal kin, spending holidays with them, sending birthday cards and gifts to them, inviting them over for dinner and special occasions. What accounts for this urban/suburban distinction concerning the conception and creation of family?

Beyond the social-class factors influencing whether one lives in suburban or urban environments, suburban lesbians and gays appear more integrated

into the predominant middle-class, Euro-American, heterosexual models of
kinship—a model strongly invested in biolegal definitions of kin (Schneider
1984). Most of the suburban respondents come from Euro-American back-
grounds, and most report that heterosexuals constitute more than half of
their friendship network. In contrast, urban gays and lesbians create social
and friendship networks consisting of mostly other lesbians and gays, with
very few urban respondents reporting more straight friends than lesbigay
ones. Frederick Lynch, in a study of suburban gay males, suggests that "the
middle-class suburban settings in which most respondents were raised, lived,
or wanted to live strongly reinforced devotion to work, home ownership/
maintenance, and continued interaction with heterosexual coworkers, relatives, and friends" (1992, 183). And while Lynch's study focuses on gay men,
it turns out that I came across more lesbians living in suburban settings than
gay men. In asking respondents about why they live where they do and what
might motivate them to move to a different setting (suburban to urban),
many of the suburban lesbian families express little desire to move to an urban location, and most said it would be difficult to afford to live in such a setting, even if desired. Lynch notes that the high cost of living encourages
some gay men to leave urban enclaves, especially when they desire to buy a
home (1992, 192–93). Due to gender inequality, lesbian families seem more
likely to face the prospect of living in suburban locations in the San Francisco
Bay Area. It seems reasonable to conclude that many lesbian families choose
to live in suburban communities in part in order to afford home ownership,
and this clearly coheres with the lower median annual household incomes of
lesbians ($49,500) than gay men ($84,500) in the sample.

While suburban residence influences the character of family life and diminishes the quantity of kin work taking place due to social isolation, the
character of kin work also changes. Suburban residents must spend more
time organizing and planning for social interaction. Many report making
special efforts to encourage friends from urban neighborhoods to visit. The
bridges and tunnels linking urban San Francisco/Oakland to its suburban
neighbors function as clear lines of demarcation, over which many urban
dwellers seem unwilling to venture. Therefore, suburban residents find that
they must make special efforts to arrange social functions at times of the
week and year that seem more amenable to urbanites. Brad O'Neil and
Jerome Steinberg live in an East Bay suburb and provide an example of this

dynamic. Brad, a computer engineer who handles much of the kin work for his family, comments:

> I try to invite people to morning and midafternoon gatherings, instead of at night, because people from the city don't want to come out here at night. It's always on a weekend; we simply don't do things on weekday nights, because no one will come. It's kind of silly, it's only ten minutes from Oakland, but people conceive of the mountains as a kind of barrier. And I tend to arrange a lot more activities in the summer; then some of our city friends want to escape the fog, then they will come.

Kin work in this suburban setting requires special considerations, an empathetic understanding of what motivates urban friends, and a more concerted and intentional effort to bring people together. Clearly this kind of kin work is labor and time intensive, as well as emotionally challenging. I met one gay-male family who had moved to a suburban community from San Francisco in order to buy a home. A year later they sold the home at a loss and moved back to a rented apartment in San Francisco. Despite their efforts to become connected in their new community, they could neither make new friends nor maintain the friendships they had prior to moving. Their sense of isolation grew. They actually had a lot less kin work to do because they could not find appropriate candidates to whom they could direct their labors.

In contrast, those doing kin work in urban settings, particularly in San Francisco's lesbigay enclaves, do significantly more kin work. Enclave dwellers often conceive of their neighborhoods as small towns where one runs into lesbigay kin, often on a daily basis. Shirley Brown, a social worker living in Noe Valley, a mixed straight and lesbigay neighborhood, captures this dynamic:

> I never know who might be coming home for dinner. Margarita will run into friends on Muni or on the bus or down on 24th Street, and before you know it we will all have dinner or go out for coffee or whatever. I often call Carol or Jeffrey at the last minute to see if they started dinner or not, and invite them over to eat with us. Carol just lives over two blocks and Jeffrey just up the hill on 24th Street. It's kind of nice, like family, I guess. People stop by unexpected, and it's cool. It's so easy to just go out to the movies with someone; I really like it here, it's like a small town.

This kind of pattern appears to be a function of both the concentration and the density of urban neighborhoods. The potential for coming into contact with gay families is much greater. This potential encourages a pattern of kin work characterized by flexibility and spontaneity. The urban dwellers don't seem to work as hard at establishing relations, but rather spend more effort managing such relations.

Lesbigay Parenting and Kin Work

The presence of children diminishes the conception of friends as family in lesbian and gay households. In four of the five households with children present in this study, neither primary partner conceives of their close friends as family. Rather, these households limit family to the primary couple, the children, and to biolegal relatives. Emily Fortune and Alice Lauer, parents of two young infants, understand family in strongly biolegal terms. Emily states: "Some people use the term *family* very loosely. I don't call friends that. The kids and our relatives, they feel like family to me. To me, my family is my biolegal family. We have a natural bond to one another." Her partner, Alice:

> My concept of family has changed a great deal in the past few months. I think before the children were born I might have considered my friends as family. My relationship with my own sister has changed since the kids were born. I have more of a sense of this family right here. I have a new appreciation for my family of origin. We can turn to them in a crisis, even though they may not be that comfortable with our sexuality.

Gay and lesbian parents appear more vested in biolegal conceptions of family, perhaps for very concrete reasons. To establish biolegal links in the American kinship structure often also establishes and legitimates economic links. Three of the lesbian families, all with infants, report relying on biolegal kin for resources, either in the form of providing housing, making loans, lending automobiles, or providing daycare. Anthropologist Ellen Lewin suggests that the pattern of intensifying relations to blood kin among lesbian parents expresses an attempt to legitimate the claim to family and to provide a stable socioeconomic environment for the children (1993, 91–94).

Moreover, the presence of children within some families distracts from the ability to maintain friends. Clarice Perry, a college professor who is also deaf, expresses her feelings about family:

My experience with family is strange. It's not easy to draw the line since I have Cheryl's children. I share responsibility for the kids, that's my idea of family. As an individual, my close friends, mostly deaf, we can't share that much because of the kids. The kids have changed my relationship with my friends. I have mixed feelings about it. I resent the kids sometimes. They took my friends away. It was not my plan to have kids, but they are now my family and I love them.

The addition of children changes one's social circumstances, both for lesbigay people and for heterosexuals. However, given that relatively few lesbigay families have children, and that parents often befriend parents in American culture, lesbigay parents may find it quite difficult to establish social links. This further encourages lesibgay families with kids to establish stronger relations with biolegal kin. The possibility exists that lesbian and gay friends may also intentionally diminish relationships with friends who have children. Some scholars find a fairly strong sentiment against children, especially among some gay men (Newton 1993).

Gender Identities and Lesbigay Kin Work

Gender appears central to explaining kin work in many settings. For instance, Di Leonardo posits that kin work reflects the influence of gender much more strongly than the influence of social class in heterosexual families (1987, 449). I can make no such unilateral claim about gender within lesbigay families. I detect gender-related concerns in terms of how lesbians and gay men both portray and do kin work, but this is complicated by the impact of socioeconomic factors. Interestingly, in this study, gay men do significantly more kin work than lesbian women. This parallels the finding of Blumstein and Schwartz (1983, 149–50) and my own research that gay men do more housework than lesbian women do. Blumstein and Schwartz argue this emerges from an effort among lesbians to avoid the low-status role assigned to housework in American society. I think additional factors play a role here.

While Blumstein and Schwartz find lesbian women shunning domestic work to avoid the low-status stigma attached to it, in the case of kin work I find both patterns of avoidance and a significantly diminished rationale for the generally less affluent lesbian families to engage in extensive kin work. When considering the economic affluence, educational level, and occupational prestige of all lesbigay households, the more affluent the household, the more educated and the more prestigious the career, the more extensive the kin work becomes regardless of gender. Dividing the lesbian families on the basis of household income into three groups (high, medium, and low) shows that those with high income report twice as many friends as those with low incomes. The same holds for males. Affluent families, regardless of gender, engage in much more extensive kin work. Due to the persistence of gender inequality, and the barriers women face in achieving higher-status, higher-paid employment, the resources necessary to sustain larger kin structures do not exist for many lesbian households as much as they do for gay men. Nor does maintaining such a network provide any economic advantage, as it does for those in occupational categories where extensive networks provide business and client contacts (lawyers, private-practice physicians, and psychologists).

Nonetheless, I am not suggesting that gender has no relevance here, but its relevance eludes easy classification. On the one hand, lesbian women may well avoid kin work activity in order to escape the devalued status associated with doing the work. After all, who wants to be "just a housewife" (Matthews 1987)? On the other hand, if one hopes to create and live within a family, then someone has to do this work. And in most lesbigay families these forms of work do occur. However, doing kin work, or failing to do it, carries different risks for gay men and lesbians. For the men, engaging in kin work produces threats to gender identity. For the women, failing to do kin work produces threats to gender identity. Making calls to family, sending cards, buying presents, inviting dinner guests and worrying about soured relationships with family all carry the potential to become gender-producing phenomenon (Berk 1985; West and Zimmerman 1987). A woman failing to engage in these nurturing/caring activities runs the risk of stigma. This "nurturing imperative" exists for women regardless of sexual orientation (Westkott 1986). I suspect that many lesbian women answering questions about kin work felt an obligation to do kin work. For instance, Melinda Rodriguez, a twenty-seven-year-old human resources administrator comments when I ask about making phone calls to biolegal relatives:

> Should I answer that the way I am supposed to or should I be more honest about it? [Laughter] I don't call too much. I feel guilty about it. But hey, my brothers don't call my parents. My mother complains to me about that, but not to my brothers.

Why should I be judged differently? I guess it's not a very feminine attitude, but I don't care. Well, I do care, but I wish they would have more realistic expectations. You know, I work a lot, as much as my brothers do. So I don't have that much time. Not like my mother, who doesn't work. She has time to call people.

Meanwhile, men engaging in extensive kin work frequently struggle with even more intense concerns about gender identity. Lance Meyter and Mike Tuzin, both in their late twenties, together for three years, and both working in the healthcare field (one in clerical, the other in higher administration), illustrate the dilemma some male couples face in negotiating kin work. Mike does most of the limited amount of kin work for their relationship. Lance feels that because Mike works at a less stressful job and has more time at home, he should do more of the "arranging of the social life." Mike, while accepting Lance's calculus, comments:

I feel kind of weird about doing this stuff sometimes. I mean, I work, basically, as a secretary because I can't decide what to do with my life. That's already kind of embarrassing and hard on my self-esteem. I like to do a lot of social-type stuff, like talking to our friends, and arranging for things, but you know, it's hard. I was talking to my mother recently, and she wanted to know what we were doing that weekend and I told her everything I had planned and she said: "My, aren't you the little housewife." She was just joshing me, but I sort of, I wanted to puke. I mean, I think it's important to do this stuff, but it's kind of embarrassing, you know? *I do go to the gym quite a bit, so I guess that sort of makes up for it* (emphasis added).

Here we see the potential for the stigmatization of men who do these activities. Mike, in attempting to manage both a feminine-defined occupation and responsibility for kin work (among other forms of domestic work), turns to the realm of athletics "to make up for it." Many gay-male families must manage the threatening character of domestic work (including kin work) to male gender identity. Let it suffice to say that there are many ways to resolve this issue, including constructing myths, using rhetorical strategies that hide the true division of domestic labor, and, for a few, simply violating conventional expectations.

Longevity and Lesbigay Kin Work

Lesbigay families living together for longer periods of time engage in more kin work than those together for shorter periods. Longer-term families more often consider kith as family. Among the thirteen lesbigay families together longer than nine years, ten conceive of kith as family. Most of these longer-term relationships involve similar kinds of kin work to those found in earlier stages of relationships, but the intensity of the work increases. For example, in comparison to shorter-term families, longer-term families engage in more gift giving, gifts for lesbigay family members and for biolegal kin. The longer-term families send more birthday, anniversary, and get-well cards, and they make more long-distance phone calls to both biolegal family and to gay family. They more frequently report lending money and providing accommodations. They organize more holiday gatherings and social occasions. They invite others over for dinner and arrange to go out to dinner more frequently.

With regard to holiday planning and arrangements, several distinct patterns emerge among longer-term families. When looking at all of the families in the study, in terms of the work related to arranging for holiday visits such as making phone calls, writing letters, and planning the itinerary, the person with biolegal connections to the family often does the work. In contrast, among longer-term relationships, a pattern of specialization occurs, where the person with more responsibility for domestic life also coordinates family activities with the gay family and the biolegal relatives of her or his partner. Rhoda Freidman, a school administrator, and her partner, Esther Kushner, a physical therapist, together for sixteen years, exhibit this pattern. Esther does much of the domestic labor in the family and also coordinates holiday gatherings with Rhoda's mother. Rhoda comments:

> I think it's great that Esther and my mother get along so well. My mother makes me crazy. Her and Esther can talk and talk on the phone. Every year, they make plans for Rosh Hashanah and Hanukkah. They decide where we will go, if we go somewhere, or if we are going to their house in New Jersey or if they are coming to our house out here. Just one big happy family. *[Laughter]*

Despite Rhoda's laughter, she reports a great deal of satisfaction with the way they celebrate holidays and feels relieved that Esther handles this kind of kin work.

In addition to holiday kin work, longer-term relationships engage in other forms of kin work often unseen among younger families. For example, another significant form of kin work involves the management and provision of medical care in the home (Glazer 1993). In this study, the provision of extensive medical care for sick people appears only among longer-term lesbigay families. Likewise, only among long-term families did I find elderly parents living in the household. In two instances, an elderly parent lives in the household or nearby, requiring some assistance, usually transportation or running errands. In four instances an adult with HIV disease lives in the household. This circumstance greatly increases kin work for one or more family members. The following family illustrates the dynamic. Nolan Ruether, Joe Mosse, and Randy Hargrove live in an affluent suburb north of San Francisco in a large split-level house. Nolan and Joe have been together for nearly two decades. Randy began living with them three years ago, shortly after being diagnosed with HIV disease. Twice Randy spent several weeks in the hospital, and he requires extensive assistance in order to stay living at home. Much of this assistance comes from Nolan, who performs much of the kin work in the family. He takes Randy to medical appointments, social engagements, worship services, and cooks for him, following a rather detailed and complicated nutritional strategy. He arranges for social occasions, monitoring Randy's energy levels to see when visits should end. Nolan answers the phone and stays in contact with Randy's biolegal relatives back East. Nolan holds a durable power of attorney for Randy's healthcare. Nolan keeps track of paperwork related to health insurance for Randy and balances Randy's checkbook. He also provides medical care for Randy, including administering intravenous antibiotic treatment once a day to help Randy avoid a recurrence of pneumonia. Without Nolan, Randy would probably need to give up living at home and move to a more institutional setting. Nolan's partner Joe works at a job that requires he put in "upwards of 70 hours a week," so he cannot provide much kin work, not to mention that Joe's income provides the financial underpinning that makes it possible to maintain their standard of living. Nolan comments on his kin work:

> I wouldn't have it any other way. Randy is part of our family. Has been for a long time. We love him and we take care of him. But I am feeling pretty overwhelmed, working 40 hours and trying to keep things together, both in terms of Randy's care and our general family life. It's hard. We now have someone coming in to clean the house and I got a garden service. I just couldn't handle it all. The most important thing right now is Randy and his care; other stuff takes a back seat. Joe's work is intense, so much of it falls on me, though he really helps out when he can.

This family illustrates the kind and extent of kin work taking place in some longer-term lesbigay families. Explaining the increase in kin work for longer-term relationships appears related to several factors. First, the longer-term families are more economically secure, and therein can engage in more kin work. And as the earlier discussion of social class suggests, affluence often facilitates a larger kin network. Second, longer-term families are more settled, living in the same community for many years. This often enables the development of wider and deeper social connections to others. Maintaining such connections entails more kin work. Finally, other research suggests that strong links to social support networks contribute to the stability and longevity of lesbigay families (Kurdek 1988).

Ethnic and Racial Distinctions and Lesbigay Kin Work

The influence of ethnic and racial identity upon kin work eludes easy analysis. The confluence of class and race in American culture often conceals distinctions between race and class (Steinberg 1989). This study captures the diversity of lesbigay families in terms of ethnic/racial identity, with over 40 percent of the respondents identifying themselves as Latino-, African-, or Asian-American. However, comparisons are limited by the fact that many of these same respondents are middle class. I know from my attempts to identify lower middle-class and working-class respondents within these groups and among Euro-Americans that lesbigays with fewer economic resources are far more hesitant to participate in this kind of research due to concerns about exposure of sexual identity. That said, let me turn to some discussion of the possible influence of ethnic/racial identity upon the extent and character of kin work.

On the one hand, because most of these families's household earnings, education and occupational identities place them in the middle class, they exhibit kin work patterns similar to their Euro-American middle-class counterparts. Most live in what Dizard and Gadlin would characterize as "minimal families" (1990). Similar to many middle-class families, and in contrast to more affluent families, these families report fewer close friends, they invite nonbiolegal kin over less often, they send fewer cards, write fewer letters, make fewer visits, make fewer long-distance calls, buy, send and give fewer presents, and organize fewer social occasions. On the other hand, Latino/Asian/African-identified lesbigay families recurrently report more extensive connections to biolegal relatives than do Euro-American families, and further, they more often than not conceive of family in strongly biolegal terms. For instance, they report greater exchange of money and material goods with biolegal relatives. A number of factors help to explain these dynamics.

First, the wide majority of African-, Asian- and Latino-American lesbigays grew up in California. This contrasts markedly with the Euro-Americans, 90 percent of whom grew up elsewhere and relocated to California. This means that, because Asian-, African- and Latino-American biolegal kin live in the area, kin relations become more extensive and more pressing. This dynamic appears more strongly related to geographical proximity than to ethnic/racial distinction. Euro-Americans who grew up in this region also exhibit stronger ties to biolegal kin. However, many lesbigay people of color strongly link conceptions of racial/ethnic identity with conceptions of kinship, something not heard among Euro-Americans. Deborah James, an African-American woman, and her partner, Elsa Harding, also African-American, both speak of their connections to biolegal family as a component of their racial identity. Deborah, who works as a daycare provider, states:

> I think that Anglo-Americans don't value family as much as Black people do. I mean, I know some lesbians who think of each other as their family, but I really don't get that. I mean, I think you gotta love your family, even if they aren't that accepting of you. For us, part of being African-American is keeping your connections to your family and your church and stuff like that.

Barbara Cho, a thirty-eight year old Chinese-American woman working as a hotel clerk, holds a similar view: "I think of my family as my relatives. I love Barbara [her partner], but she is not really a part of my relatives. I don't want to say she isn't like family to me, but she's not my family. My mother and father, and my sisters, they are my family."

Although most Asian-, African-, and Latino-American lesbigay families conceive of family in biolegal terms (many respondents use the phrase "blood is thicker than water"), not all share this conception. Ceasar Portes and Andy Yanez, together for seventeen years and living in San Francisco's Mission district, a predominantly Latino neighborhood, exhibit an alternative pattern. Ceasar comes from a large Mexican-American family, most of whom live within a half-day's drive. Andy comes from a somewhat smaller, though equally close, Filipino-American family. Ceasar, diminishing the distinction between biolegal and lesbigay kin, asserts:

> We try to include all of our family, I mean both our gay family and our blood family, who live in San Jose or in Pacifica, in our lives. We also have our religious family, you know, many brothers and sisters in the faith, who are a part of our community. We invite everyone to be here. At first, it was hard. I don't think my blood relatives really understood gay people. But they have really changed. My mother loves all of our gay family now, and so we are all family together.

Andy reports that his family, while less accepting of his sexual identity than Ceasar's family, remains strongly committed to "keeping the family together," and includes Ceasar in family activities. Ceasar says that one of his sisters thinks of Andy as a "padrino," or godfather, to her children and makes an effort to include him in family activities.

Derrick Harding and Andrew Joust, both African-American men, provide another counterexample to the notion that "blood is thicker than water." Derrick mentions two heterosexual couples at their local church whom he considers family. In response to a question as to why he considers them such, he reflects: "Why yes, without a doubt, they care about us. They are like are godparents. They adopted us. We are real close with them. They are our family." His partner, Andrew, comments on the same heterosexual couples: "They took us under their wing when we first got here. I think of them as our family, I don't know what else you would call them." These competing views of the importance of ethnic/racial distinctions upon family that exist among African-, Asian-, and Latino-American lesbigay families point to the influence of factors related to but different from ethnicity that play a role in conceptions and constructions of family life. In the case of Andrew and Derrick, they migrated to the Bay Area and established connections to a church community. Their biolegal relatives remain in the East and far away from their day-to-day lives. Andrew reports that he last spoke with a biolegal relative more than a year ago. What really seems to divide those African-, Asian-, and Latino-American lesbigay families who redefine family in non-biolegal terms from those who do is social class. All of those families who blur the distinctions between biolegal and chosen families possess bachelor's degrees, work in professional careers, and earn higher incomes. Ceasar and Derrick both work as social workers, Andrew works as a secondary education teacher, and Andy works in higher education administration.

Kin Work and the Creation of Family

In its extensiveness, its focused character, and its reflection of genuine bonds of love and affection, kin work contributes much to the creation and sustenance of lesbigay family life. The family that results from this kin work is not, as many opponents of lesbigay people would have one believe, a rough approximation of the real thing or a sad substitute for genuine biolegal relations. Nor is it just a group of friends. Far from it. The bonds created within and among these families are far more extensive than what most middle-class Americans would conventionally view as friendship bonds (Rapp 1992). Middle-class Americans infrequently take in their friends and provide them housing, food, and medical care while they are dying. Moreover, any number of the lesbigay families in this study would not dream of sacrificing the lesbigay kin ties they have created in favor of some biolegally defined entity. Not to mention that many lesbigay families don't have to make that choice because their biolegal kin have not excluded them, and therein they have been able to integrate biolegal and lesbigay kin into a greater whole. Surely, many lesbigay families are struggling to create and sustain kin ties against socioeconomic conditions that deter them, but the effort is paradoxical and often threatening to the broader culture. These families are struggling to create and sustain kin relations with the qualities associated with family ideals in American culture, but not necessarily with the forms most citizens associate with family.

consumption work
in lesbigay families

In an age robbed of religious symbols, going to the shops replaces going to the church. . . . We have a free choice, but at a price. We can win experience, but never achieve innocence. Marx knew that the epic activities of the modern world involve not lance and sword, but dry goods. STEPHEN BAYLEY, BRITISH DESIGN CRITIC

The Character of Consumption Work

When thinking about consumption, and consumerism, in contemporary American society, many people conceive of such activity as a form of leisure. To be sure, some research reveals a self-indulgent quality to consumption (Sherry and McGrath 1989). Not surprisingly, many people find it hard to conceive of visits to shopping malls, or trips to Kmart, as work. Yet many people, predominantly men, in American culture find such excursions much less than pleasurable. Research indicates that the more consumption men do, the less they like it, and that when men do consume, they are more likely to buy things for themselves than women do (Fischer and Arnold 1990). Men often become irritable and bored with the process of locating, evaluating, and purchasing products. I know from six years of working in a large retail department store, the May Company, that many heterosexual men frequently attempt to speed up the process by encouraging quick decisions. Quick decisions often requiring women to bring items back for return or exchange during their lunch hours the following week. I remember many men congregating in the electronics section at the May Company in order to watch television sporting events, attempting to get leisure, while women pursued the work of consuming. I also recall the findings from one of my first fieldwork assignments in graduate school: to follow male/female dyads throughout their trips to grocery stores, recording the activities of each throughout the shopping experience. Males often tail along for the first few aisles, but then they become bored with the process. Sometimes men suggest a quick division of labor, a narrow task focus of gathering goods separately. Sometimes they gravitate to magazine racks. Sometimes they put the heat on their female companions to speed up. In any case, the point seems clear to me, if consumption is really leisure, why do so many heterosexual men dislike so much of it? Implicit within the previous comments is the assertion that distinctions prevail between many heterosexual men and many gay men in the realm of consumption. Empirical research confirms the presence of such distinctions. Rudd (1996) reports that gay men spend more time shopping, enjoy it more, and more often view shopping as an opportunity to browse than do heterosexual men. Aaker and Dean (1993) find that gay men are more aware of visual cues in advertising campaigns than heterosexual men.

The disinterestedness of heterosexual men in consumption, in part, emerges from a lack of knowledge on the part of many such men about the consumption needs of their households and families. They do not know what items the household already possesses, what it lacks, what family members like and don't like, the clothing sizes of family members, how much money is available for such purchases, how the current products compare to those offered at other establishments, and whether or not particular items are "appropriate," given concerns about style, and class, among other factors.

Consumption work requires a careful balancing of desires, resources, product and service availability, knowledge of product performance, and social expectations. The wrong decision can create more work (for example, taking the item back for return/exchange), or can create domestic unhappiness and discontent (requiring additional emotional labor). Decisions concerning gifts for family and friends raise kin work concerns. Those who buy presents must make decisions that sustain a sense of balance and reciprocity in exchange. Buying and giving gifts frequently serves as an opportunity to enhance or diminish certain social relationships. Recent research on holiday gift buying suggests that women often conceive of the task as obligatory, as a "responsibility" (Fischer and Arnold 1990). This sense of obligation emerges from their concern about sustaining harmonious kin relations.

The activities associated with consumption constitute another example of the invisible work that many women, and some men, do in the creation and maintenance of domestic life. Weinbaum and Bridges (1976) conceive of these consumption activities as "consumption work." The typology I use to frame consumption work within lesbigay households reflects the influence of Weinbaum and Bridges conception of consumption as the work of acquiring services and material goods. Weinbaum and Bridges argue that consumption work emerges in our economic structure from the need to "reconcile consumption needs with the production of commodities" (1976, 92). Consumer capitalism produces an ever-expanding array of goods and services that simultaneously necessitates ever more sophisticated strategies of appropriately linking those commodities to individual households. It is to those strategies, the work they involve, and the patterns of consumption work among lesbigay families that I now turn.

Monitoring the Marketplace and Determining the Standards of Consumption

A central component of consumption work involves a more or less constant monitoring of the marketplace. This monitoring includes making visits to stores, reading brochures about products and services, reading catalogs and other ad materials that come in the mail or via the Internet, reading magazine and newspaper ads, attentively watching television ads or listening to radio ads, and listening to others with information about some aspect of the marketplace. Similar to heterosexual families, lesbigay families rely upon a multitude of sources to set the standards and guide them in their consumption decisions, including friends and coworkers, print media, radio and television, family members, and recommendations from sales and service providers. Lesbigay consumers appear to rely extensively on lesbigay-oriented, or at least gay-positive newspapers, magazines, radio stations, television stations, and shops. Although, as I will describe in an upcoming section, significant variations prevail among lesbigay families in their exposure to and use of gay-friendly sources. Further, lesbigay families rely extensively upon other lesbigay families to determine what kinds of consumer products and services to buy, and where to buy them.

Catalogs, Magazines, and Newspaper Ads

With the arrival of each day's mail comes another opportunity to consume, or at least to engage in some consumption work. The effort may be as simple as deciding that one doesn't want to look a catalog of a particular retailer because one knows their product line, and also knows that one doesn't need anything from that particular line right now. Or perhaps the household is running low on money, and as part of the strategy of steadying the financial ship, all catalogs automatically go into the recycling bin. Other catalogs get put into a pile for perusal at a later time—an act of planning consumption decisions for the future. Other catalogs get immediate attention. The kind of attention they receive depends upon several other forms of domestic labor, notably kin work, but others as well. If a gift-giving holiday approaches, or if someone's birthday looms, the person doing the kin work entailed in remembering and buying gifts links that effort with the work of consumption. The process of sorting through the catalogs in the mail may become an opportunity to explore possible gift ideas. Daniel Sen Yung, a thirty-five-year-old health educator with primary responsibility for things domestic in his family, observes:

> I often look through catalogs with particular people in mind. A lot of times, I don't find anything good in them, but it gives me ideas about the kinds of presents I could get for someone. I bought our friend Alex a set of garden tools from the Smith and Hawken catalog. They had a special price on this set in their Fall catalog, and I knew he wanted it, so I ordered it for his birthday.

Daniel's comment reveals the presence of a constant awareness of kin concerns that inform the process of consumption. Daniel readily knows upcoming birthdays and possesses a strong sense of things he thinks his household needs. He keeps a written list of these. He reports that when his partner suggests something for the household, he writes it on the list. Daniel keeps a calendar recording birthdays and anniversaries and he connects these social events to a constant monitoring of catalogs and magazines that come through the house. Daniel's answer reveals not only a sensitivity to and knowledge of the desires of kin, but it also reveals an awareness of expenses, a point I will return to later.

Attending to catalogs, magazines, and newspapers for information about goods and services constitutes one of the more apparent aspects of consumption work. Despite popular conceptions, when women, and some men, read the Macy's supplement in their Sunday papers, they are not necessarily engaged in self-indulgent leisure for they are often engaged in work, or in a process of creating rich patterns of domestic life while simultaneously linking their household to the broader economy and society. In this respect lesbigay families and heterosexual families would seem quite similar. I also suspect a great overlap exists between lesbigay families and heterosexual families sharing similar sociodemographic traits in the character of many of the catalogs, magazines, and newspapers that they read. However, lesbigay families report that they turn to gay and gay-friendly print media with great frequency in making consumption decisions. For instance, over 95 percent of participants report turning to a gay or lesbian magazine or newspaper to help them find some good or service provider.

Reading Brochures

Another component of consumption work entails reading different kinds of brochures provided by retailers, manufacturers, and service providers. Some brochures come in the mail, others one picks up at the retailer or service center. Such brochures frequently offer guidance on making decisions about what product to purchase. In the domestic realm, homemakers compare such information to knowledge about their particular household. Two examples from lesbigay families illustrate the process. Lance Converse, a forty-year-old healthcare administrator, describes how he decided to buy additional pieces of flatware:

> I have a little brochure that we picked up when we first bought this silverware. I read over that, and it let me know what additional pieces were available. As time went on, and we had people over, or on Thanksgiving, well, I slowly figured out

what pieces we needed. I would make a mental note, look at the brochure, and then I went down to Macy's, and I brought the brochure with me. I wanted to make sure I got the same pattern.

Another participant, Barbara Cho, comments: "The last brochure I can think of using was for those window blinds. I picked it up at Home Depot and brought it home to decide what style and color of blind to get. I showed it to Sandy [her partner] and we decided on something. I took the brochure back to Home Depot and placed the order." Gathering, reading, and reflecting upon the information provided by brochures frames one small, though not insignificant, part of consumption work.

Reading Books

In addition to reading brochures, some lesbigay consumers turn to books to guide consumption decisions. The process of buying gifts for holy unions, services of commitment, and weddings occasionally relies on these textual sources. An extensive literature exists for middle- and upper-middle-class families regarding the character and quality of gifts for different occasions. Emily Post's *Etiquette* offers its bourgeois readers an entire chapter of advice concerning the character, timing, cost, and even the return of gifts. I became aware of this chapter from one of the participants for this study, Beth Wilkerson, who turned to it to find out if monogramming a bathrobe with the initials of someone's name was "tacky" or not. She discovered that Emily Post considers it appropriate to do so, but she also learned that for a gift to a woman, the monogram should be the first letter of the first name, and for a man, the first letter of the last name. Beth considers Emily's advice sexist, but she followed it anyway.

Radio and Television

The influence of radio and television advertising upon the consumption behavior of lesbigay families extends well beyond the parameters of this study. Some empirical research investigates this topic (Freitas, Kaiser, and Hammidi 1996; Clark 1991). In terms of this study, lesbigay family members rarely refer to radio listening and television viewing as sources of information about consumption. As discussed elsewhere, more affluent families report watching television shows like *Martha Stewart Living* and indicating that such shows influence their consumer behavior. My field observations reflect a great deal of television watching, particularly on the part of suburban, and often less affluent, lesbigay families. Does this mean that television more significantly influences their consumption behavior and the standards to which they adhere? I don't know. Rarely do participants indicate that they turn to television or radio as a source of information about goods and services, nor do they mention either radio or television as influencing their decisions to buy. This might simply reflect a lack of awareness as to the influence of such media upon them. If these media do have a great influence, it appears quite hidden from the consciousness of many lesbigay consumers.

Lesbigay Families, Coworkers, and Biolegal Relatives

In contrast to radio and television, interactions with other lesbigay families, coworkers, and nearby biolegal relatives play a central role, at least in the self-understanding, in decisions of what to buy and where to buy it. Eight of ten participants indicate that they turn to other lesbians and gays for information about goods and services. Similarly, many families report going to certain shops or using particular service providers based on the advice and experience of other lesbian and gay people. Just fewer than half of participants report taking consumption advice from coworkers. Not surprisingly, most of those who do are out of the closet at work. Apparently, raising domestic consumption concerns at work, when one is in the closet, does not occur very often. Two of ten participants mention a biolegal relative in response to my question, "Who do you turn to for advice about goods and services?" For the most part, this happens among those lesbigay families with biolegal families residing nearby.

In terms of standards of consumption, lesbigay families seem to compare themselves to "similarly situated" families and individuals. By this I mean to say that lesbigay families compare themselves with families with whom they share comparable socioeconomic characteristics. Many families report making decisions to purchase certain items or services based on similar acquisitions by peers. Several examples illustrate this dynamic. Susan Posner and Carry Taglia recently bought a new dining room table. They sought the advice of several lesbian and gay friends, all in couples and all of whom owned dining room tables. The inspiration for making such a purchase, Carry comments, came from a concern about maintaining reciprocity in their social circles: "All of our close friends have dining room tables, and we get invited over a lot by many of them. I had always dreamed of having our own dining room and I love to entertain. It felt great to buy it, and it brought about a sense of balance for me, and I think, for Susan. Now we can have everyone over at our house." When Susan and Carry went to look at tables, they went to retailers suggested by their lesbigay friends. They gathered information about what their friends paid for their tables and decided on an acceptable price range, in great part based on the expenditures of their peers. Susan reflects: "When I think about what we planned to spend, I think the fact that Jeff and Michael and Jessica and Lindy had both spent between $1500 and $2000 influenced us a lot. It was more than I think we would have spent if we were completely rational about it, but it's a great table and it's an investment in our home and our life together, so I guess you pay the piper, as they say."

Wayne Osmundsen and Sterling Graves provide another example of the influence of other lesbigay families upon one another's consumption activities. Wayne indicates that the last major purchase they made was to buy a new personal computer. They had not, until recently, seen any need to own a home computer. He reports that the idea to get a new computer originated in a discussion with their close friends, Perry and Tim. Perry and Tim maintain communications with a large number of gay-male friends across the country using electronic mail. From the discussion, Sterling realized the potential to stay in touch with friends that he does not see very often, and an opportunity to create connections to new friends. The four of them, Sterling, Wayne, Perry, and Tim, had all traveled recently to a gay resort and circuit party in South Beach (a gay area of Miami Beach, Fla.). At that party Sterling and Wayne met several new friends. Sterling and Wayne realized in their discussion with Perry and Tim that many of the new friends they met in South Beach were part of a group e-mail list, and that the group maintained contact throughout the year via e-mail, and then met up with one another at the various circuit parties. Realizing that they could begin to develop a connection to this group, Sterling and Wayne decided to buy a personal computer and to get connected through the Internet. The advice and insights of Perry greatly determined the decisions made by Sterling and Wayne about what kind of computer to buy and where to buy it. Perry provided the names of computer dealers, provided directions on how to get there, told them what to ask the sales personnel, recommended America Online as a carrier, encouraged them to buy a Macintosh, told them they should get a second phone line for the computer, advised them on the cost, and went with them for the final sale. Perry monitored the local papers watching for sales on Macintosh computers and called Wayne when he saw something of interest.

The consumption experiences of Sterling and Wayne and Carry and Susan reflect a prevailing pattern among a majority of lesbigay families. These families depend upon one another and upon single lesbian and gay people for advice and information about consumption. These families compare themselves with those they view as their socioeconomic peers and make consumption decisions in light of those comparisons. There are notable exceptions to this pattern, particularly among suburban lesbigay families, most of whom compare themselves with similarly situated heterosexual families and who rely more extensively on other sources of information, including biolegal relatives and other media sources. I will say more about these variations among lesbigay families in an upcoming section. Let it suffice to say for now that a substantial majority of lesbigay families, even those in suburban communities, tend to depend upon one another in the process of making and carrying out consumption decisions.

Entering the Marketplace

In this study, one in three participants visit the grocery store more than three times a week. A similar proportion visit a department store or hardware store at least three times a month. Visits to grocery stores mostly result in purchases, but visits to department and hardware stores do not always involve making purchases. At least among many lesbigay families, and I suspect among others as well, many of these visits occur in order to get a clearer picture of what goods and services exist, to compare and contrast products offered by different stores, to gain a vision of what the household could become, and as an occasion for comparing the particulars of a given household with the options that exist in the marketplace. Many lesbigay family members who do consumption work speak of going to malls or urban shopping districts "just to look." Sometimes, families go together "just to look," but most often individuals do this alone. These consumption workers become scouts in their exploration of an increasingly complex and choice-laden marketplace. This scouting contrasts with the actual purchase of goods, especially durable goods, where adults go together to make the purchase. The scouting takes more time and energy. The individuals who just go to look, and their families, most often perceive of this activity as a result of different personality traits or interests. Perhaps this is true, but what strikes me as significant is that those family members who do more of the other forms of domestic work, notably kin work, and housework, go to the store just to look much more often than other members of their household. Bill Fagan, an artist who works in a studio out of his home, comments:

> I think I tend to go out and just look at stuff more than Rich [his partner] does. Part of that is my effort to get out of the house. I am here all the time. But it's more than that. I find that I am thinking about all kinds of stuff about our house when I go out to shop. Like, I will be thinking of presents for Rich's birthday, or gifts for my nephews for Christmas, when I go, or I will get ideas about how to improve things in the house.

Bill's observations reveal the presence of consumption work in what many might perceive as a rather individualistic pursuit. His visits to stores function as opportunities for linking the marketplace with other domestic concerns including the work of maintaining kin relations as well as maintaining his residence. I approach the questions of the division of domestic labor in an upcoming chapter, but let it suffice to say for now that scouting is not equally distributed among family members, but scouting for goods and services by visiting the marketplace, while most often invisible, plays a significant part in the character of consumption. It should also be noted that entering the marketplace with other members of one's lesbigay family can be fraught with experiences of heterosexism. For example, My lover and I recently went shopping for clothing at a suburban shopping center in suburban Palo Alto, Calif. My lover picked out and tried on several pairs of pants. A sales associate assisted him. He decided on two pairs, and handed them to me to buy with my department store credit card. The sales associate, quite perplexed, blurted out: "Gee, that's really nice that you are buying pants for him, but you probably need the cash." I didn't quite get what she was saying, so I said, "What do you mean." She replied: "Well, when he pays you for the pants, you will have cash, instead of just store credit." To this I replied, "He's my lover, and I doubt I will be seeing much cash." The sales associate turned beet red, and the rest of the encounter was rather stern. Most every lesbigay person who reads this account could provide another similar experience. In my research I have heard countless tales of such interactions with sales associates; furniture, appliance, and car dealers; and insurance providers. Other research confirms the prevalence of these dynamics (Walters and Curran 1996; Jones 1996).

Phone Calls

Making phone calls to goods and service providers often becomes one of the first steps in entering the marketplace. Seemingly uncomplicated, making phone calls requires a variety of time- and energy-consuming activities, including consulting phone books and directories, determining where to look in the phone book for the good or service you need, reading and selecting from phone book ads, arranging to call during business hours, determining the right questions to ask on the phone, and interacting with providers on the phone. Randy Ambert, explaining the last major purchase he and his partner, Russ, made, describes the use of the phone in pursuit of a waffle iron. He began by looking at a lesbigay telephone directory called the Lavender Pages. He looked under the appliances category but could not find a listing for any such business. He looked in the Yellow Pages and discovered a variety of listings including several hardware stores. This discovery sent him back to the Lavender Pages where he found one listing under hardware: Cliffs Variety, a Castro district hardware store. He then called Cliffs and inquired about waffle irons. It took a while for someone to look to see if they sell waffle irons. They did. While seemingly insignificant, Randy indicates that the effort took about thirty minutes.

Comparing Prices and Products

Comparing the cost and character of goods and services takes considerable time. The process of comparing products and services on the basis of quality, durability, cost, and other factors entails multiple trips and phone calls, attention to ads in various media, and listening to friends and family report on their own purchases. Alma Duarte, a thirty-five-year-old office manager, describes the process she went through to buy a new camera. Interestingly, Alma bears responsibility for taking family photos and organizing them. Re-

sponsibility for photos and photo albums tends to fall to the more domestically involved partner in most lesbigay relationships studied here (see chapter 3). Alma's effort to buy a camera took her to four different stores. She estimates that altogether she spent five or six hours commuting to those stores
and looking at their camera selection. She brought home brochures to share
with her partner, Rosanna, and read the ad supplements in the Sunday paper
looking for the best price on the cameras. She went to a small camera shop
owned by a gay man nearby her home where she "got the best information
about the cameras," but she actually bought the camera at a large discount
warehouse store where "the sales people didn't really know anything about
the cameras, but it was a lot cheaper." She reports feeling guilty about getting the information from "the local guy" and then buying from the discount
outfit. Students of domestic labor should not underestimate the significance
of these feelings.

In fact, Alma's feelings suggest that part of the work involved in comparing goods and services includes managing interactions with salespeople and
with service providers. This includes the work of negotiating conflicts that
exist between larger entities in the society (small businesses vs. large businesses; lesbigay shops vs. straight shops). Alma reports that the small camera
shop owner put a lot of pressure on her to buy, and she had to think of reasons not to do so, less than truthful ones. Alma tells me that she prefers to
buy from gay shops, but she won't if it will cost a lot more money: "Sometimes, I will pay the gay tax, especially if it isn't that much," in order to buy
from lesbian and gay shops. The "gay tax" refers to the widespread perception among lesbigay families that it costs more money to patronize lesbigay
businesses. I suspect this perception has less to do with "gay taxes" than it
does with the ability of large companies to reach economies of scale, as well
as the inability of lesbigay businesses to grow large enough to participate in
such economies. Alma told the camera shop owner she needed to consult
with her spouse, but in fact she wanted to see if she could get it cheaper. And
now that she knew what she was looking for, in part based on the advice of
the small camera shop employee, she could do that fairly easily at the discount store. Negotiating the terrain of the modern marketplace with its
competitions and conflicts takes its place among the various forms of work
involved in consumption. This work includes the management of feelings,
emotions, and often uncomfortable interactions produced in the modern
marketplace.

Getting Consensus

Another component of consumption work involves the efforts to achieve consensus, or at least consent, regarding the purchase of durable goods and many services. Forty of the fifty-two lesbigay families studied make decisions to consume jointly, while twelve families keep purchasing decisions strictly separate. Most of those twelve families have been together for less than five years. I recall interviewing one family where they understood every item in the house to belong to one or the other person, but rarely both. It is interesting to note that under such circumstances the participants rarely conceive of their relationship in familial ways, and also to note that four of those twelve relationships dissolved over the course of the study, including the one where every item was conceived of as separate. I now wonder if their portrayal of every item in such a fashion was not a dress rehearsal for the eventual division of property, perhaps even part of the negotiations. More established lesbigay families make major consumer purchases in a joint fashion.

When describing the process of making decisions about more expensive consumer purchases, I found that many of these decisions are often shepherded by one member of the family. These individuals often articulate the need for a good or service, locate the product or service, do the comparative pricing, and know the budget well enough to suggest an affordable time frame for making a purchase. One component of this process involves convincing other family members of the importance of these purchases. Sarah Lynch, a thirty-year-old graphic artist who works out of her home, explains:

> We go through a little ritual. I come up with ideas for things we need. She says, "No, we can't afford it." She doesn't think we need anything nor that we can afford anything. Then I have to come up with reasons why we should get something. I am strategic about it, meaning I bring it up at the moment that she is willing to hear it—emotionally, that is—and when she can see for herself that it would be nice to have a certain thing. I also know to check the budget, and to come up with a plan to pay for things.

Sarah's comments suggest the presence of a lot of behind-the-scenes effort. Sarah, in anticipating her partner's response, relies upon her knowledge of the product, her knowledge of the family budget, and her reading of her partner's emotional disposition.

Moreover, many of those who do much of the consumption work for their families also develop a strong sense of what family members like and don't like in terms of colors, patterns, fabrics, and styles. As part of the process of reaching a consensus to purchase durable goods like furniture and appliances, or "domestics" like towels, linen, and drapery, the consumer either relies upon a stock knowledge of family member preferences or must ask a variety of questions to determine these. When asking participants which one of them took more interest in the process of acquiring things for your home, a majority of lesbigay families acknowledge that one person in the relationship invests more energy and possesses greater knowledge about such matters. Even in those families where participants indicate that they take an equal interest, field research suggests this is often not true, particularly when considering more mundane forms of consumption work like selecting and buying kitchen utensils or dish towels, or buying cleaning products. In most cases, family members defer to the person who does more of the consumption work to make consumption decisions, and most decisions do not really require getting a consensus.

However, in some instances, usually when the family faces tight fiscal limits, family members cannot readily agree on making certain purchases. This sometimes leads to protracted negotiations, negotiations that often require the efforts of the consumer to provide rationalizations justifying certain choices or purchases. Michael Herrera and his partner, Federico Monterosa, have been together for four years. Michael, describing the most recent major purchase they made for their home, says:

> It was the coffee maker. It wasn't so hard deciding what kind to buy, but it was quite an effort convincing Freddy that we should get it. He doesn't drink coffee too much and didn't want to buy one, or if we got one, he only wanted a cheap one. I wanted a nice one, but I had to come up with a good reason to get a nicer one and spend more money. So, it turned out that Freddy's parents were coming to San Francisco and were planning to stay with us. Freddy's mom likes coffee, and so I made the case that we should buy a nice coffee maker to make her feel at home, feel more comfortable because it was kind of hard on her when Freddy came out to her and all. With that, he agreed and we went to Macy's and bought a decent coffee maker.

It turns out that Michael's' strategy to get consensus on the coffee maker reflects a more or less common dynamic at work in this family and many others. Because they are on a tight budget, Federico seems to play the role of keeping spending down. Michael actually encourages Federico to do this. Michael refers to Federico as the "no person," the one who prevents spending until and unless Michael comes up with a strong enough rationale to legitimate the spending.

Monitoring the Performance of Products and Services

Product and service monitoring entails a variety of efforts on the part of those who do consumption work. Much of the effort remains concealed, often hidden in the minds of those who do it. Some of this kind of work becomes more visible among those who keep records about services and products.

Mental Notes of Product Performance

Those who do consumption work often develop an extensive list of mental notes about products and services. They readily recall detailed problems with particular goods or service providers. They remember where stores and service centers are located. They can recall the repair and maintenance history of particular household items. All of these mental activities constitute concealed forms of consumption work. Some of the following examples emerge from this study: recalling the last time one replaced a filter in the air purifier; remembering to change vacuum cleaner bags; recalling what company last steam-cleaned the rugs; and recalling the last time the cat's flea collar was changed. Possessing such knowledge can reduce both expense and aggravation.

Inquiring of participants about their dissatisfaction with recently purchased products or services reveals differentiated knowledge among lesbigay family members in this arena. In the majority of households, one person could provide detailed accounts of dissatisfaction with a particular good or service while other family members, if they knew of something, had only broad and vague knowledge of the details. Together for over ten years, Cheryl Fitzgerald and Clarice Perry have three children. They live in a distant North Bay suburb of San Francisco. Cheryl works part-time for wages at a social service agency while Clarice works as a community college professor. Cheryl maintains much of the household, including most aspects of consumption work. Quite dissatisfied with an upholstery cleaning service she recently used, Cheryl offers extensive detail:

> I called this guy out, he had his own, one-man company, Bay Cleaning Services, and he advertised in the gay press, so I had him out to clean that chair . First off, the guy showed up late, like two hours late. I was quite annoyed. He said he knew what he was doing, but in fact he used too strong of a cleaner on the fabric, and the fabric totally faded. I didn't realize until several days later. The chair looked like it had been outside in the desert sun for a couple of months. I called him, but he of course denied that the cleaning had anything to do with it. It ended up costing $400 to re-cover it.

Clarice knew about the problems with the chair, but none of the detail. She did not recall that the man arrived late, nor the company name, nor that the man advertised in the gay press. All of these details reveal the different forms of work that Cheryl pursued in arranging for the chair cleaning. In the future, Cheryl will use these forms of information to arrange for future cleaning services.

Maintaining Records and Organizing Product Information

The majority of lesbigay families keep files or drawers where they store instructional manuals and service information. Some families keep records of toll-free numbers for product information and servicing. Others record on notepads, calendars, or in diaries the maintenance schedules for both products and services. Beth Wilkerson and her partner, Glenna O'Conner, have been together for five years. Among notations for people's birthdays and anniversaries, Beth records on a kitchen calendar the dates when she last replaced the cat's flea collar, the last time they fumigated the house for insects, and the last time they replaced the screens on their furnace. She expresses dissatisfaction to me concerning her perceived responsibility for organizing and maintaining these kinds of records:

> I don't really know how it happened, but I have responsibility for these things. If I don't remember, and write it down, she certainly won't. We have to keep a watch on the termites or they will do a lot of damage to the house. We didn't realize the importance at first, until we had to replace the floor in the laundry room. Very expensive. So I make sure the fumigators come out at least once a year.

Of course, such record keeping facilitates consumption activities. For each of the records that Beth keeps, she purchases a particular good or service designed to address the problem. This record keeping organizes consumption, linking this particular household to the broader structure of the economy. Similar to many other forms of domestic labor, in and of themselves, these notations appear small and not particularly laborious, yet in the aggregate these kinds of activities consume large portions of someone's energy and time.

Locating Repeat Products

Late one Tuesday afternoon with me tagging along, Lindsey Tuttle, a thirty-five-year-old woman who works part-time at a downtown San Francisco hotel, ventures out to do the weekly grocery shopping. On her grocery list, she had written "mop head," for she needs a new mop head for her sponge mop. We leave the house at about 2:30 p.m. She goes out to Patrini's Market, her usual grocery store. While in an aisle of housecleaning supplies and laundry detergents, she locates the mops. There she finds the mop that she originally purchased, but no replacement mop heads. The original mop cost fourteen dollars. Upon this discovery, Lindsey scans all of the other mop-head replacements, deliberating whether they might fit. She comes up empty. She goes to the store manager's desk to inquire about replacements. The person working the desk does not know anything about product lines but offers to page one of the managers. We wait for about five minutes. Finally, the store manager comes and Lindsey explains her need. The manager looks into a book of products the store carries and tells her that they do not carry the replacement. He recommends that she try a hardware store called Goodman's. We finish up the shopping and leave the store at 3:45. We get to Goodman's at about 4:00. We go inside, find our way to the housecleaning products section, and she begins to search for mop heads. We could not find the mop head. Lindsey asks a salesperson about it. It turns out that Goodman's carries the product line ("Quickie"), but not that particular mop. The saleswoman tells us to go to the Home Depot, a home improvement warehouse store. The nearest one is in Colma, about eight miles south of San Francisco. We leave Goodman's at 4:25. Lindsey suggests that we drop off the groceries, mostly to keep the frozen yogurt from thawing. We get back to the house at

4:45. She puts the groceries away, and at 5:10 she decides to call Home Depot. She spends about ten minutes getting connected to the right department
and waiting for someone to answer. Yes, they have one. At 5:30 we get back
into the car, and head south on Interstate 280. We get on the highway only
to discover that it's rush hour. It takes us about thirty-five minutes to get to
Home Depot.

The place is a huge warehouse. The directory signs above each aisle are
quite generic, and recessed so that one must look down each aisle to see
them. We finally come to aisle 14 with a sign that reads Cleaning Tools and
Supplies. The aisle appears the length of a city block. It takes us several minutes to find the product line and the particular mop head she needs. We get
into the checkout line. We wait in line for another ten minutes. We get into
the car at 6:30. We get back to the house at 6:45. Replacing the Quickie mop
head alone consumes nearly two hours of Lindsey's day. Lindsey feels a bit
stressed, and when we arrive home, her lover, Sue, is waiting. She asks Lindsey about the day, but Lindsey doesn't particularly feel like talking about it.
She responds: "Just the usual stuff."

The "usual stuff" for Lindsey includes the intermittent but not unusual
activity of tracking down consumer products. Examples of this kind of effort
abound among lesbigay households.

Commuting to Sources

In recent decades, with the centralization of individual shops into malls and
the elimination of smaller, independent retailers by larger megastores, the
process of visiting stores has changed. Such trips now involve longer commutes to and from retail sites. This adds to consumption work because part
of the work includes both arranging for and actually commuting to these
sites. For less affluent lesbigay families, making arrangements to visit a mall
or store often involves getting someone else to drive them. Less affluent families also seem to drive longer distances to do consumption. Partly this is a
function of the less affluent living in suburban locations in the Bay Area. But
it also reflects the lower prices offered at warehouse-style retailers, retailers
like Costco, Home Depot, and Wal-Mart. More affluent lesbigay families
frequently harbor feelings of disdain for such places, but those of more moderate incomes shop at these warehouse stores to manage costs. To do so often involves passing by local shops and commuting greater distances.

Queuing

Knowing the kind, quality, and location of the goods or services one wishes to purchase all constitute forms of consumption work. After making choices, the waiting begins. Waiting on the phone, waiting in lines at grocery stores, post offices, and department stores, and at ATM machines devours time. Frequently, consumer purchases require waiting at home: waiting for furniture deliveries, for phone installation and repair, for appliance repair, for real estate appraisers, for UPS deliveries, and for cleaning services. Waiting, while not particularly labor intensive, requires one to reschedule one's day in light of the need to wait. This sort of waiting also often assumes the capacity to be home during business hours. Waiting is a part of the work of consuming.

Matching Expenditure to Financial Resources

While locating and retrieving consumer goods constitutes a perceptible form of domestic labor, concealed behind such efforts is a complex set of mental calculations and schemes concerning expenditure and affordability. In her study of American housewives, Helen Lopata conceives of money as one of the "physical tools of being a housewife" (1971, 172). Lopata emphasizes the importance of money to the homemaker's conceptions of how to solve problems, to achieving a sense of security, to making domestic work less unpleasant, as well as to planning for the future. Extending Lopata's metaphor of money as tool, the successful use of the money tool requires a skillful manager to use the tool: the money manager. Among a majority of the lesbigay families I can identify the presence of a money manager. This kind of a role emerges most commonly among those families with joint finances. Thirty-eight of the fifty-two families in the study have joint finances. In contrast to heterosexual families, joint finances generally develop more slowly in gay and lesbian relationships (Blumstein and Schwartz 1983). This means that many lesbigay families go through a process of negotiation in the formative years of their relationship, a process during which a money manager often emerges. I do not mean to suggest that the money manager makes all or most of the important decisions about expenditures, for that is not the case. Rather, I mean to say that in most of these families someone emerges who coordinates the use of money. For most of these families the coordination of money and making consumption decisions are tightly intertwined. In order to achieve a balance of consumption choices with financial resources, one must possess a strong sense of household cash flow, available credit and new credit options, long-term financial prognosis, and an agreed-upon conception of priority purchases and/or a strategy to manage unagreed-upon purchases. Let me now turn to an illustration of this sort of consumption work.

Lily Chin and Carol Len live in a south San Francisco neighborhood known as Visitation Valley. Together for thirteen years, the couple rents a house in this predominantly working-class neighborhood. Together they earn around $45,000 a year. Lily works as an office administrator and Carol, as a social worker. Lily manages the family finances. They recently decided to buy a new futon for their place. They dislike their present couch and wanted something that guests could use more easily when they stay over. Lily and Carol went together to several futon dealers and finally decided on one that cost about five hundred dollars. Carol recalls asking Lily at the first store how much they could afford. Lily was not exactly sure, but indicated that they could finance it. She also knew that they could not increase their monthly bills by much more than $30 to $40 without cutting into the grocery funds. After visiting the first store they decided to look into stores with financing options. Lily called several furniture dealers and got the details of their credit programs. After making these calls and the getting the needed financial information, the couple visited several of the stores. Based on Lily's analysis of the family budget and her investigation of credit options, the couple purchased a futon for $500. Financed through a dealer-arranged credit program, they pay $32 a month for eighteen months for the futon. Lily's efforts, and her knowledge of family finances, successfully linked the purchase of the futon to the family's financial situation.

The Rhythms of Consumption Work

Much of the consumption work of lesbigay households reflects the annual and seasonal patterns of the wider society. Lesbigay families, just like heterosexual families, increase their consumption activity during the late fall/early winter in preparation for holidays. They plan their finances to accommodate this pattern of consumption activity. Many individuals plan particular kinds of consumption activities for particular weekends or particular dates during the year. Michael Herrera, in preparation for Christmas, plans well in advance the day that he will go to the Flower Mart to buy poinsettias. Deborah James goes to a particular shop each year in the Western Addition to buy gifts for Kwanza. Lawrence Shoong marks on his calendar when he needs to call and arrange for tickets for the Gay Men's Chorus holiday concert. Emily Fortune calls her grocer three weeks in advance to order a turkey for her Thanksgiving feast. Envisioning, planning, and executing this myriad of seemingly unrelated activities actually reflects the presence of rhythmical patterns of consumption work.

Those who do this work often maintain records of what needs to happen and when. Many use calendars to remind themselves of when to do certain kinds of consumption. As part of the research strategy for this study I asked families to share their family calendars or to indicate how they remind themselves about upcoming events and obligations. Forty-four of the fifty-two families maintain a calendar to record such events. In thirty-seven of those forty-four families, one person wrote most of the notations in the calendar, and not surprisingly that person also often bears responsibility for consumption work. Most families record on their calendars birthdays and anniversaries, including the anniversaries of commitment ceremonies and holy unions for lesbigay friends and family. These notations often serve as reminders of the need to consume and whether to simply buy a card or arrange for a gift. Cesar Portes and Andy Yanez keep an elaborate calendar recording the events of both their biolegal family and of their gay family. They and many other members of their family all receive an annual copy of the calendar. Cesar puts the calendar together and has done so for many years. The calendar records important dates including monthly family gatherings. On his own copy of this calendar, Cesar reminds himself of greetings or gifts that he needs to buy, usually making a notation ten days or so before an event. At the beginning of each new year Cesar sits down and records the major events of the next year onto the family calendar. In this way Cesar plans some of his consumption work in tune with the rhythms of the seasons and the cycle of special occasions and integrates the family.

Variations in Consumption Work

As already alluded to, the breadth and character of consumption work varies among lesbigay families most significantly on the basis of socioeconomic status, but also on the basis of whether a family resides in an urban or suburban setting, the presence of children, the length of the relationship, and possibly on the basis of gender. Let me first address the influence of socioeconomic status upon consumption.

Social Class Distinctions

Those families at the top of the social ladder do more consumption. Nonetheless, I am surprised by the amount of time and energy put into consumption by most households. For while affluent lesbigay families shop and procure the services of a much greater number, and a much wider range of businesses, those of more moderate means spend a great deal more effort on the more limited number of consumption activities they do. For example, affluent families rarely comparison shop among grocers to find bargains on food stuffs, use coupons, or pay attention to price variations among grocery product brands. In contrast, less affluent lesbigay families frequently read flyers from grocers and retailers that come in the mail and in local papers in an effort to manage costs. Affluent families rarely even read such flyers, opting instead to shop in light of other factors like greater selection, fresher meats and produce, and more stylish product lines. In general, more affluent shoppers choose stores on the basis of quality, style, service, and convenience, and while less affluent families mention these criteria, they emphasize price more strongly. This pattern occurs not only for grocery shopping, but also for the consumption of the household appliances, linens, towels, clothing, dishes, cookery, home-repair supplies, and furniture.

Accordingly, this concern with price results in lesbigay families with fewer economic resources shopping in different locations. Most often, this means trips to megastores promising lower prices and offering less service. As already indicated, the less affluent travel greater distances to make consumer purchases. Partly this is a function of less affluent families living in suburban locations, but even among urban dwellers, less affluent families travel to the nearer suburbs to shop at megastores like Target, Home Depot, Costco, or Bed and Bath. It is only recently that stores like Costco acquired space in the city of San Francisco proper. And even though these stores built within the city, many affluent families report avoiding such outlets. I heard many a derisive comment from more affluent lesbian and gay consumers about Costco and "the kind of people who shop there" (that is, poorer people). More affluent families buy more goods and services from smaller, nearby, more up-scale firms. Clear patterns emerge here. Among those families reporting annual incomes above the sample median ($58,500), one finds that the last major consumer purchase occurred at a large urban retailer (Macy's, Nordstrom, Neiman-Marcus, the Emporium) or at an urban specialty shop in seven of ten cases. In contrast, among those families below the median, the last major purchase occurred at a less prestigious, less expensive, often sub-urban retailer (Sears, Montgomery Ward, and J. C. Penney) or at a megas-tore (Home Depot, Target, Bed and Bath Superstore) in nine of ten cases.

Another distinction that prevails between more and less affluent families concerns the sources of information about consumption. More affluent fam-ilies rely on the advice of friends more extensively in making consumption decisions. This reflects both the greater numbers of social ties among the wealthier families, as well as their more limited exposure to popular media outlets, notably television. More affluent families spend their evenings in other places than in front of televisions. As I have said already, television functions for less affluent lesbigay families as a reprieve from work, a restful occupation. More affluent families disproportionately spend their evenings in gyms, at church and synagogue meetings, at community board meetings, political club meetings, in classrooms, at concerts and performances. Rest-ing in front of a television seems less necessary, or at least less desirable for the affluent. This changes the nature of consumption decisions for the afflu-ent. Due to their extensive social interaction, prosperous families rely more extensively on friends to guide their consumption work.

By the same token, the more prosperous also rely more upon magazines and mail-order catalogs than do the less prosperous. For instance, the pros-perous are much more likely to subscribe to magazines. As a part of the in-terviewing and the fieldwork for this research, I recorded the magazines left out on tables and counters in lesbigay households. I also asked families to re-port to which magazines they subscribed. The less affluent the family, the fewer magazines they received, and vice versa. The coffee tables and kitchen counters of the affluent are adorned with magazines. Common magazines (the magazine appeared in more than three households) found in affluent households include *Consumer Reports, Architectural Digest, Metropolitan Home, Gourmet, Sunset, Martha Stewart Living, Better Homes and Gardens, Art News, Food and Wine, Interview, GQ, Details, Travel and Leisure,* the *Atlantic Monthly,* and *The New Yorker.* Not only did I observe more magazines of this sort, but

I also observed more mail-order catalogs and specialty store catalogs among the affluent. Common catalogs (again, more than three families display or subscribe) include Crate and Barrel, the Pottery Barn, Brooks Brothers, L. L. Bean, International Male, IKEA, Chef's Catalog, Macy's, and Eddie Bauer. More affluent families report relying on these print sources of information much more often in making consumption decisions. Less affluent homes depend on local newspapers for consumption information. It is also of interest that the more affluent households are much more likely to display and/or subscribe to lesbigay magazines like *The Advocate*, *Out*, *10 Percent*, and *Genre*. In this study, thirteen families subscribed to *The Advocate*, three to *Out*, and one to *Genre*. Of these seventeen subscriptions, twelve occurred among households earning above the median income of the sample.

Further, these subscriptions to lesbigay publications mirror a broader distinction between more and less affluent lesbigay families in terms of consumption. More affluent families more extensively rely on lesbigay sources for consumption. There are several dimensions to this. First, affluent lesbigay families rely on advice from other lesbigay people or lesbigay family members much more frequently than do the less affluent. Second, the affluent buy goods and services more often, and with greater resolve, from lesbigay businesses. This pattern persists both in terms of frequenting local lesbigay shops and in terms of relying on national lesbigay magazines and lesbigay-oriented mail-order catalogs.

By "greater resolve" I mean to point out that concerns about boycotting certain companies or patronizing other companies due to lesbigay issues, occurs much more often among more prosperous lesbigay families. Two examples illustrate this point. As I indicated in the housework chapter, I asked families to share bank transactions for one week prior to the interviews. In recording these transactions I asked the name of their bank. On many occasions family members made comments concerning the lesbigay boycott of the Bank of America. The Bank of America, California's largest bank, provides funding to the Boy Scouts of America, an organization that officially discriminates against lesbians and gays. This led to the boycott. Many of the more affluent and more urban lesbigay families made some comment about the Bank of America boycott when I inquired about their bank. Strikingly, only one family earning above the median income patronized the Bank of America, and one partner in this family expressed feeling guilty for doing so, when asked to identify the bank. Eight families earning below the median income of the sample use the Bank of America. Only one person in such a family commented to me on this, a lesbian living in a northern suburb of San Francisco. She was aware of the boycott but expressed her dependence on suburban ATMs, of which the Bank of America has many. While this may simply be coincidence, I suspect that given the greater exposure to lesbigay culture (through magazines, organizations, and through living in the lesbigay ghettos), more affluent lesbigay families are simply more aware of such matters.

A second example reflects the same pattern. Patronizing certain businesses due to their perceived support of the lesbigay communities appears much more common among the more affluent. Two people commented on making purchases from IKEA, a furniture and housewares dealer, because of their advertising to the lesbigay community and because of their portrayal of lesbians and gays in that advertising. Both people live in affluent households. Rarely did I hear of such efforts among the less affluent, more suburban participants. Finally, the more affluent are also more likely to shop in the lesbigay ghettos and pay the higher prices that come with that decision.

Urban/Suburban Distinctions

For the most part, distinctions between social-class status and the location of one's residence prove difficult to make because the two factors conflate so often. Most prosperous lesbigay families live in the city, and often in lesbian and gay neighborhoods. A few live in the suburbs. Likewise, for the most part, the less affluent live in the suburbs or in more distant, or more transitional, urban neighborhoods. Looking at prosperous suburban families, or at families of more humble means who live in the lesbigay ghettos, suggests that location operates independently of social class in terms of consumption work. A number of distinctions exist between suburban and urban dwellers.

First, and for obvious reasons, urban dwellers patronize lesbigay businesses with much greater frequency. Most lesbigay businesses are located in or near lesbian and gay neighborhoods. Second, urban dwellers turn to the lesbigay press for consumer information much more often. This happens because of the profusion of such media in or near lesbian and gay neighborhoods. Third, urban dwellers more often rely on other lesbigay people to guide and inform consumption decisions. Again, in part, this happens because so many lesbian and gay people live nearby the urban dwellers. Turning to lesbigay neighbors and store owners for consumer information is a part of living in a lesbian or gay enclave, regardless of one's socioeconomic status.

While all of these sexual identity issues influence distinctions in the character and prevalence of consumption work between urban and suburban residents, other distinctions also endure. Suburban families use the automobiles for consumption much more than urban dwellers, and they travel greater distances to do their consuming. This entails greater time obligations from suburban family members to do consumption work. Amy Gilfoyle and her partner, Wendy, live in a distant suburb. They own both dogs and cats. In order to get the food their veterinarian recommends for their overweight cats, Amy drives nearly fifteen miles (roughly thirty minutes one way) to pick up the food from a pet store. Margareta Lopez and Shirley Brown also have fat cats. They use the same cat food. They live in the Noe Valley district in San Francisco. Shirley walks three blocks to buy the same food.

On a similar note, for urban dwellers living in lesbigay areas, major retailers are but a few subway stops from home. Grocers, dry cleaners, pharmacies, hardware stores, clothiers, liquor stores, bakeries, tailors, flower and card shops, thrift stores, bookstores, optometrists, banks, coffee shops, copy shops, gyms, jewelers, pet stores, nurseries, and video rentals are no more than a few blocks from home for most urban lesbigay families. Suburban residents must often travel, and sometimes rather great distances, to procure all of these goods and services. All of this implies much more effort at consumption on the part of suburbanites, and for any given consumption activity, suburban life seems to mean more time and more work for the consumption worker. This partially explains why among the few affluent lesbigay families living in suburban locations, there is usually one person who cuts back paid-work hours significantly in order to do consumption work and the other forms of domestic labor—-a point I develop in the upcoming chapter on the division of domestic labor.

In addition, suburban residents make greater use of media sources like television, radio, and newspapers and less use of neighbors and friends to steer consumption decisions. Again, as earlier chapters have suggested, suburban lesbians and gays are more isolated from those who live around them, and this influences how they get information about consumption. Further, suburban dwellers report that they turn to colleagues and biolegal relatives with greater frequency for information and advice about goods and services. They also patronize megastores with greater frequency. Part of this reflects concerns about cost among the less prosperous suburbanites, but it also reflects the fact that suburban dwellings are larger than urban ones, and therein suburban dwellings offer greater room for the storage of bulk purchases. For instance, I went shopping one day with Tim Reskin, who lives in a distance East Bay suburb. We went to the Costco. He bought a twenty-four-pack of toilet paper, an eight-pack of paper towels, four cases of iced tea, a sixty-four-ounce container of Pace picante sauce, and a four-pack of dishwasher detergent. This bulk buying saves his family money and time, but most urban dwellers of similar socioeconomic means could not make such purchases because they would not have the space to store these items.

Consumption Work and Children

Lesbigay families with children encounter a unique set of consumption concerns and of work associated with those concerns. Before attending to some of the unique aspects of child-related consumption for lesbigay families, let me briefly note some of the similarities. First, and readily apparent, families with kids do more consumption work to provision their children with food, clothing, furniture, health and dental care, transportation, and daycare. This magnification of consumption produces an equally magnified load of consumption work in most of the aforementioned forms. These families make more trips to more stores, read more ads and brochures, compare more prices and products, maintain more mental notes about such products.

Reflecting on the unique aspects of consumption work for lesbigay families with kids, several dynamics deserve comment. First, the process of going to stores to make purchases or bringing services into the home entails the potential for experiencing heterosexism. Many lesbigay families, with or without children, come up against heterosexism in the marketplace in a multitude of forms. But lesbigay families with children face unique challenges in these consumption encounters. They must not only take into consideration how they and the sales personnel might experience and react to such situations, but they also consider the perspectives of their children. This reality encourages families with kids to make a special effort to seek out safe marketplaces where they can go with their children without harassment. Therein, lesbigay families with kids exhibit a deep reliance on other families for getting information about "safe" service providers and stores. Emily Fortune, one parent of recently born twins, comments: "When we were searching for daycare out here, I asked several straight friends, who are also parents, about the options. I had to tease out of them what the reactions might be to lesbian moms, and after I started making some contacts, I had to just be real honest, and ask providers about it up front. We found a place, and it seems to working out okay. We'll see what happens."

Concerns about heterosexism simply amplify the amount of work consumption requires. Note the effort Wendy makes to "tease out" information about the intensity of heterosexism she might confront in a daycare provider. She must pile this concern on among all of the others in her effort to secure daycare. In like fashion, many lesbigay parents report that they try to shop in "safe" places, and yet do so on a budget. Many report shopping for children's clothing, toys, and furniture on 24th Street in San Francisco's Noe Valley neighborhood. This urban shopping district caters to families with children, and is known for its inclusionary outlook. Many lesbigay parents also consider it an expensive place to shop. Much like those lesbigay consumers choosing to patronize lesbigay shops, lesbigay parents must balance concerns about relative safety, and their commitment to inclusivity, with efforts to stabilize the family budget.

Consumption Work and Relationship Longevity

Consumption work expands as relationships age. However, this occurs for the most part due to the fact that economic affluence buttresses relationship longevity and durability as much sociological research suggests (Cutright 1971, 292; Spanier and Glick 1981; *Family Planning Perspectives* 1985; Stacey 1990, 252–54; Rubin 1994, 121). In other words, economic stability leads to relationship stability, and in the process, consumption work expands. However, it also appears that certain forms of consumption must wait until the relationship reaches a certain level of maturity, regardless of economic affluence.

Buying a house together constitutes a particularly apt example. The process of buying and furnishing houses involves extensive and varied forms of consumption work. In this sample most every family that bought a home together did so only after they had developed a strong sense of relational stability. Quite simply, this means that all of the work entailed in buying homes occurs among relationships of longer duration. Other examples include the remodeling of houses, the purchase and furnishing of vacation houses, and the arrangement of elaborate travel plans. Each of these events encompasses extensive consumption work. And, as I will discuss in the upcoming chapter on the division of domestic labor, the expansion of such work among longer-term families also explains why such families produce a greater specialization of roles for family members and a greater lack of parity in the division of domestic work.

Gender and Consumption Work

On the surface, a number of gender-related distinctions in consumption work readily appear among lesbigay families. Included among these are a stronger affinity to consumption among gay men, and that gay men do significantly more consumption work. I say "on the surface" because, due to the conflation of class and gender and the all too prevalent denial of class differences in American culture, there exists no easy way to distinguish class and gender dynamics. Because of the segregation of the workplace by gender, and the resultant wage gap between women and men, gay men have more income than lesbians (though less than straight men; see Badgett 1995), and therein gay men do more consumption. Comparing and contrasting affluent lesbian households with the more meager gay-male households suggests the significance of class with affluent lesbian households engaging in much more consumption work and, in some cases, surpassing that done by gay men of similar socioeconomic status.

While socioeconomic status appears central, questions of gender and sexual orientation identity are present. There exists among many urban gay men a strong association with retail institutions and the processes of consumption that take place therein. Historically, department stores and their predecessors, apothecaries, played a significant role in the development of gay-male subcultures (Trumbach 1977; Ruggiero 1985). Historian George Chauncey notes that department stores in New York City became one of the sites where gay men could both meet one another and work in a relatively tolerant environment (1994, 274–75). Chauncey also notes that display windows of department stores became one of the sites where gay men could legitimately linger and meet one another (1994, 190).

The cultural association of gay-male identity and retail continues today. Examples abound. Popular culture images of gay-male employees in retail serve as one example. The gay character Mr. Wilberforce Clayborne Humphries in the British comedy show "Are You Being Served" comes quickly to mind. The show, broadcast by PBS in the United States, focuses on the daily activities of a department store and relies extensively upon stereotypical images of gay men in retail. Another example from San Francisco reflects the same dynamic: back in 1994 the San Francisco Gay Men's Chorus offered their annual holiday concert. As a part of that performance the chorus created a musical variation of the traditional "Twelve Days of Christmas" entitled "The Twelve Floors of Macy's." In the years since that performance I have heard countless recollections of it but rarely a criticism of its stereotypical image of gay men as avid shoppers. Another example comes from the recently published humorous guide to being gay, entitled *The Unofficial Gay Manual: Living the Lifestyle*, by Kevin Dilallo and Jack Krunholtz. The manual provides advice on where to shop for consumer products like furniture, linen, and kitchen utensils. While seemingly tongue-in-cheek, the manual provides detailed advice on the appropriate stores. Even if unwittingly, the manual sets the standards for where gay men should shop: "If you *must* shop at a chain, be prepared to see your prized possessions *everywhere*. Approved chains include Pottery Barn, Williams-Sonoma, and Domaine. Of course, for a more generic (though acceptable) look, there's always Crate and Barrel and Ikea" (1994, 112).

The affinity to retail resonates with many, though obviously not all, gay men. Easy explanations of this affinity elude us. My own research reveals at least part of the answer. The affinity to shopping emerges from the reality that relationships and family life require consumption work. In most middle-class heterosexual families, women do consumption work and therein relieve men of the task. In gay-male relationships, like most others, consumption work remains a central part of settling down or "nesting," and one or both of the men must do the work of consuming. This puts gay men into the marketplace in ways that many straight men never experience. The gay-male presence in retail establishments becomes more conspicuous in part because it represents a violation of the "female" character of consumers in many retail sites. Research does suggest that gay-male couples often confront more neglect and greater hostility from sales personnel than do either straight couples or lesbian couples (Walters and Curran 1996). This suggests the visibility as well as the taboo character of gay-male consumption. I wonder if the humorous treatment of gay-male consumption in American culture doesn't function to alleviate the awkward sentiments that both gay men and others feel about this male presence in the market. This suggests that consumption work, like other forms of domestic work, when done by men, requires careful management (in a Goffmanesque sense) in order to protect men from threats to gender identity.

Sustaining Lesbigay Families through Consumption Work

Consuming goods and services produces and sustains families. There are several dimensions to this. First, one can see this in the understanding of joint consumer purchases as symbolic of the relationship. Many lesbigay families, and surely many heterosexual ones, consider joint purchases, and particularly either the first joint purchases, or later, the major joint purchases (furniture, autos, and houses), as representative of the relationship. Lesbigay family members invest these forms of consumption with transcendent meanings. Consider the following examples from field research: a new house, an antique armoire, and a newly planted apple tree. Family members used each of these items as metonyms for their relationship, and I suspect that other people (friends, family, coworkers, real estate agents, and so on) read these items as indicators of relational commitment and stability. In a sense, the relationship gets socially constructed through this process. From purchasing their first futon to selecting a home for retirement, lesbigay families conceive of these consumption work-laden acts as symbols of family and relational solidarity. Take note that this process assumes a foundation of consumption work. Even the apple tree sapling required multiple phone calls to identify a nursery that sold them; a trip to several nurseries to compare prices and quality; reading about its feeding, lighting, and pruning; not to mention the actual work of planting it, watering it, pruning it, and monitoring it for disease. The work itself became an enactment of the commitment to the relationship.

A second dimension of constructing/sustaining family identity involves relative levels of consumption. In most cases the greater the level of consumption and the concomitant consumption work, the stronger the perception of the relationship as a family. Obviously, one cannot consider consumption work in isolation from the various other forms of domestic labor in terms of their family-producing capacity. However, consumption work plays an essential part in the cultural production of family—perhaps a growing part, but an essential part. Among those lesbians and gays with a solid sense of their relationships as family, mostly among the affluent, consumption abides. When these lesbigay families talk about what makes them families, besides an appeal to romantic notions of love, they point to their houses, to their jointly created living quarters, to shared expenses, shared investments, and joint purchases. Most of these symbols of relationship require consumption work.

5

the division of domestic
labor in lesbigay families

Sterling never cleaned toilets, he still doesn't clean toilets; he intends to clean the toilets, but right about the time when he gets to it, I have already cleaned the toilets. WAYNE OSMUNDSEN, 35-YEAR-OLD SOCIAL WORKER

The common metaphorical use of laundry, as in the phrase "to air their dirty laundry in public," connotes several things about actual laundry, most notably a common expectation that dirty laundry should remain hidden. This chapter violates that common expectation, in both a metaphorical and in a literal sense.

Stigmatized and oppressed communities often struggle with the menacing question of how to deal with "dirty laundry." Many lesbian and gay authors feel the need to present ourselves, and our communities, to the dominant culture in ideal terms, a feeling that I have

⚹ present gay culture in "ideal" terms

often shared. These portrayals, as opposed to the empirical realities, often reflect the efforts of lesbigay people to provide a respectable image of ourselves in a society often bent on devaluing and marginalizing us. Undoubtedly, the observations made here regarding the division of domestic work in lesbigay families violate the expectation that dirty laundry remain closeted.

The public portrayals and presentations of egalitarianism among lesbigay families do not cohere with the household realities that prevail among them. Two components of the research strategy used here expose the gap between public portrayals and empirical realities. First, the use of back-to-back interviews instead of joint interviews produces discrepancies in answers to the most routine of questions about domesticity. As Aquilino (1993) reveals, interviews often produce much higher estimates of spousal contributions to domestic work when the spouse is present than when he or she is not. Second, the fieldwork component of this research offers behavioral observations that reveal significant gaps between what participants say in interviews and what participants do in everyday life. The commitment to the ideology of familial egalitarianism within the lesbian and gay community, and among the subset of lesbigay families, is palpable. Yet, the empirical reality for many of these families is something quite different, something much more akin to patterns among heterosexual families (Gerson 1985; 1993). Moreover, when a particular family achieves something close to parity in the distribution of domestic activities, this almost always occurs under unique social conditions: great affluence, relative impoverishment, or among a distinct minority of couples with significantly diminished senses of themselves as family. In this chapter I examine each of these exceptions and what motivates lesbigay people to portray their relationships in ideal terms both to themselves and to the outside world. I will also consider what factors seem to most significantly influence the actual division of domestic labor among lesbigay families.

The Egalitarian Myth

There exists among the lesbigay families studied here a prevalent and persistent commitment to viewing both one's own relationship and those of other lesbians and gays as egalitarian. Most participants in this study, when asked to describe in general terms how they divide up household responsibilities in their relationship, relied upon the language of egalitarianism. Typical responses included: "Oh I would say it's fifty-fifty around here," or "we pretty much share all of the responsibilities," or "everyone does their fair share," or "it's pretty even." These perceptions persist even in the face of obvious empirical observations to the contrary. Many lesbigay family members fail to make much of a distinction between what they consider equal and what they consider fair. The blurring of these two quite distinct matters is necessary to maintaining the myth of egalitarianism.

I will never forget the moments during an interview with one member of lesbian relationship, a relationship where both family members are deaf. For this interview I hired someone adept at American Sign Language to translate. Midway through the interview the translator paused, somewhat confused by a subtle shift in meaning. In American Sign Language, the gestures for *equal* and *fair* are the same. The participant begin to make a shift in describing how the family organized domestic work from equal to fair. The shift in usage came in response to a series of probes exploring the work of feeding this family. The inequality in the division of feeding work was apparent to the three of us, and I suspect created some awkward feelings for the participant. The fact that the translator had to stop and seek clarification exacerbated the dynamic. The translator later told me he sensed great discomfort on the respondent's part, and he felt like he had done her a disservice through stumbling over the subtle transition she was making. Despite his feelings of betrayal, the stumble revealed something that exists in many families, a perception that what a family considers fair, they also consider equal. Her clarification of *fair* led to a defense of the "fairness" of the distribution of feeding work in their family, a defense premised on the difficulty and demands of her paid employment when compared to that of her partner.

Consequently, one must remain aware of the distinct possibility that intense pressures exist upon a participant's answers to questions about the division of domesticity. I think these pressures go a long way in explaining why lesbigay families, when asked about domestic activities, particularly in public settings, often joke about the matter. The humor masks the awkward feelings such questions produce. And after a few humorous exchanges, and possibly a little dig or two, the families make a concerted effort to reestablish the perception of equality. The research of Hochschild (1989) indicates that heterosexual families do exactly the same; they construct myths of egalitarianism. But there is more to the story among lesbigay families than meets the eye.

The Model-Minority Effect

Similar to other minority groups in American culture, lesbian and gay people are highly aware of the public images of ourselves. Strikingly similar to many Black Americans in the 1950s, contemporary lesbian and gay Americans go to great lengths to see, and reflect upon, the media images of us within the broader culture. The African-American documentary film producer Marlin Riggs notes in his film *Color Adjustments*, a film tracing images of Blacks in television, that during the 1950s many Black people remember calling families and friends any time a Black person was to appear on television. These viewers understood that those images would shape the broader cultural understanding, if not the self-understanding, of Black Americans. Black Americans hoped for positive images, images that would advance the civil rights struggle. Lesbian and gay people maintain a similar vigil. Witness the near obsession surrounding the coming out of Ellen DeGeneres on the ABC situation comedy "Ellen" in 1997. As a part of this concern, lesbigay families portray themselves using the ideals put forward by American culture, ideals propagating the myth of the egalitarian middle-class family. Appealing to those ideals obfuscates the truth about real lesbigay families that they, like all other families, struggle with real world concerns about how to balance work and family obligations, and that the dynamics that produce inequality in heterosexual families also produce inequality within lesbigay families.

The Management of Gender Identity and Domesticity

Gender looms as a significant matter in the portrayal as well as the organization of domesticity in lesbigay families. Like many other scholars of gender, I find that domestic work results not only in the creation of goods and services but also in the creation of gender (Berk 1985; West and Zimmerman 1987; Coltrane 1989; Hochschild 1989; Ferree 1990; DeVault 1991; Petuchek 1992; Brines 1994). The potential for domesticity resulting in the construction of gender identity means different things to lesbian women and gay men. For lesbians, the capacity of domesticity to construct gender carries important consequences for partners whose paid-work obligations prevent them from engaging in much domesticity. Examples abound. Many of the lesbian women employed in time- and energy-consuming occupations expressed guilt about, and made much humor of their inattentiveness to and lack of participation in, domesticity. Their partners often provide cover for them, assigning credit for domestic tasks that they really did not do, or emphasizing some femininity-producing activity that compensates.

In a number of lesbian families, that compensation comes in the form of personal appearance and fashion. One of the families I studied up close provides a vivid example. Arlene Wentworth, a successful attorney, and her partner, Dolores Bettenson, also an attorney, illustrate the dynamic. Both women work full-time, though Arlene works many more hours than Dolores. While this family relies upon cleaning services, garden services, and restaurants for much of their domestic life, many of the remaining domestic activities fall to Dolores. One of the striking differences between the two women is their personal styles and sense of fashion. Dolores leans toward more gender-neutral fashion. She greeted me at the door for the first time wearing jeans and a T-shirt. She wears professional attire for work, but emphasizes staid colors, "sensible shoes," and little makeup. In marked contrast, Arlene greeted me the first time in a bright teal-blue dress, high heels, makeup, and jewelry. The distinction was persistent with Arlene attiring herself in such a way most everyday. I remember one evening when Dolores and Arlene were to go out to a cocktail party, Dolores, sitting next to me on the couch while waiting impatiently for Arlene to finish dressing, commented: "These lipstick lesbians are certainly high maintenance, huh?" I replied: "Yea, what's that all about?" "Oh, I think it's her way of getting in touch with her womanhood. She doesn't really get any other chance to do that. Being a prosecuting attorney doesn't leave much room for that." Dolores's observation underscores the impact of one's paid work upon one's identity. Arlene expressed guilt and discomfort with the fact that Dolores did much of the domestic work in their family. Dolores placed special emphasis on the contributions Arlene did make, such as pointing out the particularly feminine bed linens that Arlene had chosen for them, as well as emphasizing Arlene's participation in occasional baking. The management of gender identity is a collective concern in many lesbian and gay families—not surprisingly, for how many of us really would want the world to think of our loved ones as deviants of one sort or another?

The Invisibility of Domesticity and the Egalitarian Myth

Much of domesticity is invisible. Many of the forms of domestic labor rest upon a foundation of unobserved efforts that consume an individual's time and energy. Monitoring the house for cleanliness, monitoring the calendar for birthdays, monitoring the catalog for appropriate gifts, monitoring the cupboard for low supplies, monitoring the moods of one's spouse, and monitoring the family finances all are expressions of domesticity, and all are mostly invisible. The vast stores of accumulated knowledge about domestic things go unobserved by most: the knowledge of a family member's food tastes, dietary requirements, clothing size, the last gift one bought for them, work schedule, and the last time the cat received a rabies shot are all forms of domesticity and are hidden in the heads of those who hold responsibility for doing these things.

This invisibility, even to those who do it, sometimes produces seemingly inexplicable feelings of anger and resentment. Domestic work often becomes the site of enduring conflict between partners in relationships. Joe McFarland and Richard Neibuhr have been together for just under four years. Their relationship is "on the rocks," as Richard puts it. They reluctantly agreed to an interview. The family recently bought a house together, using money from Joe's inheritance from his previous lover, who died in the late 1980s. Both Richard and Joe conceive of their domestic relationship in strongly egalitarian terms despite what to me resembles a clear pattern of specialization with Richard doing much of the domestic labor in the family—not just much of the invisible work, but the visible work as well. Richard is not happy about the situation, although he has difficulty finding the words:

> I think things are pretty equal in the relationship, although I wish Joe would appreciate my contributions more, and maybe be a little more helpful. It's hard to describe, but I feel like I do a lot of stuff to make our life better, but he doesn't really care about that. I think he thinks I'm just nagging him. If I ask him to do certain things, like, for instance, I asked him to call someone about going out to a movie on Friday night. He got annoyed. He says that if I want to go out to a movie with

someone, then I should call. He thinks that's my interest. It's funny, though, because if I don't do it, he will ask how come we're not doing anything, and complain that we don't really have many friends. I get sort of frustrated about it, but I don't push it too much. He feels like I am dominating his space, imposing on his free time too much, not respecting his boundaries. He's very big on boundaries, he gets that from his therapist, who thinks that he needs to keep his own space.

A similar conversation took place with Joe. Notice how the advice of the therapist actually influences the division of domesticity:

cc: Tell me about continuing discussions/points of conflict or unresolved feelings with your spouse over these kinds of cleaning tasks.

JOE: My therapist is of the opinion that Richard lacks empathy for me, and/or maybe empathy for people in general, and doesn't understand that for me, time down and time alone is a chance for me to think my own thoughts, feel my feelings, expand my emotional life through reading or television. Richard doesn't have any appreciation for that. Consequently, the therapist thinks he lacks empathy. He asks me to do things that are his interest, and that's not fair to me.

cc: What kind of things?

JOE: Well, like stuff for the house. I mean, I paid for the house, or at least mostly, and I don't really care that much how the house looks. I mean, I want it clean, but a little messy is not a big deal. If he wants it a certain way, he can do it. I need my space.

Richard feels frustration because Joe won't help with domesticity. If Richard expresses those sentiments, they actually become illegitimate because they are understood as an imposition of Richard's "interests" upon Joe. Both Richard and Joe conceive of their relationship as egalitarian with the differences over domesticity actually reflecting different individual "interests." The advice of the therapist, or at least the way it gets understood and deployed in the relationship, legitimates Joe's claim to private time and relaxation, and delegitimates Richard's desire for help.

Several months after these interviews I ran into Richard at the gym. He had just joined, and we talked for a while. He told me he was coming back to the gym to "get in shape, and get a man." He then reported that he and Joe had broken up, and that I was part of the reason. He said he wanted to thank me for helping him to get out of his relationship. I felt perplexed, guilty, mortified. Here is my rough approximation, scribbled on the back on my workout card, of what transpired that day at the gym:

cc: I am very sorry; I certainly didn't intend any harm.

RICHARD: Oh, it's okay, it's not really about you, but what you helped me learn about myself.

cc: What do you mean?

RICHARD: Well, that interview helped me to realize just how much I actually do, and did for that jerk.

cc: Like what are you thinking of?

RICHARD: Well, like all those questions about going out and buying things for the house. You know, I did all of that. And I did it because I wanted us to have a nice home, to be a family. But, being a family, he thinks, is all about me and my needs. He says I am codependent. He just couldn't appreciate what I was doing for us. The interview made it so clear just how much I had taken for granted. I actually sat down and wrote a list up, thinking of the things that you asked about. Then I realized, I confronted him with it, but he basically thinks those things are my interests, and if I want to do them, that's all about me. Well, I knew I had to get out, and find someone else who appreciates me more.

The sociologist as homewrecker was not quite what I envisioned for myself. But this situation led me to wonder about why so much of domesticity is hidden from those who do it through discourses about individual "interests" and in narrow conceptions of what domesticity actually is. Families hide much of domesticity, closet it, and drape the door with the ideological veneer of egalitarianism for quite practical reasons. First, as previously suggested, they do it to avoid the stigma associated with violating gender expectations. Second, and perhaps more significantly, they do it to avoid conflicts and to preserve relationships existing in a broader socioeconomic context that does not enable families to actually produce much equality. When thinking about Joe and Richard and the demise of that relationship I can see the dilemma that many relationships face. Joe really does need "down time"; he needs his TV for relaxation. Here he describes his paid work:

JOE: Well, it's high stress. I am working about fifty-five to sixty hours a week. I have to travel down to L.A. every other week for at least a couple of days. I constantly get called at home if things aren't going right. The project director is a total asshole—oops, sorry, I guess I should say he's difficult to deal with. Ask Richard. I vent at Richard about the guy all the time. He's your typical straight white-male loser. He is constantly second guessing everyone, micromanaging us, and is highly insecure. You just have to learn to deal with him.

cc: Travel?

JOE: Yeah, as I said, I go to L.A. every other week for a couple of days. I actually like it, it gets me out of the office, and gives me a little breathing room. It gives me that space I need.

CC: What hours do you work?

JOE: I usually get home about 7 or 7:30. I go in at 8:30, leaving here at about 8.

CC: Do you work evenings?

JOE: It depends on the cases. If a project is due, it's due. Sometimes, that means I work all night. I can be at the office till midnight, it just depends.

CC: Weekends?

JOE: It's the same. I usually work on Saturday mornings. I try to get some time at the gym on both Saturday and Sunday, but that doesn't always happen.

CC: How long a commute to work?

JOE: About 30 minutes.

CC: Do you think of yourself or as Richard as more committed to work/career? How come?

JOE: I think I am. I don't know why exactly. He's not into it as much. He likes his work, but he's not driven by it like me. He also works in a more pleasant environment. He doesn't have to deal with as much obnoxiousness.

CC: What does your partner think of your job?

JOE: Well, I suspect it's a love/hate thing. I think he resents that I travel, because he thinks I am having fun, and he gets stuck keeping things going around here. I do feel a bit of guilt about that, but it really is my job that takes me down there. I also think he respects what I do, and I make good money at it. That makes our life better, especially trying to live in San Francisco. It takes a lot of money to maintain a life here, and so I really try to make sure we are earning enough. Not that I don't think Richard doesn't work hard—I know he does—but if we both worked in jobs like his, we couldn't live here, or at least we couldn't have a house of our own.

A fairly clear picture emerges here, one that many families experience. The character of Joe's and Richard's paid employment greatly determines the organization of domesticity. Richard works in human resources, as a benefits counselor, for a suburban community. He works thirty-nine hours per week in a public-sector job with extensive family-friendly benefits, mostly negotiated by his union. He works mostly with heterosexual women, many of whom also hold responsibility for family life. Richard earned $31,000 dollars in 1993. He earns much less than Joe, who earned $52,000 the same year. Joe's work exhausts him, allowing little time, much less energy, for doing family. His work frequently seeps into family time. Concealing domesticity in the language of "interests" prevented Richard and Joe from reflecting upon paid work and family conflict. In fact, concealing the matter allowed them to avoid hard choices, including the possibility of Joe seeking alternate employment, with the potential for a reduced standard of living. They also could have acknowledged Richard's specialization in domestic matters, something they both seemed unprepared to accept. Richard understood their conflict in terms of personality, without much awareness of the impact of paid work upon what happened to them.

The Egalitarian Pattern

A minority of lesbigay families do achieve a rough equivalence in the distribution of domestic work, even using a broad and inclusive conception of domesticity. Roughly 25 percent (thirteen) of the families I studied approach this rough parity. The participants in these families appear to take responsibility for, as well as spend similar amounts of time on domestic matters. Interview data and field observations reveal patterns of specialization among many of these families, although they still approach equity. For instance, in several families, one person pursues much of feeding work while another manages housework and kin work. Some families go to great lengths to achieve this parity. For example, three families use quite extensive "chore wheels." Chore wheels list many of the major housework items—and in one family much of the feeding work was listed as well—but none of them listed consumption, kin work, or status work-related chores. These families share a number of distinct sociological characteristics explaining much of the parity in the division of domesticity, and to those characteristics I will now turn.

Egalitarianism: Reliance on the Service Economy

Wealthier lesbigay families often purchase much domesticity in the marketplace, therein enhancing the egalitarianism within the relationship. In contrast to working/service-class and middle-class lesbigay families, these affluent families rely extensively on the service economy, or upon an army of low-paid workers without fringe benefits who provide much of the domestic labor. This pattern closely resembles one detected by Hertz (1986) in a study of upper-middle-class, dual-career heterosexual families who achieved greater equity in their relationships through reliance on service workers. Eight of the ten wealthiest families in this study hire someone to do housework for them. Four of those eight hire Latina women who work for an hourly rate without benefits. No family earning less than the study's median income hires someone to clean. Seven of the wealthiest ten families frequently rely either on laundry services or include laundry as a responsibility of the domestic workers who come to clean. Two families earning below the median income take laundry on a consistent basis to a laundry service. Six of the wealthiest twenty families hire someone to care for their lawns or gardens. Four families, all earning above the median income, hire someone to walk their dogs during the day. As mentioned in an earlier chapter, one in five lesbigay families eat at least four meals per week in a restaurant. Sixteen of those twenty-one families earn above the median income.

A very clear picture emerges here. Some lesbigay families achieve partial equity in their relationships through reliance on the labors of mostly working-poor people. One can see some of these workers behind the counters of taquerias, laundries, pasta shops, coffee shops, and delis in lesbigay neighborhoods, although many others one cannot see because their labors are more hidden (domestics, gardeners, laundry workers, daycare providers). These workers are for the most part Latino-, Asian-, and African-American women, and young gay men and lesbians. Their labors contribute much to the achievement of egalitarianism within the families of the affluent.

Egalitarianism and Female-Identified Professional Occupations

The egalitarian pattern emerges with notable strength among those families where both individuals, regardless of gender, work in traditionally female-identified professional occupations: primary/secondary teaching, social work, healthcare assessment (nurses, dietitians, occupational therapy), librarians, school counseling, social work, and public-sector human resources jobs. A disproportionate number of lesbians and gay men in this study work in these professions (see table B6). It remains an open question whether this pattern reflects the broader population of lesbigay people (Badgett and King 1997). Popular mythology holds that lesbigay people are everywhere, and perhaps they are, but lesbigay people in long-term relationships don't seem to be. It may well be the case that these forms of employment actually nourish longer-term relationships, providing at least one, and in the case of some egalitarian families, all family members the opportunity to pursue family matters more readily. When the primary partners in relationships work in these fields they establish a greater degree of equality between them in the distribution of domesticity. Why?

These forms of employment often feature *real* forty-hour work weeks, and they often offer paid vacation, paid holidays, more holidays, family leave, paid sick days, flex-time, flex-place, as well as employee assistance programs offering services to families facing alcohol, drug, and domestic violence concerns. All of these family-friendly policies create a somewhat more conducive environment for doing family work. In contrast, lesbigay people working in other professional occupational categories infrequently receive such benefits, or they seem reluctant to take advantage of them, even if offered. Moreover, very few people in these professions report working more than forty hours per week for wages. This is not to say that these forms of employment are all dandy. In fact, they often feature short career ladders, glass ceilings, lower wages, and less control over the content of one's work than do male-dominated professional jobs (Glazer 1991; Preston 1995). In a sense, discrimination relegates lesbigay professionals into the female-dominated professions and enables them to do more domesticity. When looking at lesbigay professionals in the male-dominated occupations, including the engineers, physicians, attorneys, and middle-level managers, a starkly different pattern emerges, one encouraging a clear division of labor within the relationship. Moreover, most of the female-dominated professions do not require one to use one's residence in order to serve clients, or to entertain them very much. This reduces the amount of housework, feeding work, consumption work, and kin work within such households.

Egalitarianism and Downsizing the Family

There is one other form of the truly egalitarian family: the downsized family. These families, mostly composed of male couples, engage in relatively little domesticity. Similar to the affluent egalitarians, these families also rely on the service economy to provide domesticity, although they rely on it much less extensively. These families often live in urban environments, usually sharing a living space with multiple adults. These guys, mostly in their late twenties or early thirties, are often in their first relationship. They spend very little time in the places where they live, instead hanging out in cafés, bars, restaurants, gyms, and dance clubs. They don't put much effort into feeding work, eating out at cheap taquerias and hamburger joints throughout much of the week, or eating instant ramen noodles or microwaved frozen dinners. If they engage in body building, as many seem to, they eat simple meals of vegetables, bread, and pasta when they eat at home. They don't do much consumption work, although they do make joint purchases of CDs, linens and towels, and some used furniture. These joint purchases often become emblematic of their relationships. These couples do very little kin work, calling biolegal relatives mostly, but usually on major holidays or at Mother's Day, with each person responsible for his or her own biolegal relations. Even in these austere circumstances, domesticity often comes to play a crucial role in the creation of the relationship. For instance, several of these young-male couples understood the time they spent together doing laundry at laundromats as expressions of their relational identity, particularly when they mixed clothing items together for washing and drying.

The Specialization Pattern

One person specializes in domesticity in roughly three of four (thirty-eight) of the lesbigay families studied. This pattern actually parallels Blumstein and Schwartz's finding that longer-term families frequently consist of one person who places more emphasis on domesticity and one who places the emphasis on paid work (1983, 172). In this study, the longer the family has been together, the more pronounced the specialization becomes. For instance, only among families together longer than nine years (twenty-one families), and mostly earning higher incomes, do I find someone working part time by choice in order to handle domestic activities (seven families), or someone engaging in homemaking full-time (three families). Interestingly, these highly specialized, longer-term lesbigay families conceive of their circumstances as *equal*, although I suspect they really mean *fair*. They consider things fair in light of a whole series of spoken and unspoken matters ranging from the number of hours someone works for wages to the pleasures one garners from domesticity. Let me now turn to some of the central factors encouraging specialization in domesticity or in paid work within lesbigay families.

Paid employment exerts the greatest influence upon the division of domesticity in most lesbigay families. The number of hours paid work requires, where the work takes place, the length of the commute to work, the pay, the prestige, and difficulty of the work all conflate to encourage a pattern of specialization. The relative resources that each person brings to the relationship from paid work influences the division of labor. In most cases the person with less earning potential, or with less occupational prestige, picks up a disproportionate share of domestic labor. This finding parallels the "relative resource" model put forward to explain the division of domestic labor among heterosexual families (Blood and Wolfe 1960; Brines 1994). The pursuit of such resources (money, benefits, stock options, prestige, and networks) also takes time, usually leaving the pursuant with little time left to handle domesticity. In this sense, my findings parallel the "time availability" explanation (Hiller 1984; Coverman 1985; Acock and Demo 1994) of the division of domestic labor. However, unlike some resource theory, my analysis does not conceive of domesticity as a great unpleasantness that the person with more resources (e.g., income, prestige, and education) forces onto the person with fewer. Such a view reduces domesticity to its unpleasant aspects and conceals its attractive ones, therein leaving us with no convincing explanation of why some people prefer, and orient themselves toward, domesticity (Ferree 1976, 1980). Rather, I detect a pattern of family members attempting to maximize the quality of their household lives both through providing income and through providing domesticity. Among the affluent participants, each family member pursues income, and the family purchases meals, laundry, housecleaning, and so on in the service economy. Most lesbigay families can't afford this, even with both working full-time, and therein, they must pursue a different strategy. Longer-term families recognize the importance of domesticity to relational and family stability, and many of them pursue a strategy to attain both domesticity and financial well-being. The most obvious strategy consists of encouraging the family member with the greatest economic opportunity to pursue paid work vigorously. This has its limits, but the pattern occurs in the majority of households, and becomes stronger over time.

Gravitating toward Domesticity

Practical economic concerns and occupational characteristics play the largest role in determining who gravitates toward domestic involvement. In a few instances those who gravitate toward domesticity "choose" employment that compliments their family commitments. In most instances the character of one's paid employment facilitated participation in domesticity, with very little "choice" or much reflection on the matter. Some people appear to make conscious choices about domesticity, but the choices are constrained by economic and occupational realities. For instance, only among affluent families does the choice exist to work part-time for wages, devoting the remaining time to personal and/or family life. Similarly, those in professional careers frequently find it easier to merge work and family concerns together. Recall the professionals making phone calls to friends and family from work, as well as arranging their work schedule to pursue domestic matters. Working- and service-class lesbigay families don't have these options. I want to emphasize the importance of context to the question of "choice" here. Some participants choose to ensconce themselves in domesticity, but few really possess that option. Some participants choose to take on a disproportionate share of domestic labor, but most simply find themselves doing the work without much sense of choice. That doesn't necessarily mean they feel unhappy or conceive of things as unfair—some do, and some don't. Rather, they often simply adjust in light of the expectations and opportunities associated with their own paid work and the paid work of other family members.

Family-Friendly Careers and Jobs

Many of the women and men in these specialized families are employed within traditional female-identified occupations (teaching, nursing, and so on). They take on a disproportionate share of domesticity, especially when they are in relationships with individuals in professional, managerial, or executive positions. The pattern is quite apparent among school teachers. The summer recess, holiday breaks, the capacity to do schoolwork at home, and lower salaries all conflate to encourage teachers to pick up a disproportionate share of domestic life. Few of the teachers anticipated this state of affairs at the beginning of their relationships. The experience of one teacher, Andrew Kessler, illustrates the dynamic. In the summer of 1997, at a northern California gay resort area popularly known as the Russian River, I ran into Andrew, a third-grade teacher, whom I originally interviewed back in 1994. He has taught school for eight years now, and is in a relationship with a computer software consultant. During casual conversation he commented on returning home from vacation to begin his "summer housewife stint." I asked: "How is it that you came to play that role?" Andrew responded:

> Well, it's kind of strange. I think it happened because I have the summer off. I wasn't really that into domestic things when we first got together. I was just out of school and I was very gung-ho about my teaching. Part of it has to do with Darren's job. He works a lot and he works pretty hard, and so I think I feel a little bit of obligation to try to ease the burden on him. He earns a lot, and that makes our life pretty great. It's funny, though, I don't really feel like I was forced to do the house and stuff. More like, I came to like it over time. I felt a certain accomplishment about it, about keeping it nice. Darren couldn't really do that much, given the hours he works, and he travels some. So I think it fell to me to create more of a sense of home for us. Some of it's quite boring, of course, but I like some of it too.

Andrew's experience is actually quite common among lesbigay families. Andrew did not really choose to become domestically oriented; rather, over time, he gravitated in that direction. Andrew's explanations of why he prepares evening meals, meets service and delivery people at the house, and does much of the consumption work all point to paid work, either the relative flexibility of his own career, or the inflexibility of his partner's career. In Andrew's case the pull toward domestic involvement began early in his work experience, and in some ways this left him less cognizant of the ways that work influences family life. For others, the pull came later, and they have a much stronger sense of how work influences family life.

Fanny Gomez, now forty-four and in her second long-term relationship as well as her second career, recently finished school and began working as a social worker. In her first relationship she did very little in terms of domesticity. She worked sixty hours per week as an accountant for a large commercial real estate firm. After her first relationship broke up she decided she wanted to make a lot of changes in her life. Mostly she wanted to pursue a career that made her happier, and one that would "make some contribution to improving other people's lives." When she and her new partner, Melinda Rodriquez, moved in together, she realized that neither of them was particularly adept at domestic tasks. They wanted to eat meals together at home, but "the meals didn't seem that satisfying." Fanny decided to spend some time learning how to cook. She bought some cookbooks and attended a cooking course on Saturdays, something she "would not have had the energy to do when she was working at the real estate firm." Her new job, doing social work with elderly Latinos as part of a city-funded program, is stressful but it has more limits. Fanny says she works thirty-eight hours a week and "not an hour more," unlike her old job, where they knew no limits, where "my whole life was about that firm." She also receives more holiday time and more vacation time. She doesn't earn as much as she used to, but she's happier. Fanny noticed that her new job, and her new relationship with Melinda, a midlevel sales manager for a computer technology firm, brought new responsibilities on the home front:

FANNY: We've had some fights about housecleaning over the past couple of years. She says she doesn't have time to do the stuff, and I sort of understand that, but I don't think it's fair that I have to do it. But, I think I realized that if I didn't, then nobody would. And I am here more often than she is. I get home earlier, and I leave for work later. Because I get home earlier, it's easier for me to cook, and to stop by the store and stuff.

CC: How is this different from your first relationship?

FANNY: I never would have done that sort of thing in my first relationship. In fact, I've sort of gone through a transition. I had no interest in cooking when I was with Janet. But in this relationship, it seems more important to me. I guess I missed the meal time that I had with Janet, and I wanted to have that again with Melinda, but Melinda wasn't into doing it, so I sort of picked it up. I think Melinda appreciates it though.

On the one hand, Fanny contributed to her new involvement in domestic life through choices she made about work. On the other hand, Fanny's work and the work of her new lover, Melinda, changed Fanny. Fanny's search for more fulfillment in her career brought her into an occupational context that facilitated more domestic involvement.

Fanny, a social worker, and Andrew, the teacher, are not alone. Of the twenty-eight professionals that work as nurses, primary/secondary-school teachers, counselors, social workers, librarians, and community college instructors, eighteen are more domestically involved than their partners while six appear equally involved and four of those six are in relationships with partners in similar occupations.

In addition to the female-identified professional career tracks that seem to encourage domestic involvement, those individuals who work at home as artisans, writers/editors, or independent service contractors, as well as those who are students, retired, or underemployed, also bear a disproportionate share of domesticity. Twenty-four participants do much of their paid work at home—work ranging from accounting services to daycare to running a bed and breakfast to book editing to building furniture. Of these twenty-four participants, eighteen carry a greater share of the domesticity. These participants often weave their paid work with their family work. Mary Ann Callihan, an artisan, builds custom Arts and Crafts style furniture out of her garage. She recounts her activities for the day I interviewed her:

> Well, I started off eating breakfast, and then loaded the dishwasher and started it. I came out to the garage to check on a custom headboard for a bed I am working on. I applied a stain to the maple last night, so I wanted to see how it turned out. Then I went back into the house and sorted some laundry and put a load in. Let me think. Then I went back out and cut some pieces of maple for the footboard that goes with this bed I am working on. That took a couple of hours. I think I went into the house a few times. I know I changed the laundry over several times. Right about lunch time, I ran down to the Castro to get some glue. I stopped by the store and picked up some groceries for dinner on the way. I got back up here, and I ate some lunch, watered the garden, and then continued working on the footboard for a couple of hours. About 4:00 p.m. I went down to deposit a check at the bank in Castro. I talked to some friends I saw in front of the bank. I got back up and folded most of the laundry. Margie got home about 5:00 p.m. I guess I started dinner just before she got here. She kept a watch on dinner while I took the car and ran over to Restoration Hardware, where they special-ordered some hinges for one of my projects. I got home and put the finishing touches on dinner. We ate, and now you're here.

Surprisingly, Mary Ann portrayed the division of domestic labor as "about fifty-fifty" at the beginning of the interview. In contrast, her partner, Margaret Jackson, felt that Mary Ann probably did more mostly because "she's around the house more, and I think she's just more aware of what needs to be done, and she often does it." The interviews made fairly clear that Mary Ann tends to do much more domesticity. Margaret works as a personnel manager for a retail clothing store, often working into the evening and every other weekend. Margaret reports working about fifty-five hours per week. Determining how many hours Mary Ann works is not easy, given the blending of domestic life with her furniture work. She made $22,000 in 1994 from her furniture sales and other carpentry jobs. Her partner Margaret earned slightly more, about $25,000 the same year. Mary Ann's specialization in domesticity appears to result from the fact that she works at home, a circum-

stance that for her, and for many of the others who work at home, encourages greater involvement in domesticity.

In sum, many participants gravitate toward domesticity not out of choice,
or because of a strong interest in domestic pursuits, or even because they possess certain skills. Rather, they gravitate toward domesticity because the character of their paid work and that of other family members encourages their involvement. Many of these domestically involved individuals have not made a
big decision to focus on family life. Rather, because of many small decisions,
they gravitated toward the domestic. The decision to start the evening meal
because one arrives home earlier than others facilitated increased feeding
work. For those who work at home, the decision to clean the bathroom or do
the laundry during the day led them into increased housework. For those with
more flexible work schedules, the time to shop for consumer goods led them
into increased responsibility for consumption work. Some participants do
make a conscious commitment to greater involvement in domestic and family matters, and I will address them in the next section, but most do not. Their
domestic careers appear to develop residually, accumulating slowly and unreflectively over the course of their relationships. They then become the experts
and begin to feel the responsibility for domesticity.

Domestic by Choice

Few individuals actually choose, in a particularly conscious manner, to become more involved in family and domestic affairs. However, some do, and
for a variety of reasons—reasons often reflecting growing disenchantment
with paid work, or concern about maintaining an endangered relationship,
or simply a love of domestic life. However, the nature of theses choices varies
dramatically across social class. The two men who conceive of themselves as
homemakers are notable examples of choosing domestic involvement, as
well as one woman, Virginia Kirbo, who works ten hours per week. All three
made conscious choices to forgo paid employment in favor of concentrating
on family and community life. All three are in relationships with highly successful, well-paid individuals. These families dwell in exquisite yet labor-
intensive homes. I found the daily schedules of all three quite stunning, for
not only do they maintain homes thick in domesticity, but also these three
people expend great energy volunteering in the nonprofit sector.

John Chapman, forty-seven years old, once worked as a successful graphic artist. Over the past decade he gave up his successful graphic art practice in favor of "keeping the house" and "doing good things for the community." He consciously decided that "some of the fun went out of his work, especially serving so many corporate clients." He felt that serving corporate clients created a "factorylike feel" to what he thought of as an "artistic and creative enterprise." The factorylike character of the work distracted from his satisfaction with his work, and he decided he wanted to do more work for nonprofit organizations. The rising income and career success of his partner, Theodore Fairchild, made it possible for John to do more of this kind of work, and eventually he stopped taking on new contracts.

John now does graphic work only as a volunteer. He serves on the board of directors of two of San Francisco's largest AIDS service providers. For one, he edits the monthly newsletter and maintains the website. He spends two mornings a week volunteering at a hospice for people dying of AIDS-related diseases. He has served his local Episcopal church in almost every leadership and volunteer capacity over the last decade, most recently chairing a ministerial search committee for the parish. He volunteers as a guide every other Saturday at the Conservatory of Flowers, in Golden Gate Park, where he blends his personal interest in gardening with his sense of public service. He spends two nights of every month working for the Stop AIDS Project, where he takes to the streets of the Castro and "gets to tell the young ones how to practice safer sex." John and Theodore live in a spectacular Victorian residence in the Presidio Heights section of San Francisco. John maintains the house and an elaborate garden. They entertain often, and always have meals at home, something that John feels is very important to their relationship. John's experience is quite unique, for few lesbigay families earn enough money to make such choices.

Hindered Work Opportunities

While some of the more affluent participants became disillusioned with their careers and "chose" to emphasize domestic life instead, many other participants found themselves unable to get onto career or promotional tracks or ran into glass ceilings and consequently shifted to a domestic focus. The lack of job/career opportunities resulted in a greater emphasis on domesticity for at least eleven of the families I studied. Five of these families came to San

Francisco due to an employment opportunity for one member of the family. These families migrated with hopes of finding suitable employment for both partners, but this didn't always happen. Carey Becker, forty-three years old and working part time as a radiology technician, shares her life with Angela DiVincenzo, a special education teacher. Five years ago they moved to San Francisco from New Jersey. A suburban Bay Area school district offered Angela a position creating a new curriculum and program for special education. Carey, who worked as a full-time radiologist in back East, discovered that she lacked the proper credentials for employment in California, and that few employment opportunities existed. Carey took a part-time position with hopes of finding something full-time. She never did. Initially, Carey picked up a larger share of the domesticity:

CC: Describe the impact of significant job changes on your relationship.
CAREY: The move to San Francisco had a major impact, and I think it still does. I am still trying to get into the kind of work I would like to do. Although, I don't know if it's possible now. The market for radiology techs is not very hot. I have thought about what else I could do. Angela just wants me to be happy, and she hasn't put any pressure on me to find something else. The part-time position actually is thirty hours, and now that Angela's school district offers domestic partnership, I don't need to worry about going without insurance.
CC: Did the move change what you do in the relationship?
CAREY: In some ways, it did. I do a lot more of the housework and stuff now. I don't really mind it too much. Angela works pretty hard, and I try to contribute what I can to our relationship.

Following a similar pattern, Julie Avilla moved to San Francisco with her partner, Teresa Rivera, in 1986. They came after Teresa received an offer for a midlevel management job with a San Francisco hotel. Julie found work as an attendant at a group home for severely disabled adults. Julie hated the work and switched to a sales position with a health food store for a couple of years. During the past three years she worked as a sales associate for a large bookstore. She really dislikes the work, and thinks about going back to school, but "feels a bit old to be trying a whole new career or something" and doesn't really know what she would study, much less whether they can afford for her to go. Asked whether she thought their incomes influence the division of household chores in any way, Julie responded:

Sort of, but not directly. I mean, Teresa doesn't say or ever even imply that because I earn less I should do more household chores. I mean, I think I do more because it means more to me, I really get something out of it, a sense of accomplishment, of contributing something. I sure don't feel that way at work. I feel exploited there. We tried to unionize recently, and it was just ugly. The whole thing left a bad taste in my mouth, about how much the corporation that owns the store just doesn't appreciate its employees. At home, I feel appreciated. Teresa values what I do at home. She notices when I reorganize the furniture or take care of some small thing.

The poor quality of Julie's paid worklife, in combination with the relative success of her partner, nourishes Julie's identification with domestic life, an arena where she feels more appreciated.

In a similar fashion, some lesbians and gay men ran into the proverbial glass ceiling at work and consequently reconceived of their careers as jobs, set limits on how much work could encroach on family life, and developed a new interest in domesticity. This pattern emerged with marked strength among lesbigay professionals and managers working in predominantly heterosexual contexts. Brad O'Neil, in his early fifties, spent much of his life in computer engineering. Over the past decade he has attempted to break into an upper-level management position with his current employer. He responded thus to questions about his sexual orientation and the impact of being gay on his job:

cc: Does your employer know of your sexual orientation?
BRAD: Yes.
cc: Describe the impact of this circumstance on you.
BRAD: I don't know what to say. I feel like for a long time I tried very hard, I did all the right things, I worked and worked, staying late, going in on weekends. Somehow, they kept passing me by for promotion. I suspect that the old straight boys think that I will not fit in, not make the decisions that they would make. I mean, maybe I am not really cut out for a high-level position. It's hard to tell. Are they discriminating against me? I think they are, but they would deny it. I look at some of the people that have moved into executive management positions, and I really wonder. In the last few years they have moved a couple of women into those positions, but I think they did that reluctantly. And I am not saying that those women shouldn't be there, they should. But you know, I think I should also be there. Maybe there aren't enough spaces for everyone who's qualified. But the reality is, when I look around at top management, it's all straight white males and a few token straight women.

cc: How has this situation impacted your relationship?

BRAD: Over the past few years, my viewpoint changed. Like I said, I realized I was not going to move up, not unless I went to another company. So I began to set some limits. I no longer go in on weekends, and I try to leave by 5:30 now. I do a lot more at home. I am trying to lift some of the burden off of Jerome, who is younger, and trying to get his career going. I do much of the cooking at home, when we eat at home, and I do a lot of the social planning for us. Jerome used to do more of that kind of stuff, but I do a lot of it now.

In like manner, Randy Ambert, a flight attendant for the past fifteen years, realized that upward mobility was not really a possibility for him, and over time he became more vested in domestic pursuits. Listen to Randy's comments about his commitment to career:

cc: Do you think of yourself or your partner as more committed to work/career?

RANDY: I think he is.

cc: How come?

RANDY: He gets more out of his work now than I do. When I first started flying, it was different. I had a real sense of it as a career, and that maybe I would move into management or something. But there really aren't that many opportunities for flight attendants to move up. And you certainly don't move to higher echelons of the company. I have never met a gay executive at Transglobe Airlines, in fifteen years, not one. So I think I lost interest after a while. A lot of people fly for a few years and then get out of it. For me, it's a job. I do what I need to do to get through it, and I find meaning in my life by doing other things.

cc: What kind of things?

RANDY: Oh, the house and our friends. I collect furniture from the 1950s, and I maintain the yard, and I cook a lot. Things like that.

Unsuccessful efforts to enter or progress in paid work, whether due to lack of credentials, discrimination, or to short career ladders created disenchantment with notions of meritocracy and undivided commitment to work. As a result, the affected individuals shifted focus and infused greater effort and meaning into family matters.

Preserving Relationships

Finally, another dynamic bolstering active participation in domesticity springs from efforts to preserve a cherished relationship. At some point in their life together, several lesbigay families faced hard choices of maintaining two careers or maintaining the relationship. In most cases, these longer-term lesbigay families struck a deal. Sometimes the deal included someone turning down a promotion; in other cases the deal included a diminution of work involvement for one while the other put more into paid work. Narvin Wong and Lawrence Shoong, together for just over five years, faced just such a crisis about a year before I interviewed them. Narvin, a healthcare consultant, made the decision to do independent consulting. He saw a lucrative economic opportunity and the chance to exert greater influence over his work, and he decided to take it. The decision also meant a great increase in the number of hours that he would work. Meanwhile, Lawrence had taken a promotion to a nursing position with a large, well-funded research project. The position entailed a pay increase and was much more prestigious, given that the project was associated with a major medical research center. The position required Lawrence to work many evenings with research subjects, and diminished the amount of time he could spend at home and with Narvin. About six months into their new work situations conflict began to develop at home. The conflicts initially circled around housework, but eventually expanded to questions about emotional availability, and the energy available for sexual interaction. Lawrence reflects on a question about the impact of work on his family life:

cc: Describe the impact of significant job changes on family/relationship.
LAWRENCE: Narvin's choice to go into independent consulting created some big changes, changes in his attitude, and changes in our life together. He has very high expectations for himself. He went to an Ivy League business school, and I think he puts lots of pressures on himself to succeed. The problem was that I felt left out, sort of abandoned. I took the position at the medical center, and suddenly I wasn't around in the evenings, and I felt like our relationship just went into a spiral. I loved working at the medical center. I got to work with really great people, and the work was interesting, and I was putting in quite a few hours, more than I used to at Marin General. But after a while I began to feel like I no longer had a life with Narvin. We talked about it, and I asked about him about working less on weekends, and maybe trying to have a little more energy for us being together. He was pretty stubborn, though.
cc: What was he stubborn about?
LAWRENCE: His career and his consulting work. He just felt so strong about trying to make it go.
cc: How did that make you feel?

LAWRENCE: It felt terrible. For a while, I thought maybe he was no longer interested in me. I started having these fantasies that while I was at the lab, he was here, and instead of working, he was having an affair with someone. I would call, and he would get annoyed because he was trying to get work done. We talked about it, and I realized that he wasn't really having an affair, but he was just committed to his work. I think he was pretty worried about finances as well. I mean, we just bought this house, and he was giving up a good salary, and it's not like nurses make a whole lot. I mean, even with my promotion, I wasn't earning but a fraction of what he was earning.

CC: So, what did you guys do?

LAWRENCE: Well, I gave up the job at the lab. I mean, we talked about it, and I realized that I still wanted a relationship with him. He was in a tough place. It wasn't like he could easily go back to the hospital where he was; not at that level, you don't really go back. After a few months Narvin was making decent money, and I just decided I would rather be here at night. So I applied for a day shift position at St. Stephens, and they took me. They were a little surprised that I was leaving the medical center, but the woman who hired me was pretty understanding. I mean, I told her that I needed more time for my relationship. Once I got back onto the day shift, things really improved. I was able to come home at a decent hour, and keep things going around here, and be with Narvin, even if he spends most of his time in his office, I can still go in there and talk to him, and we can have dinner together.

CC: What else did you mean by "keep things going around here"?

LAWRENCE: Just taking care of stuff.

CC: What stuff do you mean?

LAWRENCE: Everything, from laundry to shopping. I am trying to get the house to feel more like a home, more lived in. Of course, he thinks I am spending too much, so I have to watch that, but yah, just doing a lot of stuff around here to keep things going, and to take the pressure off of him.

CC: Did Narvin change anything after you gave up the lab job?

LAWRENCE: Not really around his work. He couldn't, really. But we did agree to set times for dinner, and we always take time for brunch on Sunday, and then do something together. So, yeah, I guess he gave up a bit of work time. I don't mind though. I mean, he's happy. I thought of leaving him for a while, and I think he really dreaded that. He probably would have thrown himself into his work, but I don't think he wanted that. So I made a sacrifice. He says he'll make it up to me, and he does seem a lot more responsive to my needs now than before.

Lawrence and Narvin preserved their relationship, but not without Lawrence's willingness to place more emphasis on family life. Both of them view the choices made as practical, and both anticipate a financial gain from Narvin's commitment to his consulting business.

On the whole, those individuals who gravitate toward greater domestic involvement than their partners often share common socioeconomic characteristics. Frequently they share their lives with partners who earn more, have greater career opportunities, work more hours, and work outside the home. In addition, more domestically involved participants often work in occupations that offer real forty-hour work weeks, more flexible work schedules, the ability to work at home, more holiday and vacation time, and affiliation with colleagues who also share family obligations. Domestically involved participants seldom recognize the confluence of factors encouraging their domesticity. Instead they rely on the vocabulary of individual choice, psychological disposition, and "interests," ignoring the social context in which such dispositions and interests develop.

Gravitating toward Paid Work

The old adage "nothing succeeds like success" applies to many of those participants who gravitated toward work and career. Interesting and challenging work, stable and in some cases lucrative financial opportunities, as well as ample opportunities for promotion or new positions in other settings all contributed to some participants gravitating toward paid work. Both they and their partners recognize the opportunity structures available to them, and their partners frequently encourage them to pursue those opportunities. Moreover, for a few lesbigay employees, work offers more than just a place to achieve personal and financial goals; it sometimes offers a working environment that can feel just like a family.

Career Conditions

Those gravitating toward paid employment often work in occupations and institutions that afford higher incomes, long career ladders, notable pay increases, and the potential for a great deal of agency in one's work. Returning to the case of Joan Kelsey and Kathy Atwood one can see the influence of such factors. The week I spent living with Joan and Kathy provided a clearer picture of Kathy's career. She works as an accountant with a prominent San Francisco bank earning around $85,000 (in 1994). Kathy reports four promotions over her eleven-year career at the bank. For the past two years, she received pay raises of 7 percent each year. She expects 8 percent at her next review. However, she also works fifty-five to sixty hours per week. She awakes at 6:30 each morning in order to get to the train at 7:25 and to work by 8:00 a.m. During the week I stayed with Joan and Kathy, Kathy arrived home between 7:30 and 7:45 every night. Commenting on the hours, Kathy says:

> I know it's a lot. But I love it. I am highly respected at the bank. People look to me for leadership, and as someone who understands the fine points. The bank has re-warded me with several promotions, and they really do appreciate my commit-ment. You've got to do those kinds of hours to really gain their respect, and I have done that, and it's paid off. I love my work, and we have a nice home and a great life because of it.

Kathy shares some common experiences with other participants gravitat-ing toward paid work including a history of upward mobility at work. Among those thirty-eight families with a discernible division of labor, when com-paring the thirty-eight people who gravitate toward paid employment with the thirty-eight with greater domestic involvement, the former report twice as many promotions with their present employers than do those gravitating toward domesticity. Further, among the thirty-eight work-oriented partici-pants, eighteen report taking new jobs during the course of their present re-lationship while only eight domestically oriented participants took new jobs. In most cases the new jobs were upward career moves to new firms for higher pay, more authority, and/or with greater control over work content. This in-cluded four participants who started their own businesses.

While a greater opportunity for promotion characterizes the work envi-ronments of those who gravitate toward paid work, those environments also feature higher salaries and other benefits, including stock options and domestic-partnership benefits. With regard to income, twenty-nine of the thirty-eight work-oriented participants earn more than their respective spouses. Of the eight participants in the study with stock options, six are among those families with a specialized division of labor. The remaining two are among the highly affluent egalitarians who purchase much of their do-mesticity in the service economy. At the time of the interviews, twelve of the employers of the thirty-eight work-oriented participants offered domestic-partnership coverage. Only three of the domestically involved participants worked for employers offering such benefits. Among the twelve participants receiving those benefits, four opted to use them for their partners. None of the domestically involved participants utilized their domestic-partnership benefits for their families.

Family Support

While a positive set of work conditions encourages one to identify with paid work, the support and respect of other family members also contributes. Asking participants what their partners think of their jobs reveals something quite telling. The work-oriented respondents often speak of garnering respect from their spouses. Asking the question "What does your partner think of your job?" to the thirty-eight work-oriented participants elicited no fewer than twelve respondents asserting their partners "respect" their work. The reverse did not occur, with only five mentioning respect as part of their answer. Consider the following answers to the question "What does your partner think of your job?"

ATTORNEY: I think he is very respectful. I don't really know beyond that.

ARCHITECT: I think he enjoys the work I do and expresses an interest in what I do. We talk a great deal about my daily activities and what I do at work. He seems to express a fascination with it, and respects me for it.

BANK MANAGER: Well, I think she knows it's hard work, and that it takes a lot out of me. She respects how hard I work. She has said that.

Note what the more domestically involved partners of the above three have to say to the same question:

FLIGHT ATTENDANT: Seriously, he pokes fun at it because of the stereotypes. Within the gay community even, we are perceived as cupcakes and mindless blond babes. And unfortunately he has met quite a few flight attendants who seem to fit into this stereotype. I keep looking at this and can't quite figure out why it happens. He knows that the work is hard, and that the hours are long, and the frustrations can get intense. It is not work that I particularly look forward to or enjoy. Sometimes, he forgets, and treats it like a picnic.

VISITING NURSE: I get two messages. There are times that he is amazed by it, and proud of it. Other times, I think he feels it's not work, because I do a lot of things that don't seem like work. He doesn't take it seriously, and assumes that I can do things because I don't have enough to do.

COUNSELOR: Well, I don't know. I think because I work at home, she wonders how much I really do. I work hard, and my days are plum full. I think she envies the flexibility I have.

The above answers suggest something about the ways in which the characteristics of jobs influence dynamics within families. Higher-status jobs with higher earning potentials generate feelings of respect from family members. The reverse does not occur. Perhaps some of the discrepancy is explained by the demands of the jobs. The domestically involved participants do work slightly fewer hours for paid wages. The thirty-eight domestically involved participants worked an average of thirty-eight hours per week, with a median of forty hours. The full-time homemakers and the seven part-time workers bring the average down. The job-oriented participants report forty-six hours on average, and a median of forty-four hours. I now wish I had pursued what "respect" actually meant to participants, but I did not ask. I suspect, that in many cases, it meant that the job, its demands, and its various rewards, both to the individual and to the family, afforded a certain amount of power to the holders of such jobs.

In many cases, both among those families where I conducted fieldwork and among those I interviewed, a kind of deference is paid to those with high-demand, high-status jobs. I recall an incident one Thursday afternoon where Sarah Lynch, a graphic artist who works at home, was busy doing the laundry, among other things. I spent much of the day hanging out at her house, and she was, to say the least, busy. She would try to answer my questions in between answering phone calls and running down the hall to change the laundry over every forty-five minutes. At around 5:30, with a huge pile of unfolded laundry on the bed, she began folding at a quick pace. I asked what her hurry was:

CC: What's the rush?
SARAH: Oh, nothing really. I just want to get this done, and out of the way, before Andrea gets home.

CC: How come?

SARAH: I just don't want her to have to deal with it. I really like us to be able to have quality time when she gets here. She has enough pressure to deal with at work, so I try to keep this kind of stuff out of the way.

CC: Do you follow this same pattern of folding the laundry before she gets home, every week?

SARAH: Yep! I like getting it done. It feels good.

Seemingly, Sarah works as many hours as Andrea does. If one counts the domestic work, Sarah actually works many more hours than Andrea does. Sarah earns less. She works at home. Sarah was one of the respondents who earlier expressed a feeling that Andrea might harbor doubts about how much she actually does during the day. Sarah works to produce that invisibility. They both consider their relationship quite egalitarian. This led me to wonder why Sarah wanted to hurry up and get the laundry done and out of sight. Was there something that Andrea did in a similar fashion, some domestic chore hidden from Sarah's view? I could identify nothing. What I could identify was a perception on Sarah's part that Andrea deserved respite from her paid work. The fact that Sarah does laundry in such a fashion reveals the presence of a great deal of support for Andrea's commitment to her paid work.

Work as Family

Finally, a few participants gravitate toward their paid work because of a pleasant and almost familylike atmosphere at work. This doesn't happen with much frequency for lesbigay people, due largely to discrimination and the heterosexual orientation of the workplace (Woods 1993; Friskopp and Silverstein 1995), but six participants described their work life in quite familial terms. Four of those six participants were among the thirty-eight gravitating more toward paid work than toward domesticity. All six share the common experience of working with many lesbian or gay colleagues in work environments affirming of lesbigay people. Carry Taglia, a human-resources professional, working for a San Francisco-based clothing manufacturer, comments on her work environment:

I work in employee benefits. It's great. I love it. The company is so supportive of its lesbian and gay employees, you know, nondiscrimination, domestic partner-

ship, diversity programming, etc. . . . And I get to work with lots of other gay people. It feels good to go to work. The people there, I mean, I really care about them,
and they care about me. And I have met so many great people, gay and straight
people, there. Everyone has such a positive attitude, and even though the company
is going through a restructuring, it's so clear that they want to treat everyone well,
like they are people with real lives.

Carry went on to describe the extra hours she works, the commitment
that she feels toward her employer, and the sense of gratitude she feels because her employer affirms her and the value of her contribution to the company's success. Carry uses the metaphor of a mother-daughter relationship
to describe her working relationship with her immediate manager. Carry's
gravitation toward paid work makes a lot of sense. Few lesbigay people experience such an encouraging relationship with their employer. But when
they do, they respond. However envious we might feel about Carry's working conditions, we should probably maintain some critical distance, for as
Arlie Hochschild's latest research, *The Time Bind: When Work Becomes Home
and Home Becomes Work* (1997), suggests, the motivations for employers to
create familylike atmospheres at work are mostly self-serving and rarely permanent.

In a similar fashion, Wendell Moncado works as an accountant for a nonprofit AIDS-education agency. He reports working up to sixty hours per
week, and feels a great passion for his work, and a strong sense of solidarity
with his coworkers. He understands his coworkers in familial terms. Wendell
depicts his work environment:

> I really like it. I feel like I'm able to maintain a commitment to my values and get
> paid for it. And the people I work with are amazing. We are like a family. We look
> out for each other, listen to each other. Every week we have a meeting just to check
> in with everyone else, to see what's going on in their lives. It's very important to do
> that when you do this kind of work because there can be a lot of pain, and if you
> don't talk about that, about the losses, and a sense that you are not doing enough
> to inform people accurately about their risks, well, that can be quite a burden. It's
> something you've got to talk about. So I feel very good about my work, and espe-
> cially good about the people I work with.

Wendell's work environment encourages him to put in sixty hours, often
working on weekends and socializing with colleagues. In some sense, work
had become family for Wendell. Not that he did not experience family with

his partner, Daniel, for he did. But Wendell and Daniel both experienced some sense of family through Wendell's paid work. Most of their common friends, and much of their leisure time, revolved around Wendell's employment. Wendell's work commitment also left Daniel with much of the responsibility for maintaining much of their domestic life. Daniel expressed resignation, but not bitterness, about this:

> I have mixed feelings about it. I don't really bring it up. His work is very important to him, and it is very important work, I know that. Given how intensely he feels about it, there's not much room for changing things, and you know, I don't really push it. If he were doing something else, maybe I would feel different. But for now, I am willing to deal with it.

In both Wendell's and in Carry's cases the pull of meaningful and affable work environments encourages them to gravitate toward paid work.

Pragmatic Choices and the Sense of Fairness

I have seen a practicality in the ways that lesbigay families sort and arrange domesticity, whether the family is egalitarian or specialized. Such practicality does not create equality, however. True equality, measured with a plumb line, eludes many of these families, but that has little to do with the families per se , and much more to do with the character and quality of employment opportunities that avail themselves to these families. If the reality is that only one member of the family can make money in a fulfilling way, then lesbigay families adjust to that reality.

Many lesbigay relationships don't survive, for a wide variety of reasons. I would add to that list the dilemmas of domesticity—not just the conflicts over who does what but the often overlooked fact that the opportunity to pursue domestic things is not available to everyone. If all of the family must toil at unpleasant and poorly compensating work in order to make ends meet, they do, and they try to fit domesticity in where they can. Of course, these are the families that often don't make it, and that should not be so surprising because without the resources, time, and energy to create family, it withers.

conclusion:

domesticity and the political

economy of lesbigay families

Love, the strongest and deepest element in all life, the harbinger of hope, of joy, of ecstasy; love, the defier of all laws, of all conventions; love, the freest, the most powerful moulder of human destiny; how can such an all-compelling force be synonymous with the poor little State and Church begotten weed, marriage? EMMA GOLDMAN

On a sunny afternoon in the fall of 1996 at a Castro district coffee shop, I sat down next to Henry Zamora, whom I had interviewed back in 1992. Henry and his partner, Joe Solis, had been together for fourteen years. In the conversation with Henry that day I discovered that their relationship had ended in late 1995. Henry described the breakup in detail, attributing the demise of the relationship to an affair Joe had had with his secretary. (Joe works as an attorney for a prominent financial services company in San Francisco.) As I talked with Henry, the details of their domestic life started to resurface in my mind. Henry and Joe lived in Marin County, just across the Golden Gate Bridge from San Francisco, in a small cottage nestled in a grove of redwood trees. Henry worked part time (thirty hours per week) as a nursing assistant in a nursing home for mostly affluent elderly. Henry and Joe shared a domestic life that I would later come to characterize as a "specialized" family where Henry, in his own words, "tends to hold down the fort" while Joe "brings home more of the kill."

The kill was good. In 1991 Joe brought home $110,000 in annual income; Henry earned $28,000. Not surprisingly, Henry invested himself in their domestic life: monitoring, managing, envisioning, and performing feeding work, housework, kin work, and consumption work, as well as providing emotional solace to Joe, whose job, Henry reported, "took a toll on Joe." Joe, by his own account, as well as by Henry's account, worked sixty to seventy hours a week. Throughout their fourteen years together, the couple shared their money, with Henry doing much of the everyday management of that money. However, "their" home was owned and financed by Joe.

As we talked, Henry described his move back to the Castro district in San Francisco, reporting the struggle he went through to come up with $1,000 to put down as a deposit and first month's rent for a place to live. He talked about what it was like to suddenly have three roommates after fourteen years of having a house to himself for part of the day. He had gotten a full-time job in San Francisco at a recently constructed residential-care facility for the elderly. He indicated that he had to go without healthcare insurance until he could begin coverage with his new employer. When he and Joe were together, Henry had an individual health plan that cost about $150 a month. Since the breakup, Henry felt that he could not afford the premium, given how little he was earning. His part-time job at the nursing home in Marin offered no benefits for part-time workers. Henry had a few personal belongings, mostly clothing and a few items of furniture, that he brought with him to his new apartment. I recalled an elaborately furnished home in Marin, but as Henry said that afternoon, "Much of that really belonged to Joe. He did buy it, after all." Henry had no savings or retirement funds because he had planned to retire with Joe. Joe had saved 8–10 percent of his salary in a 401(k) throughout the years of their relationship.

Henry had invested his energy, his labor, and his time into creating family for Joe and himself, and now he had little or nothing to show for that effort. What truly perplexes me is that Henry felt no sense of entitlement. He accepted, with a few lingering doubts, that he didn't contribute anything of economic value to that relationship. He felt that he could make no claim to the resources that had accrued during those fourteen years. Joe earned the money, owned the house, the furniture, the 401(k) accounts, and Henry was left with practically nothing. Amid the lingering doubts expressed by Henry was a distinct feeling that perhaps he had invested too much in the relationship and should have put more energy into his job, and into his "own self-development." In a confessional manner, Henry expressed his "codependency," holding himself accountable for his misfortune. And yet, a few minutes later, Henry expressed a hope in finding a new relationship, and of establishing a new home and family life. In fact, he desired it more than anything else.

Satisfying this desire for family requires a great deal of domestic work, even though the extent of the work is not always acknowledged by the parties involved, and can often entail significant sacrifices for those who do the work. The extent of this work and the determination of who will do the work depends on a number of factors, notably the availability of resources and the characteristics of one's paid work. Doing domestic work often involves sacrifices, such as Henry's, on the part of one or both parties. What drives people to make these sacrifices? What prevents some people from making them? Why should the cost of making such sacrifices be so high? What if *no one* makes those sacrifices?

Family Aspirations

Many lesbigay family members desire a stronger sense of family in their lives. The sentiment saturates lesbigay families, and was very palpable among the families with whom I lived. I think the sentiment partially underlies the political effort to achieve same-gender marriage. In contemplating Henry Zamora's aspirations to begin family anew, as well as the similar aspirations of so many other lesbian and gay people to create home and family, I find Marjorie DeVault's (1991, 77–78) discussion of the origin of family ideals in American society instructive. DeVault begins her discussion of how heterosexual women construct family through feeding work by addressing the ideal notions of family held by the nineteenth-century middle and upper middle classes. DeVault cites historical research suggesting that women in such households tried to create a perfect order, and understood housework as an effort in making meaningful patterns: patterns creating orderly and elegant meals, comfortable and pleasant rooms, and peaceful and harmonious social interaction. Few families have actually achieved this highly mythologized package (Barrett and McIntosh 1982), either in the present or in the past (Davidoff and Hall 1987; Coontz 1992). Nevertheless, most lesbigay families aspire to achieve them.

DeVault observes that many contemporary heterosexual women in families no longer strive for the perfect order but continue the effort to make meaningful patterns, and in the process to create some sense of family. These women struggle against economic and social conditions that impair and limit their efforts. The same holds true for those who make meaningful patterns for lesbigay families. Lesbigay family members desire perfect order and meaningful patterns, both in material and in emotional terms. For better or for worse, the ideals lesbigay families aspire to attain are often quite similar to those of their heterosexual peers.[1]

The Political Economy of Constructing Family

Constructing a fulfilling and durable family takes resources. Approximately one in three of the households studied here have achieved something approaching their ideal. Among more educated and more affluent subjects I heard many speak glowingly of their lesbigay families, their chosen families (Weston 1991). Those families who feel content with their chosen families also tend to fall toward the higher end of the socioeconomic ladder. The greater availability of resources, including time, makes the investment in domesticity—the building blocks of family—much more possible among the affluent, and consequently expands the opportunities to do family with satisfaction. These are the lesbigay families that marketers portray to the lesbigay communities themselves and to the broader public.[2] Clearly, domesticity becomes more comprehensive and ample among those with greater socioeconomic resources. Such families maintain more relationships, engage in more extensive social interaction and community participation, hold jobs offering more flexible time, possess more money to spend and, consequently, can invest more effort in the construction and maintenance of family. Those lesbigay families who possess these things lead richer, more fulfilling family lives. I have taken quite a bit a flak for this assertion, but I refuse to romanticize the struggles of lesbigay people to build and sustain family, and the reality is that they often fail, not because of some inherent defect but due to social and economic realities that pare down their capacity to do family. Too much recent analysis of disempowered groups, including lesbian, gay, bisexual, and transgendered people, emphasizes the successful efforts by these groups to sustain family, religious identities, and cultural traditions in the face of oppression. Left out of such analysis is the brute fact that many such groups get trounced economically, which has consequences for their ability to build stable identities, families, and communities.[3]

The resources available to these more prosperous families has enabled them to construct a somewhat alternative conception and practice of family, one that is organized more strongly around "choice."

Domesticity and Family: Who Gets to Do Family?

One of the critical lapses in the contemporary debate over lesbigay family life concerns the socioeconomic inequalities that prevail between different lesbigay families. I find it striking how differentiated the ability to do family is among lesbigay "families." Even the assertion that lesbigay relationships constitute family seems linked to socioeconomic resources. As resources accumulate, participants begin to think in familial terms about their lesbian- and gay-defined household lives. They have the resources required to create more elaborate domestic regimens, and more stable families. Family construction requires a combination of time, money, ideology, and relationships (friends and/or biolegal relatives). For instance, some of the more affluent lesbigay families had the money, the relationships, and even a commitment to notions of "chosen family," but insufficient time. Their work hours, commutes, and travel obligations made a more elaborate family life something they perhaps envisioned but rarely experienced. In these households there were well-furnished dining rooms, fully equipped kitchens, and inviting spaces for entertaining, but they were rarely used. They sat idle most of the time because in order to obtain them, their owners had to work for wages constantly, and when they were not working for wages they were exhausted and preferred to grab a burrito and rent a movie rather than to entertain themselves or guests with a big production. This scenario was most common

among the affluent egalitarians I described in the last chapter. As Susan Posner, a twenty-nine-year-old lesbian, put it: "We bought this dining room
table, and now we are too tired to use it because we spend all of our time trying to earn the money to pay for it." In contrast to the few affluent families
without time, there are a multitude of lesbigay families of more moderate
means who lack time, money, kin networks, and the energy to create family.

The Minimal Lesbigay Families

The general sense of satisfaction among the more affluent households contrasts markedly with the isolation and disappointment I heard in the many
other lesbigay households about family life. Most participants spoke of de-
siring more friends and more community, and of hopes of healing soured
or rotted relationships with biolegal relatives, and even with former lesbigay family members. Many lived with an uneasy sense of how they would secure themselves financially, expressing doubt about ever owning their own
homes, obtaining adequate healthcare, or having a secure retirement. These
families live in walk-up or basement apartments that have no space for
guests, or they live in suburban apartments where they have minimal interaction with their neighbors and only occasional interactions with other lesbigay people or with biolegal relations. Their employers do not offer domestic partnership benefits, and even when they do, those benefits are often
not extensive enough to consider them "family friendly," assuming that
means that such policies enable the recipients to put more emphasis on constructing and maintaining family. Their employers expect constant overtime
and undivided attention to work when they are at work—a common experience among the service/working-class participants, as well as a majority of
the middle-class participants in this study. When they arrive home they do
not have the energy to plan birthday parties, cultivate gardens, have conversations with their partners, cook interesting food, create and maintain photo
albums, visit friends, or participate in a host of other family-building activities. Many participants were too tired from exhausting workdays to spend
much time cultivating chosen families, and instead collapsed in front of televisions seeking relaxation. When their relationships do falter, these families
cannot afford a therapist to adjudicate domestic conflicts. Most of these lesbigay families find themselves struggling to do family against a set of social
and economic conditions that impede their efforts.

Whether due to extensive and exhausting work schedules, inflexible work hours, small homes, high housing costs, soured relations with biolegal relatives, or a limited sense of obligation to significant others, most participants live within an attenuated family, or what Dizard and Gadlin (1990) call a "minimal family." Most lesbigay families experience at least some isolation from biolegal relatives and have yet to develop and fortify alternative family structures. Of course, many heterosexual families increasingly face a similar predicament. Jan Dizard and Howard Gadlin (1990), in a recent monograph concerning the status of family in our society, use the term *familism* to refer to the processes and functions of what to them constitute the essential core of family. They argue that familism consists of

> a reciprocal sense of commitment, sharing, cooperation, and intimacy that is taken as defining the bonds between family members. These bonds represent the more or less unconstrained acknowledgment of both material and emotional dependency and obligation. They put legitimate claims on one's own material and emotional resources and put forth a set of "loving obligations" that entitles members of the family to expect warmth and support from fellow family members. In addition, these bonds are assumed to be deeper and more lasting than those that exist in other, non-familial relationships. Familism embraces solicitude, unconditional love, personal loyalty and willingness to sacrifice for others. Familism makes the home a base to which you can always return when your independent endeavors fail or prove unsatisfactory. (1990, 6–7)

Dizard and Gadlin note, however, that many families increasingly have difficulty performing these functions and meeting these basic human needs. The economic demand that most families now include two full-time wage earners, along with the separation of paid work from family life, makes it difficult for many families to act in familistic ways, including many lesbigay families. Recognizing the difficulties more and more families face, Dizard and Gadlin call for the adoption of a public familism (1990, 204–19) in which the state and/or employers provide some of the basic needs previously found in families. The provision of comprehensive healthcare or publicly funded preschool would be beneficial to heterosexual families as well as to lesbigay families. It remains an open question as to whether such basic needs will be met. Even if such benefits are achieved, they will only partially assist in the creation and maintenance of family life. In order for more lesbigay families to invest more in the work that constructs and sustains them, we need to work toward political goals that reduce the risks and lower the costs of making the sacrifices that domesticity currently entails.

Contemplating the Risks of Doing Family Work

Given the fact that domestic work doesn't pay much of a wage, engaging in it necessitates risks, the kind that are clearly seen in the life of Henry Zamora. These risks vary from person to person, depending on one's gender, race, educational level, and other factors. As we have seen in earlier chapters, lesbian families do less domesticity than their gay-male counterparts. Of course, notable exceptions exist (recall the affluent Kirbo-Pendleton household described in the housework chapter). In the main, lesbian families, as well as individual lesbians, earn significantly less money than do men (straight or gay). For many lesbians, achieving economic security precludes the option of making a significant investment in family work. Many of the lesbian families in this research face unique disadvantages in the struggle to create family. Due to the persistent nature of gender inequality in access to socioeconomic resources, lesbian families have fewer such resources (money, time, living space) to construct a durable family life.[4] Paradoxically, this partially explains the greater degree of equality within the lesbian relationships studied here—there was less domesticity to do and a greater sacrifice entailed in doing it. For many of the lesbian families of moderate means, the choice to invest a great deal of energy into domesticity would mean a sacrifice of wages that they cannot afford to lose. In contrast, the longer-term affluent lesbian families studied here are thick in domesticity, and they are either specialized in their division of labor or they rely on domestic service workers to provide some domestic labor.

Similar dynamics are at work in the family lives of many people of color. A disproportionate number of African-, Asian-, and Latino-American participants dwell in working/service-class families (see table B9). I do not think this is an artifact of sampling procedure, but rather a reflection of the greater economic constraints that operate in the lives of these participants. This lack of resources partially explains the stronger tendency of African-, Asian-, and Latino-American participants to conceive of family in biolegal terms. Recall Barbara Cho, the Chinese-American woman who could not conceive of her partner as part of her family. Barbara's proximity to her biolegal Chinese-American relations (her parents lived less than a mile away), along with her economic ties to them (her parents owned the apartment building in which she lived), partially prevented Barbara from constructing a lesbigay family. Barbara's biolegal relations know that Barbara is a lesbian but they prefer to keep the matter concealed. Part of this reflects the legacy of compartmentalizing sexual matters as private in many Asian cultures (Chan 1989; Murray 1996, 264–65), but part also reflects the legacy of the economic ties that bind people (particularly women) to the patriarchal family.

Moreover, the legacy of economic marginality for people of color in the United States, combined in some cases with sociocultural traditions that conceive of the patriarchal family as the only means of economic viability, reinforces an ideology linking individuals to biolegal relations, particularly in periods of economic crisis (Amott and Matthaei 1996). Many people of color have not had the freedom to construct chosen families, although many have had to turn kith into kin, often a strategy of resisting poverty (Stack 1974). This economic marginality continues and prevents many lesbigay people of color from creating the kinds of family life (chosen and/or biolegal) that they prefer to lead. To make a greater investment in domesticity entails economic and social risks. Barbara Cho could insist on a stronger acknowledgment of her lesbian life, say, through inviting everyone to an event honoring her anniversary with her partner, Sandy. She might also get thrown out of her apartment. Moreover, the hours that Barbara Cho and Sandy Chao work for wages, along with the frequent swing shifts—Barbara works at a hotel covering night shifts three days a week and Sandy works at a daycare center, arriving at 6:30 a.m. to meet the first parents with their kids—prevent either of them from investing a great deal of energy into their domestic lives. For either or both of them to reduce work hours would entail a significant economic risk that neither is really prepared to take, not to mention that Barbara has a strong commitment to making herself economically independent of her biolegal family.

For affluent, often Euro-American, lesbigay families, economic independence and a reliance on service workers diminish the risks to members of the family; each can pursue employment with less chance of exploitation of other family members. Certainly, as indicated earlier, many of the affluent lesbigay families create a greater sense of equality between the partners through reliance on the service economy, or in other words, upon the poorly paid labors of others, notably women of color and younger, less-educated gay men and lesbians. As indicated in the housework chapter, financial resources enable many of the affluent lesbigay families to purchase several forms of domestic labor (laundry, housecleaning, gardening, routine meals) in the marketplace, and this allows such families to invest more time and energy in the more pleasant forms of family work (for example, kin work, ceremonial cooking, and the more pleasing forms of consumption work). This parallels patterns that exist among affluent heterosexual families (Ostrander 1984; Hertz 1986). These expenditures create greater equality within the family.

But is equality that is premised on the exploitation of outsiders a worthy ideal? Even if some find it so, this leaves the majority of lesbigay families who cannot afford such services in a dilemma. For them, creating family demands domesticity, while at the same time the reigning ideals demand egalitarianism. The two are not so easily merged. Conflict is inevitable given these contradictory expectations. One of the potential outcomes of this conflict is the diminution of domesticity in the lives of lesbigay families, which contributes to the emergence of minimal lesbigay families. I suspect this diminution frequently involves diminishing emotional needs as well as domestic activities. Lesbigay people are already experts at emotional asceticism, trained to conceal our most fundamental feelings, needs, and sentiments by the persistent potential of physical and psychological violence against us (Garnets, Herek, and Levy 1990). It seems quite plausible that lesbigay people feel less entitled to caregiving from other family members than do many heterosexuals. Is it really a sign of strength that lesbigay people live with reduced expectations of care from significant others?

Potentially, the combination of domestic needs and egalitarian expectations can lead to the demise of the relationship. Those who would place lesbigay families on the egalitarian pedestal need to come to terms with the fragility of lesbigay relationships (Blumstein and Schwartz 1983; Kurdek 1992). Fully aware of this fragility, many lesbigay family members who might invest more energy in domesticity probably do not, instead putting more energy into paid work and consequently reducing the quality and the long-term durability of their family relationships. In his angrier moments, Henry Zamora now wishes he had done so.

Now You See It, Now You Don't: Gender and Domesticity

Too many scholars have pinpointed gender as the crucial variable in creating egalitarianism in lesbian and gay relationships. Many have argued that because there are not both men and women in lesbigay families, the traditional assignment of domesticity on the basis of gender cannot take place, and therefore lesbigay families must negotiate domesticity, which leads to a more equitable division. This is simply not the case among longer-term families.[5] As we have seen, lesbigay families carefully stage information about domesticity, as well as the performance of domesticity itself, in order to prevent stigma. Recall Rich Chesebro's effort to prevent people, including me, from thinking of his partner, Bill, as a "housewife, or something" by constantly emphasizing Bill's artistic career, or Dolores Bettenson's strategic emphasis on the "feminine bed linens" chosen by her partner, Arlene, an emphasis that partially attempts to conceal the reality that Arlene works as a prosecuting attorney seventy hours a week and has little time for things domestic. Recall the nearly universal assertion of participants claiming they split domestic work "fifty-fifty" when the empirical reality is that they do not.

Lesbigay family members strategically emphasize those behaviors that conform to and affirm the reigning ideals concerning gender and family in American culture. For a modern lesbigay family to portray their family and/or gender identities in the ideals of an earlier time (butch/femme, instrumental/emotional) now seems anachronistic, if not uncivilized. I don't think that lesbigay families have changed as much as the official ideology has changed. Kennedy and Davis, in their social-historical study of the lesbian community in Buffalo, N.Y., make the following observation about lesbian domestic life in the 1950s: "Narrators who came out in the 1950s also had a variety of approaches to dividing housework, although there seemed to be a tendency for fems to do more of it" (1993, 290). Of course, the "fem's" participation in housework probably made her more "fem." I suspect that if the ideals of that earlier era made a comeback, few of the families I studied would have much difficulty reportraying their relationships in light of those older ideals. Such a portrayal might even be more honest and accurate, but certainly not any less true than the widespread assertions of egalitarianism that are now heard.

Many scholars of late have argued that lesbigay families carry the potential to undo the gendered ideology and inequality of midtwentieth-century family life because of their supposed egalitarianism (Stoddard 1989; Hunter 1991; Schwartz 1994, 1; Okin 1997, 54–56). These scholars offer the lesbigay family as a model for the future. My research seriously challenges the effort to place the lesbigay family in the vanguard of social change, a model of equality for others to emulate. Such assertions are based on the ideology

of egalitarianism, not on its actual existence, and on the invisibility, devaluation, and diminishment of domesticity. The minimal family and the
familized corporation (Hochschild 1997) may well be the path of the future
but it is not a path to equality, fulfillment, and happiness for most lesbigay
people, nor for most other people.

Devalued and Invisible: Lesbigay Domesticity

Returning to the demise of Joe Solis and Henry Zamora's relationship and
comparing their circumstances with the laws and customs that govern
heterosexual relationships, one realizes that domesticity is potentially even
more devalued and exploited within lesbian and gay relationships than it is
within the context of heterosexual marriage. Joe and Henry are not a typical
lesbigay family. Given Joe's affluence, the gap between their wages, and the
long period they were together, they are atypical. However, the demise of
Henry and Joe's relationship gives rise to several observations concerning
domesticity that pertain to many lesbigay families.

First, the devaluation of much of domesticity, even among those who do
it, encouraged Henry's perception that he was entitled to little compensation
for his efforts. Henry, like millions of other people who toil at domestic
work, had devalued and romanticized his contributions; neither he nor Joe
could conceive of them as work. Henry understood much of his domestic involvement as a natural expression of his more "nurturing" personality, an extension of his "personal interests" rather than as necessary work worthy of
some form of social compensation.

Second, much of Henry's contribution was invisible. Henry did not
possess much of a vocabulary for articulating what he had done for much
of those fourteen years. He spoke of "holding down the fort," and when
prompted he could identify specific household tasks he performed in great
detail. But, as many do, he lacked a set of categories that would reveal and organize much of his domestic effort. At one point in our initial interview in
1992 Henry answered a question about who cleans the bathtub/shower: "We
tend to share that. We clean it twice a month or so. I get Joe to do it once a
month, I guess. I tend to do it a little more thorough, like getting to the mold
and mildew that grows on the ceiling in there. He doesn't tend to notice that
as much." Henry knows that he must "get" Joe to do housework, that he does

housework "a little more thorough," and that he "notices" that it needs attention, but he failed to recognize these efforts as significant. He portrays an equality that conceals the fact that he facilitates the domestic work, sets the standards, monitors the house in light of those standards, and makes a plan to achieve the standards. These energy- and time-consuming efforts remain invisible in most families, including most lesbigay ones.

Third, and quite similar to many other lesbigay families, the character and organization of domesticity within Henry and Joe's household reflected the influence of paid work. The effects of paid work upon lesbigay family life remain largely invisible and undocumented. I noted in the introduction the dearth of research on this matter. In part this invisibility occurs due to an overemphasis on individual volition when thinking about family life. We too often assume that the hours that someone works for wages, the energy they put into that work, and their subsequent capacity to make themselves available to family and domestic life is simply a question of individual values or personality. Such an emphasis fails to acknowledge the structures of constraint (Folbre 1994, 51) at work in people's lives, particularly in the lives of working/service-class families, where choices are greatly constrained by economic necessity. Neglecting the effects of paid work on family life leaves pressing political and economic questions unaddressed. Questions like, Why should most salaried workers be exempted from the forty-hour work week? Or, Why should household work go uncompensated, or when compensated, without benefits like healthcare?

In sum, lesbigay families are not as distinct from heterosexual families as many seem to believe. Taking the wider view, looking at domesticity in its myriad forms, examining it, and depicting it in its detail, as I have tried to do, creates a portrait of longer-term lesbian and gay family life that more often than not resembles patterns seen within heterosexual families. This raises a set of provocative questions about how lesbigay families and communities either resist or accommodate the broader cultural context in which they live. A debate rages about what constitutes gay and lesbian culture, and whether that culture does or should accommodate or resist the social practices and discourses of the broader society (Faderman 1989; Herdt 1991). My research and observations about domesticity suggest a significant pattern of accommodation to the predominant social structure of American society among lesbigay families. Much of that accommodation goes unrecognized, notably the seclusion and devaluation of domesticity. Some of that accommodation is denied, as in the case of the many gay men who conceal domesticity performed by themselves or other family members, or in the case of the domesticity that contributes to the creation and maintenance of social-class distinctions. Some of the accommodation is recognized by lesbigay people but undocumented and untheorized by researchers, as exemplified by the dearth of research exploring the effect of paid work upon the organization and character of lesbigay domestic life.

Marriage and Lesbigay Domesticity: Who Will Be Bound by the Ties That Bind?

Contemplating and discussing with others the demise of Henry and Joe's relationship, I have heard many people, both straight and gay, advocate legal marriage as a solution to what seems to many an inequitable circumstance. Most appear to believe that Henry was entitled to a just and equitable settlement of some sort, and that legal marriage would provide him an avenue to justice, or at the very least a legal ritual "that takes apart our relationship as deliberately as we put it together" (Duggan 1997). Of course, the deliberate construction of family in all but the most exceptional cases takes considerably more effort than its deliberate deconstruction, and most significantly to the argument here, much of the work that went into building the family goes unrecognized during its demolition.

For example, divorce proceedings also often assume the invisible and devalued status of domestic work (Graycar and Morgan 1990). Moreover, American family law leaves the determination of the "value" of domesticity provided during the course of a relationship to a judge to decide.[6] Considering the resistance of legislatures and courts to acknowledge heterosexual women's contributions to their husbands' job performance as a divisible marital asset (Singer 1997), I am quite circumspect as to how the judiciary would appraise the value of similar contributions performed in lesbigay families. Does one suppose that Henry Zamora could successfully argue in divorce court that he should receive the prevailing wage[7] for the domestic services he provided for more than fourteen years, let alone half the household earnings? For the sake of argument, and in violation of much of what I have discovered in this research, let us reduce Henry's domestic contribution to ten hours per week. Compensation for those ten hours per week for fourteen years at the prevailing wage would entitle Henry to nearly $60,000. In Henry and Joe's case, such wealth exists in the form of property. It is possible that legal marriage would have provided Henry with some compensation (maybe even enough to pay for his health insurance premium?).

However—and herein lies the problem with thinking that legal marriage would prevent the exploitation of one's domestic labor—most lesbigay families do not own their homes, and they contribute only meagerly to retirement funds. Most would end their relationships with debt, not assets. From what source of capital will compensation come for those who worked their ten hours a week but who have no assets? Many in our society would argue that Henry made his choices and now he must live with the consequences. But to those of us who advocate lesbian and gay liberation, as well as gender equality, this set of circumstances is not just. Henry should not have been in such a predicament. For affluent lesbigay families, marriage would provide some security, allowing individuals within such marriages to reduce the risks of investing time and energy into domesticity, and this undoubtedly would result in happier, more enduring family formations for some.

Nonetheless, legal marriage will prove a Trojan horse for many other lesbigay families, as well as the multitudes of single lesbigay people. Those who marry will find themselves faced with the expectations associated with legal marriage, including expectations for more domesticity (Denmark et al. 1985), without any additional resources. Sociological research suggests that even after controlling for children and paid work, marriage creates more domestic work (Shelton and John 1993; South and Spitze 1994). The advent of lesbigay marriage will usher in an expansion of domesticity. Yes, friends and family will attend a wedding ceremony to acknowledge one's relationship, but they will also expect thank-you cards for the wedding presents, cards that are bought by someone, addressed by someone, organized by someone, and stamped and mailed by someone. If legal marriage brings the social status to lesbigay relationships that marriage advocates desire, it will bring with it new expectations for domesticity in a variety of forms. Biolegal relatives, as well as lesbigay family, will expect greater participation in kin networks along with the attendant kin work. They will expect greater participation in the gift-exchange networks, thus expanding consumption work. They will expect to visit and to come for dinner, thus expanding housework and feeding work. Do not misunderstand me. These are wonderful things that families aspire to achieve, but marriage will not make it any easier to provide them.

Marriage will create expectations without changing the capacity of most lesbigay families to meet them. The additional work will not bring additional compensation.[8]

Nor would legal marriage reduce the economic risks involved in pursuing domesticity. In fact, legal marriage might well encourage caregiving individuals to take those risks, to invest more in domestic life without providing substantive resources (time and/or money) to create that domestic life. Note, for instance, that most of the economic benefits of marriage pertain to those who are affluent. Examples include the right to spousal support or alimony in case of divorce, the presumption of joint ownership of real estate, the right to dower, the tax-free transfer of property, and inheritance rights. While such benefits will protect the property interests of more affluent lesbigay families, they will not contribute much to sustaining everyday family life for most lesbigay families. Moreover, those benefits associated with legal marriage that might meaningfully contribute to the sustenance of lesbigay families would mostly accrue to the more affluent. Examples include health, dental, and life insurance benefits, reduced auto insurance rates, family discounts for health club memberships, married rates for family-owned business licenses,[9] family-leave benefits, and reductions in the legal costs of adopting children.[10] Many middle-class and most working/service-class lesbigay families work for employers who do not provide health and dental care insurance. They often rely on public transit systems, they can't afford health club memberships, they don't own businesses, they can't afford to adopt or conceive children, and they certainly are in no position to take unpaid time off to care for children, elders, or the sick. Legal marriage won't provide much of substance to these families.[11] In the main, the supposed economic benefits of legal marriage won't contribute much to creating durable and happy lesbigay families.

For single lesbigay people, lesbigay marriage will mean that those in married relationships will begin to accrue some economic benefits at the expense of their unmarried neighbors. For instance, in some states, legal marriage entitles one to lower automobile insurance rates based on the statistical probability that those in marriages drive more safely. In lesbigay neighborhoods in urban centers, where auto insurance rates are quite high, this could amount to substantial savings. But the judiciousness of this seems highly suspect. Why should my best single friend, living in the same neighborhood with a clean driving record, pay more for his car insurance than I do because I am in a relationship? Or why should I be able to join a grocery buyer's club with my partner for the same cost as what my friend will pay for just one person? The logic of marriage in these cases, and in many others, is little more than a rationalization of privilege and will contribute to greater, not less, inequality within the lesbian and gay communities, as well as in the wider society. Clearly, in those families where at least one member works for an employer who provides health and dental care benefits for dependents, legal marriage will bring concrete economic benefits to that family. For single lesbigay people, particularly for the mass of service/working-class and many middle-class workers who work for employers who do not provide such coverage (including those who work for most of the small businesses in lesbigay neighborhoods), the extension of coverage to the legally married will diminish their chances of expanding access to healthcare. This will happen because some of the political and social support for universal healthcare that now exists within lesbian and gay communities will erode as the married gain access. Once the affluent elite within lesbigay society have their benefits, the struggle for universal access to healthcare will become even more difficult. Proponents of lesbigay marriage acknowledge that greater economic benefits will accrue to affluent lesbigay families (Eskridge 1996, 83) but appear oblivious to the potential sociopolitical consequences of such a development.

Too many advocates of same-gender marriage view marriage as the elixir that will finally bring happiness, fulfillment, and inclusion of lesbigay people. They imagine that the sociolegal status of marriage will bring acceptance and inclusion of lesbigay people through making lesbigay people more like our heterosexual counterparts. But, we must ask, at what price? I have already noted that single lesbigay people have little to gain from this strategy and a lot to lose, including the additional onus of stigma that is likely to become associated with singleness if some lesbigay people attain a new married status. But my greatest concern, the one rooted in my investigation of domesticity within lesbigay relationships, focuses on the consequences for those who take the risk and do the work of constructing family life. Many of these individuals will contribute their free labors to creating family only to find themselves tied by legal and economic binds to stultifying, emotionally destructive, and unpleasant relationships, or even to relationships that have simply lost their passion, and will have few options to free themselves or to protect themselves if their family collapses. Undoubtedly, a structure of legal marriage would make these relationships more stable, but it would not necessarily produce greater happiness for everyone involved.

Those who have put lesbian and gay marriage at the front of the political agenda have lost their way: they have no vision of what a fair and just society entails for all lesbian and gay people. One notable gay proponent of gay marriage, Andrew Sullivan, former editor of *The New Republic*, persuasively argues against any form of public discrimination against homosexuals. He argues that the rights and responsibility that heterosexuals enjoy by virtue of the state, including legal marriage, should be extended to gay people (Sullivan 1993, 24–26). The problem with Sullivan's conservative, supposedly pro-gay politics is its willingness to address public forms of inequality as the sole legitimate path to lesbigay inclusion in Western society. His analysis fails to address the private consequences of a public act like marriage. Moreover, Sullivan seems oddly unknowing of the complex and constantly shifting relationship of the public/private spheres in Western societies (Nicholson 1986). The identification of domesticity with the private sphere resulted from social, political, and economic interests that benefited immensely from artificially dividing social life into such spheres (Hartman 1981; Jaggar 1983, 143; Connell 1987; Glazer 1993, 211). Assuming the legitimacy of the private/public distinction and leaving the inequalities that prevail in the private sphere unaddressed in the effort to achieve lesbian and gay inclusion into the public sphere is an ethically barren political strategy. Sullivan wants to make marriage universally available as a way to do away with discrimination against lesbigay people. But participation in marriage will legally reinforce inequality within lesbigay relationships and drive social wedges between single and married lesbigay people. Advocacy of legal marriage, as that marriage currently exists in American society, is a strategy that is willing to sell out the interests of the typical lesbigay family, and of the broader lesbigay communities, in order to obtain the privileges of married heterosexual society for a few, mostly affluent lesbigay families. If the goal is to make the world more inclusive of lesbigay families, then we must recognize that legal marriage is inadequate to the task at hand. We do not need civil ties that bind individuals into nuclear dyads. Rather, we need civil ties that bind all of us to one another, recognizing our mutual responsibilities for the whole of our communities and for each individual within them. We must continue to work toward a "public familism" (Dizard and Gadlin 1990). We need civil ties that recognize the complexity of our real family lives, not off-the-shelf models imposed upon us by the affluent elites, including lesbigay elites, who have no real interest in changing the quality of lesbigay family life but are rather more interested in securing their own place at the table of the privileged.

Do not misunderstand me. I am not arguing against binding ties between caregivers and those who need care (for example, guardians and children; guardians and those who are dependent upon them). However, placing the burden of caregiving upon the family unit leads to an unfair distribution of work and resources within families. It is highly problematic to rely upon the unpaid labors of women and some men (including many of the gay men in the families studied here)[12] to provide caregiving. It fosters inequality within relationships and requires too much sacrifice on the part of caregivers; it also fosters privatism and an extreme preoccupation with one or two individuals that eclipses the concerns of the wider community. In our public policy and political organizing we should emphasize the public responsibility to create and sustain social institutions that provide care (daycare centers, schools, nursing facilities, home healthcare programs, hospices, social security) over expectations of care from legally defined family members. And within families we must figure out ways to compensate those who provide domestic labors, whether through procuring domestic services from fairly paid domestic-service workers or through paying wages to family members who provide these labors.

Moreover, I am not arguing against legal mechanisms for identifying guardians in case of incapacitation, or establishing visitation rights in case of incarceration or hospitalization, but there is no reason to attach such rights to legal marriage. Rather, we should strive to make such rights universally available to each person. Let each citizen decide who will serve as their guardian, who will inherit their property, who may involuntarily hospitalize them, and who may visit them in prison or in the hospital. Arguments asserting that it is not practical to offer these options to all are simply elitist. If these rights are so important, should we not figure out practical ways to extend them to each person in light of his or her desires? For instance, if we can register to vote at the same time that we renew a driver's license, why shouldn't we be able to establish powers of attorney on that same occasion? Lesbigay people are well aware of the capricious and unethical character of biolegally sanctioned definitions of kin. Many of us who lived through the worst years of the AIDS epidemic can recount stories of biolegal relatives marching into the lives of gay men, asserting their status, and summarily ignoring the social bonds that actually meant something to the person, particularly in cases where the individual had become incapacitated or had died. Lesbigay marriage would prevent some of this, but only for the married.

What Do Lesbigay Families Need to Prosper?

Clearly, many lesbigay families need greater social support in crafting happy and durable family formations. In a sense, lesbigay families need work—feeding work, housework, consumption work, kin work, interaction work, and emotional work. These are the essential labors of a successful family life. Yet the creation of such families also takes energy, time, and money, networks of loving and caring individuals, family-friendly public and corporate policy, as well as acknowledgment of and compensation for doing family work. A limited number of lesbigay families have many of these resources and they have created family formations that are often both happy and durable, and occasionally equitable, as my research has shown. So the question arises as to how to achieve this state of affairs for a wider range of lesbigay families without exploiting individuals within lesbigay families or contributing to greater inequality within the lesbigay communities or the wider society? How do we move from minimal families to maximal families in a manner that advances individual happiness, familial happiness, and a broader *public* happiness?[13] Advocates of familial happiness for lesbigay families should recognize our common interests with many other American families. The same policy and political options that will make most families happier and more durable will do the same for lesbigay families as long as we fight for inclusive definitions of family. Family-friendly policy suggestions abound,[14] but I would like to highlight a few sweeping policy changes that would contribute much to making lesbigay family life more pleasant, successful, and equitable. I realize that these suggestions are broad and politically difficult, but such proposals would contribute the most to making happy and lasting lesbigay families. Then I will turn to some of the particular policy options that currently exist in the political arena, notably the domestic partnership efforts, and suggest why they offer the most hope to the majority of lesbigay families.

In terms of sweeping policy suggestions, and confluent with the interests of most American families, lesbigay families need shorter work weeks so that they can invest more time into their family and community lives. American families, including lesbigay families, are working for wages too many hours per week to successfully sustain family life (Coontz 1997, 44ff; Hochschild 1997, 246; Rubin 1994, 244). The American lesbian, bisexual, and gay movements should align with progressive efforts to reduce work hours for American employees. The forty-hour work week has slowly eroded for many workers whether through forced overtime for many working-class employees and through deceptive redefinition of job categories (for example, hourly workers redefined as salaried workers, thus exempting them from the forty-hour rule) for many middle-class employees (Schor 1992). Lesbigay family advocates should join the effort to reduce work hours and restrict the capacity of employers to exceed the forty-hour work week (Schor 1992, 142).

In addition, a limited number of affluent lesbigay families would benefit from inclusion in the Family and Medical Leave Act of 1993. The law should be extended and the family member(s) should be whomever one chooses to so define (that is, "fill in the blank"). Expanding eligibility is important, but inadequate. Amending of the Family Leave Act to provide *paid* time off from jobs in order to provide care for newborns, elderly parents, and sick family members would be of much greater use to the majority of lesbigay families. Moreover, like many families, lesbigay families need access to affordable and meaningful healthcare regardless of their marital or employment status. Further, they need access to family-assistance programs that will assist them in their struggles with chemical dependencies and counseling services that will enable them to sort out the psychological and relational matters that concern them. Obviously, all of these provisions cost money, and it remains a matter of political struggle to determine who should pay, but it is disingenuous to claim that the wealthiest civilization in human history cannot afford such provisions while most of the rest of the industrialized world, including our leading economic competitors, routinely provide such benefits (National Research Council 1991, 155). I do not accept, nor should other lesbigay family advocates, the assertion that the United States cannot afford family-friendly policy until we take care of other seemingly more pressing concerns (like balancing the federal budget and stabilizing social security) that currently dominate American political culture (Reich 1998).

In a similar vein, lesbigay families need the services of *fairly paid* domestic-service workers who will provide some of the domestic work needed to create family life.[15] It is a disturbing and unpleasant reality that much of the equality achieved by affluent lesbigay couples comes about through their utter reliance on poorly paid domestic and service workers. In terms of social policy we need greater emphasis on developing and enforcing fair labor practices for domestic workers. Clearly, a national system of healthcare would greatly improve the lives of these workers and diminish some of the exploitative character of their employment.

Finally, the efforts to establish domestic partnership legislation, as well as corporate domestic partnership policy, provide us with an unprecedented opportunity to contribute in a meaningful way to the happiness of lesbigay families. Some legislative and policy initiatives have significantly expanded eligibility to a wider range of relationships. San Francisco's landmark domestic partnership legislation offers a glimmer of what the future could hold. Within the San Francisco policy, employees may choose to provide health, dental, and other benefits to a wider range of relationships. Under the terms of the policy, if one wishes to provide one's granddaughter, spouse, or domestic partner with healthcare, one may choose to do so. Conservative and corporate interests attempted to limit the policy to same-sex domestic partners only based on the notion that domestic partnership is really only a rough approximation of marriage and should be limited to only those who are excluded from legal marriage. Corporate interests wanted to limit costs through excluding unmarried heterosexuals and limiting eligibility to only biolegally defined direct dependents. Advocates of a more inclusive partnership policy prevailed, much to the dismay of corporate interests. There exists a certain amount of irony in how the San Francisco policy actually evolved. The Equal Benefits Ordinance requires that all entities that contract with the city to provide goods and services offer the same kinds of benefits to employees regardless of the employee's marital status or sexual orientation. For example, a company that offered health insurance to heterosexual married employees would need to provide the same coverage for gay unmarried employees. Strangely, some opponents of domestic partnership for lesbian and gay people, intending to sustain contractual relationships with the city, actually devised institutional policies that expanded the field of eligible candidates for coverage in order to avoid having to institutionally recognize lesbian and gay relationships. The Catholic Archdiocese of San Francisco and the Bank of America both took this route. Many lesbians and gays found this disturbing because they desired symbolic recognition of their covenanted relationships.

I do not find this move disturbing at all. I consider it a meaningful step toward providing family-friendly policies to a broader range of relationships. In fact, I think the Equal Benefits Ordinance and similar corporate policies should veer away from attempting to define the attributes of those who become eligible for coverage. Employees should be able to designate anyone whom *they* choose to receive those benefits. Employers conceive of such benefits as compensation, and given those employees earn that compensation, why should employees not decide how to allocate who receives it? Offering health, dental, vision, life, and long-term disability insurance are not required by law, so why should the law attempt to narrowly define who is eligible for these benefits? Opponents of such an inclusive domestic partnership policy would assert that this would make practically anyone eligible. Exactly. Why exclude? It is incumbent upon those who want to exclude to offer compelling reasons for doing so. Expanding domestic partnership policies in this manner will contribute much more practical assistance to real lesbigay families than legal marriage could ever provide. For instance, I know of many gay-male families where individuals would like to extend medical benefits to family members with HIV/AIDS, but because our family members are not our "domestic partners" and they lack biolegal status, they are not eligible. A broadly defined domestic partnership policy would recognize the kin ties that actually exist within lesbigay families. Such policy would also contribute much to the emergence of fulfilling and happy family lives among all American families, and it would do so in a way that would actually diminish rather than exacerbate broader patterns of social inequality.

appendix a: interview guide

A. Background on job/career.
   1. History.
      a) List.
      b) Job searches or career changes/promotions during this relationship.
      c) Describe the impact of significant job changes on family/relationship.

B. Impact of work on family/relationship.
   1. Current job.
      a) Tell me about your job.
         1) Travel?
         2) What hours do you work?
         3) Evenings?
         4) Weekends?
         5) How long a commute to work?
      b) Do you think of yourself or as your partner as more committed to work/career? Why?

      c)   What does your partner think of your job?

      d)   Does your employer know of your sexual orientation? Colleagues? Clients?

          1)   Describe the impact of this circumstance on you.

C.   Impact of family on work.

    1.   Cross-cutting responsibilities.

      a)   Do you work extensively at home?

      b)   Does your partner ever help you with that work?

      c)   Do you do much job-related entertaining? At home? With partner?

      d)   In what ways has your relationship either enhanced or limited your job/career pursuits?

    2.   Information sharing.

      a)   Do you discuss your day at work with your partner? How often?

      b)   What kinds of things do you talk about?

      c)   Who usually asks about work, you or your partner? Example?

      d)   Who talks more about their work? Why?

    3.   Partner's influence on your work.

      a)   Does your partner influence decisions you make at work? If so, how?

      b)   Do you influence your partner's work decisions?

    4.   Partner's impact on job choices.

      a)   Would you relocate with your partner?

      b)   Have you discussed relocating?

      c)   Negative impact on you by your employer if you refused to relocate?

    5.   Views of the employer.

      a)   Does your employer hold an image of the "ideal spouse"?

      b)   Does your partner fit the image?

      c)   Does your employer support your relationship? In what ways?

      d)   Does your employer provide benefits to your family/ relationship? Children? You?

D.   Housework.

    1.   Household chores.

      a)   Describe in general terms how you divide up household chores in your relationship.

b)   Tell me about the household chores you completed today.

2.   Specific household chores.

a)   Who in your relationship last cleaned the kitchen?

1)   The oven?

2)   The refrigerator?

3)   Tell me about the typical pattern of cleaning up the kitchen.

4)   How long does it take?

b)   Who last cleaned the bathtub/shower? Typical?

1)   Toilet? Typical?

2)   Sink? Typical?

3)   Why this pattern of cleaning the bath?

4)   How long does it take?

c)   Who last did the laundry?

1)   Typical? Why?

2)   When and how often does laundry get done?

3)   Who normally washes the bed linens and towels?

4)   How much time per day do you spend on laundry?

5)   How many loads does your household wash per week?

d)   Who last made the bed, changed linens?

e)   Who last vacuumed or cleaned floors? Why?

1)   How much time does this take per week?

f)   Who maintains the garden/yard? Why?

1)   Who cares for indoor plants? Why?

2)   How much time per week do you spend on this?

g)   Who last dusted/polished furniture?

h)   Who last took out garbage/recycling? To the curb?

i)   Who last cleaned the automobile(s)? Why?

j)   Who straightens up the living/family room?

k)   Who usually brings in the mail and sorts it?

l)   Who generally sews and mends clothing?

m)   Tell me about continuing discussions/points of conflict or unresolved feelings with your spouse over these kinds of cleaning tasks.

3.   Purchasing domestic labor.

a)   Do you have a cleaning service ever come in to clean? How often? Who comes? Gender/race of worker?

  b) Do you take laundry to a laundry service? How often?

  c) Do you take in a lot of dry cleaning? How much? How often? Who?

  d) Do you use a yard/garden service?

  e) Do you hire anyone to care for children or elderly or sick members of your kin or family?

  f) Who usually arranges these services?

  g) How much do you pay for these services per month:

    1) Laundry/dry cleaning?

    2) House cleaning?

    3) Yard?

    4) Child/elder care?

  h) How do/would you feel about paying for such services? Your partner?

4. Household management.

  a) Who takes responsibility for home repairs or upkeep?

  b) Who usually meets service or delivery people at the house? Why?

    1) Anyone come in the last month? Who? Six months? Who?

  c) Who keeps tabs on which cleaning supplies you need?

  d) Do you feel like you need to prod your partner to help with or to do household tasks?

  e) Where do you turn to get information about housework?

  f) Tell me about the standards you follow for housework.

    1) From where do you think do those standards come?

5. Financial management.

  a) Do you share money? All of it?

  b) If separate, how do you handle joint responsibilities like rent or groceries?

    1) If together, who maintains the joint expense accounts?

  c) If together, how do you divide the task of paying bills?

  d) How do you decide to spend money for:

    1) Clothes?

    2) Sports/hobby equipment?

    3) Entertainment?

    4) Furniture?

        5)   Cars?

        6)   Housing?

    e)   How do you manage longer-term investments? Who? Why?

        1)   Do you have joint savings for purchasing a home or any other goal?

    f)   How do you handle business-related expenses? Who? Why?

    g)   Have you always had this system of finances in your relationship?

    h)   Tell me about how you maintain financial records.

    i)   Do you plan out a budget for the household and/or for individual expenses?

    j)   Tell me about continuing discussions/points of conflict over the management and/or spending of money.

    k)   Do you think that your incomes influence the division of household chores in any way?

    l)   Would you be willing to share with me all of the financial transactions you made in the last week?

E. Feeding work.

    1.   Meal preparations.

        a)   Who last cooked dinner at home?

            1)   Typical?

            2)   Why?

        b)   Breakfast?

            1)   Typical?

            2)   Why?

        c)   Lunch?

    2.   How do you decide what to eat?

        a)   Do you read magazines that focus upon food?

        b)   Do you read the food section of a local paper?

    3.   Do you plan for meals each day? Week? Longer?

    4.   Do you often eat evening meals together? If so, what does that mean to you?

        a)   Did you make a conscious decision to do this?

    5.   After you decide what to eat, do you usually find a recipe?

        a)   Tell me about the process of cooking.

b) Do you take health considerations into account when deciding what to eat?

c) What kinds of concerns?

d) Do you know the things that your partner will not eat?

e) Do you know their favorite meal or kind of food?

f) What foods do you most enjoy?

   1) What foods do you dislike?

6. Do you have close friends/kin with whom you eat evening meals on a consistent basis (more than once a week)?

a) When was the last time?

   1) What do they like to eat? Things they don't like?

7. How often do you eat evening meals out?

a) How do you feel about eating out?

b) How often do you get takeout food?

8. Tell me about continuing discussions/points of conflict over food or meal preparation.

9. How often do you go to the grocer?

a) Who went last?

b) Typical?

c) Why?

d) Do you take a grocery list?

e) Who writes the list and/or checks to see what is needed?

   1) Why?

f) If you go, how do you decide what to buy at the store?

g) Do you clip coupons? Your partner?

10. Where do you shop?

a) Why?

b) How much do you spend on groceries each week?

c) How much do you spend on eating out each week?

F. Home products and services consumption.

1. Do you purchase furniture or appliances jointly for your home?

a) Tell me about your most recent purchase.

b) Tell me about how you decided to buy what you did.

2. Who takes more interest in the process of acquiring things for your home?

a) Why?

3. Do you choose and purchase linens and towels jointly?
   a) Dishes?
   b) Cookery?
4. Where do you usually buy such products?
   a) Why?
   b) Do you go out to shops and stores to just look?
   c) How many times in the last month did you visit a department store?
   d) How many times in the last month did you visit a hardware store?
   e) Where do you turn for information about products?
   f) Who do you turn to for advice about goods and services?
      1) What is their relationship to you?
   g) Do you go to more than one store to compare prices on household goods?
5. Can you recall a product or service you felt dissatisfied with recently?
   a) If so, describe the problem and what you did about it.
6. Does the decor and style of your home reflect more your tastes or your partner's tastes?
   a) How do you feel about that?
   b) What factors do you consider in purchasing furniture for your home?
7. Tell me about the last time you bought a present for someone for a holy union or service of commitment or a heterosexual wedding.
8. Do you read the home or garden section in the newspaper?
9. Do you subscribe to or consistently buy magazines about art, interior design, gardening, or housekeeping?
   a) Which of these magazines do you read most?
10. Do you subscribe to lesbian- and gay-oriented magazines?
    a) Do you pick up the local lesbian and gay newspapers.
    b) Do you turn to either lesbigay magazines or to lesbigay newspapers when looking to purchase goods or services?
11. Tell me about the last brochure or instructional manual you read about some item in your home.
12. Tell me about the artifacts/art you display in your home.
    a) Where did you get them?

      b)   What do you think it says about you and/or your partner?

13. Do you experience much conflict with your spouse over purchases?

14. What sport or leisure activities do you engage in by yourself?

      a)   With your partner?

G. Kinwork

1. Do you have close friends who live in the area?

      a)   How many "close" friends?

      b)   Who met them first, you or your partner?

      c)   Of these, how many are gay and how many straight?

2. Do you share the same friends as your partner?

3. Do you consider your close friends as "family" or "kin"?

      a)   Why?

      b)   What attracts you to them?

4. Do you spend a lot of time with any one person other than your spouse?

5. Do you invite people over for dinner or brunch?

      a)   How many times in the last week/month?

      b)   Who did you invite recently?

      c)   What else did you do on that occasion? Who thought of it?

      d)   Who cleaned up after the event?

      e)   Who prepared for and cooked the meal?

      f)   Did you discuss the occasion with your partner afterward?

      g)   How did you both feel about it?

6. Who usually contacts and invites people to come over?

      a)   Why?

7. What kind of food do you typically serve to friends/family when they come over?

      a)   Tell me about how you think through what to serve to guests.

8. Do you go out to dinner often with close friends? Who normally arranges for this?

9. Do you keep in touch with friends out of town? Do you call? Write?

      a)   Biolegal relatives out of town? Do you call? Write?

      b)   Do you do more of this kind of thing for friends or for biolegal relatives?

      c)   Why?

10. Did you send holiday greeting cards last year?
    a) Did you send them jointly?
    b) Who purchased the cards?
    c) Who filled them out?
    d) Did you send a note/newsletter in them?
    e) Approximately how many did you send?
11. Do you buy birthday presents for anyone on a consistent basis? For whom?
12. Birthday cards? For whom?
13. Anniversary cards? For whom?
14. To whom did you last send flowers?
    a) How often do you send flowers?
    b) Do you send them jointly?
    c) Who actually makes the call to order them or goes to the florist?
15. Where did you spend the winter holidays you celebrated last year?
    a) Were you together?
    b) Who made the arrangements?
    c) Where did you spend Thanksgiving?
    d) How do you feel about the ways in which you celebrate holidays?
    e) Do you like the people you spent them with? Why?
    f) Do you celebrate other holidays throughout the year in any way?
16. Have you taken any vacations in the last year? Where?
    a) Who made the arrangements?
    b) Why?
17. Who spends more time talking on the phone to friends?
    a) Why?
    b) How many long-distance calls do you make per week? Who do you call most often?
18. Who cares for pets? Feeding? Walks? Brushing? Baths? Vet appointments?
    a) If cat(s), who changes litter?
    b) If dog(s), how often do you walk?
        1) Partner?

19. Have you registered as domestic partners with the City of San Francisco or Berkeley?
    a) Did you or your partner push for this?
    b) What does it mean to you?
    c) Do you have a will that recognizes your partner as a beneficiary?
    e) Do you have a power of attorney or durable power of attorney for your partner in case of incapacitation or death?
    f) Did you or your partner push for power of attorney?
    g) Who did most of the research on wills and power of attorneys and handled the paper work?
    h) Why they do it?
20. Do you do any volunteer work for any organization or group?
    a) Which one?
    b) How many hours do you put into that per week?
    c) Do you provide assistance to elderly or sick friends or family of any sort?
    d) Describe what you do.
21. How often do people stay over night in your home? Who did so last? How long did they stay?

H. Childcare
    1. Do children live with you?
        a) If so, tell me about your childcare arrangements.
        b) Who normally makes the arrangements?
        c) If the children do not live with you, how much time do you spend with them? Your partner?
        d) Tell me about the children's housework responsibilities.
    2. Tell me about making purchases for or arranging for services for your children.
        a) Toys?
        b) Clothes?
        c) Furniture?
        d) School supplies?
        e) Daycare?
        f) Insurance, healthcare, dental care?

I. Conceptions of gender/family.
    1. Tell me about your attitudes toward traditional roles for men and women in the family in our society.
    2. Do you feel like the prescriptions for such roles influence or shape your relationship? Why?
    3. In what ways would you like your relationship/family to more closely resemble the relationships/family life of heterosexual marriage?
    4. What would you think of your partner or yourself engaging in homemaking full-time and working for wages only partly or not at all?

J. Conception of ethnicity and domesticity.
    1. What influence does your ethnic identity have upon your relationship with your spouse?
    2. How does it influence the kinds of household tasks and responsibilities you each do?

K. House data section.
    1. Approximate floor area of residence?
    2. Number of rooms?
    3. Number of baths?
    4. Dining room?
    5. Yard?

L. After-interview data sources.
    1. Photo of grocery list(s).
    2. Photo of living/family room.
    3. Calendar(s).
    4. Budget.
    5. List of financial transactions for the past week.

appendix b:

sample characteristics

TABLE B1.   PRESENT FAMILY CLASS DESIGNATION

	Female	Male	Total
Working/service class	10	4	14
· *Family incomes: $20,000–$45,000*			
· *Educational level: high school/some college or community college graduate*			
· *Wages: hourly wages*			
· *Occupations: retail sales; lower-paid craftspeople; clerical; drivers of commercial and public transportation vehicles; service workers*			
· *Housing: rental apartments costing $600–$1,000 per month*			
Middle class	11	10	21
· *Family incomes: $45,000–$70,000*			
· *Educational level: some college or college graduate*			
· *Wages: salaried workers*			
· *Occupations: lower-level managers; lower-status professionals (nurses; teachers; social workers; librarians); higher-paid craftspeople*			
· *Housing: rental houses and apartments costing $1,000–$1600 per month; a few homeowners*			
Upper middle	5	12	17
· *Family incomes: $70,000 plus*			
· *Educational level: college graduates mostly with postgraduate study*			
· *Wages: mostly salaried workers with occasional flows of capital from stocks and/or bonuses*			
· *Occupations: upper managers; higher-status professionals (attorneys, architects, physicians, college professors; computer and business consultants; dentists)*			
· *Housing: luxury apartments costing $1600 per month or more; homeowners*			

NOTE: The conceptions of class I use to classify lesbigay families mirror those designations developed by Gilbert and Kahl (1993), with family income, educational level, and occupational prestige serving as the major indicators of class identity.

TABLE B2.   ANNUAL INCOME: FAMILY AND INDIVIDUAL

Annual Income	Family	Individual*
$0–$9,999	0	8
$10,000–$19,999	0	10
$20,000–$29,999	3	16
$30,000–$39,999	7	31
$40,000–$49,999	11	14
$50,000–$59,999	10	12
$60,000–$74,999	6	6
$75,000–$100,000	6	5
Over $100,000	9	3
Total	52	105

*Non-wage-earning children under 18 not included.

TABLE B3.   FAMILY AND INDIVIDUAL INCOME BY GENDER

Annual Income	Male Family	Female Family	Male Individual	Female Individual
$0–$9,999			2	6
$10,000–$19,999			5	6
$20,000–$29,999	1	2	6	10
$30,000–$39,999	2	5	14	16
$40,000–$49,999	3	8	10	6
$50,000–$59,999	5	5	5	4
$60,000–$74,999	4	2	6	1
$75,000–$100,000	4	2	3	2
Over $100,000	7	2	2	1
Total	26	26	53	52

TABLE B4.   ETHNIC/RACIAL/CULTURAL IDENTITIES

	Women	Men	Total
Black/African-American	7	6	13
Asian-American			15
Chinese-American	3	4	
Vietnamese-American	2	1	
Japanese-American	1		
Korean-American	1	1	
Filipino-American		2	

Continued on next page

TABLE B4. *Continued*

	Women	Men	Total
Euro-American			63
Anglo-American	7	9	
German-American	4	5	
Irish-American	5	4	
Jewish-American	4	3	
French-American	3	3	
Italian-American	2	4	
Other Euro-American	5	5	
Latina/Latino-American			15
Mexican/Chicano-American	4	7	
Cuban-American	1		
Puerto Rican-American	1	2	
American Indian			2
Osage	1		
Cheyenne		1	

NOTE: I asked participants to identify their primary ethnic/racial/cultural identity. Many participants actually descend from multiple ethnic/racial/cultural groupings. The significance of these designations holds some meaning for some participants in some dimensions of domesticity, including the content and character of feeding work. Children are included.

TABLE B5. OCCUPATION BY GENDER IDENTITY

	Male	Female	Total
Homemaker	2		2
Student	1	2	3
Retired	1	1	2
Service workers	3	3	6
Craftspeople	2	4	6
Clerical	4	1	5
Sales workers	6	3	9
Technical workers (includes computer programmers, trainers, and consultants)	3	4	7
Administrators/management/small business owners/human resources/public relations	6	9	15
Professionals (see next table)	23	23	46
Executives	2	2	4

TABLE B6.   PROFESSIONAL OCCUPATIONS BY GENDER

	Male	Female	Total
Accountant	1	2	3
Architect	1	1	2
Attorney	3	3	6
Clergy	1		1
Counselor/therapist	2	3	5
Dentist	1		1
Engineer	1	1	2
Librarian	2		2
Optician	1		1
Physician	1	1	2
Professor		3	3
Registered nurse	4	2	6
Teacher	3	5	8
Social worker	2	2	4

TABLE B7.   EDUCATIONAL LEVEL BY GENDER

	Male	Female
Some high school	1	
High school graduate	1	3
Some college	4	12
Community college graduate	7	3
College graduate	21	18
Masters	11	11
Ph.D., J.D., M.D.	8	5
Total	53	52

TABLE B8.   LENGTH OF RELATIONSHIP BY GENDER AND CLASS

Number of Years Together	Female	Male	Service/Working Class	Middle Class	Upper Middle Class	Total
2–4	9	6	6	7	2	15
5–8	9	10	6	9	4	18
9–11	4	4	2	3	3	9
12–15	3	4		2	5	7
18–21	1	1			2	2
22 plus		1			1	1

Working/service-class families
   Troy Diablo∞ and Jeffrey Richards♣
   Sue Murphy♣ and Lindsey Tuttle♣
   Amy Gilfoyle♣ and Wendy Harper♣
   Carey Becker♣ and Angela DiVincenzo♣
   Sandy Chao⊗ and Barbara Cho⊗
   Elsa Harding♦ and Deborah James♦
   Tim Cisneros∞ and Paul Leal∞
   Fanny Gomez∞ and Melinda Rodriguez∞
   Lily Chin⊗ and Carol Len⊗
   Shirley Brown♣ and Margareta Lopez∞
   Tim Reskin♥ and Phillip Norris♣
   Michael Herrera∞ and Federico Monterosa∞
   Marilyn Kemp♣ and Letty Bartky♣
   Mary Callihan♦ and Margaret Jackson♦

Middle-class families:
   Rhoda Friedman♣ and Esther Kushner♣
   Cindy Pence♣ and Ruth Cohen♣
   Jessica Thyme♣ and Letty Feldman♣
   Lance Meyter♦ and Mike Tuzin♦
   Wayne Osmundsen♣ and Sterling Graves♦
   Jerome Steinberg♣ and Brad O'Neil♣
   Rosanna Metz♣ and Alma Duarte∞
   Linda Yee⊗ and Sucheng Kyutaro⊗
   Russ Pena∞ and Randy Ambert♣
   Susan Posner♣ and Carry Taglia♣
   Emily Fortune♣ and Alice Lauer♣
   Cesar Portes∞ and Andy Yanez⊗
   Carl Maynard♣ and Scott Hale♣
   Andrea Sayers♦ and Sarah Lynch♣
   Derrick Stonecraft♦ and Andrew Joust♦
   Raquel Rhodes♦ and Danielle Wood♦
   Wendell Moncado⊗ and Daniel Sen Yung⊗
   Gary Hosokawa⊗ and Scott McKendrick♣
   Bill Fagan♣ and Rich Chesebro♣
   Teresa Rivera∞ and Julie Avilla∞

Upper-middle-class families:
   Greg Fuss♣ and Matthew Corrigan♣
   Cheryl Fitzgerald♣ and Clarice Perry♣

Continued on next page

TABLE B9.   *Continued*

Glenna O'Conner♣ and Beth Wilkerson♣

Joe Solis∞ and Henry Zamora∞

Dolores Bettenson♣ and Arlene Wentworth♣

John Chapman♣ and Theodore Fairchild♣

Robert Bachafen♣ and Greg Sandwater♥

Joe McFarland♣ and Rich Neibuhr♣

Virginia Kirbo♣ and Clarice Pendleton♣

Kathy Atwood♣ and Joan Kelsey♣

Lance Converse♣ and Casey Nivens♣

Narvin Wong⊗ and Lawrence Shoong⊗

Steven Beckett♣ and Anthony Manlapit⊗

Nolan Ruether♣ and Joe Mosse♣

Billy Swanson♣ and Greg Ellwood♦

Brent Navan♣ and Christopher Saylor♣

Henry Goode♣ and Lawrence Sing⊗ and Jimmy Depaula♣

NOTE: All names are pseudonyms to protect participant anonymity. ♦ = Black/African-American; ∞ = Latino/a-American; ⊗ = Asian-American; ♥ = American Indian; ♣ = Euro-American.

notes

Introduction

1. I suspect that my mother, and presumably others, have wondered if my gay identity did not emerge out of this unconventional childhood. Of course, cause and effect are not easily discernible in such cases (Green 1987; Bailey 1995).

2. Kurdek readily acknowledges the difficulties with self-reported data, particularly with reference to gender concerns. In a research article concerning relationship quality among lesbian and gay couples, Kurdek writes: "The assessments used in this study were exclusively self-report: therefore, the higher scores for lesbians may be due to gender-related biases in reporting interpersonal and intimate events" (1988, 114).

3. One hundred eight individuals, including three children old enough to talk to me. The odd number of adults (105) results from the inclusion a one male family with three adult members. This threesome has been together for nine years.

4. By "socioeconomic context" I mean something akin to feminist economist Nancy Folbre's conception of structures of constraint: "sets of asset distributions, rules, norms, and preferences that empower given social groups. These structures locate certain boundaries of choice, but do not assign individuals to a single position based on ownership of productive assets. People occupy multiple, often contradictory positions because they belong to multiple groups" (1994, 51).

5. Instead of identifying the gender, class, and ethnic/racial identity of each individual in the text each time a participant appears, figure 1 provides such identities for each participant.

6. I use the term *biolegal* to distinquish traditional conceptions of family, those based on biological and/or legal criteria, from conceptions of family based on the character and quality of social interaction. This distinction allows one to recognize that many lesbigay people do not conceive of "family" as consisting primarily of biolegal relatives. Carol Stack (1974) used the term *fictive kin* in her study of African-American kinship to point to a similar distinction.

7. The Yankelovich Monitor Survey of 1994 reports that close to two-thirds of lesbigay people live in cities with populations exceeding one million residents (Lukenbill 1995, 100).

8. Comparisons to New York, Seattle, Denver, Boston, and Chicago (all experiencing economic health and intense gentrification) are perhaps more apt than comparisons with Detroit, Miami, Philadelphia, or Los Angeles.

Chapter Two

1. Blumstein and Schwartz (1983, 149–50) observed the exact same pattern in their research on American couples.

Conclusion

1. Of course, such aspirations reflect the influence of economic interests, notably in the form of corporate advertising that encourages citizens to associate a wholesome and happy family life with any number of consumer products.

2. Consider a recent Subaru advertisement as illustrative of this. The ad features two men (presumably gay) washing their brand new Subaru Outback Station Wagon in the driveway of their single-family house while the family dog romps through the suds. This kind of marketing image contributes to the widespread perception that most lesbigay people are affluent (Gluckman and Reed 1997), despite empirical evidence to the contrary (Badget 1995; Lukenbill 1995, 96).

3. For evidence of the economic inequalities faced by lesbians and gay men, see

Badget (1995) or the results of the Yankelovich Monitor 1994 survey summarized in Lukenbill (1995). The Yankelovich Monitor survey provides the most reliable and valid empirical data to date on this matter, and reveals that lesbigay household income consistently lags behind heterosexual household income.

4. Empirical research contradicts the widespread myth of lesbian relational stability, finding roughly equivalent rates of dissolution among gay men and lesbians (Blumstein and Schwartz 1983; Kurdek 1992).

5. Perhaps, this negotiation creates more equality early in the relationship, and the negotiation outcomes give way to other factors over time. Many of the studies from that 1970s and 1980s finding egalitarianism in lesbigay relationships also report large numbers of nascent relationships. In Blumstein and Schwartz's groundbreaking work *American Couples*, slightly over half of the lesbians and close to one-third of the gay men were in relationships less than 2 years old. Two-thirds of the gay men, and three-quarters of the lesbians were in relationships less than 5 years old. Other widely cited studies finding lesbigay egalitarianism also report on nascent relationships. Peplau and Cockran (1988) report a median length of relationship of 15 months; Lynch and Reilly (1986) report a median of 2.9 years together; Tuller (1978), a median of 2 years. All participants in my study were together at least 2 years, with a median length of slightly over 7 years.

6. The Uniform Marriage and Divorce Act (sect. 307), as well as the wide majority of state laws (see *Family Law Reporter: Reference File*, Washington, D.C.: BNA, loose-leaf, 400:001-453-001) grant to the courts enormous discretion to redistribute spousal property upon divorce, regardless of title, in a way that seems equitable to a judge. This discretion is more limited in California, a community property state, where redistribution would be limited to marital "acquests" (property acquired during the relationship).

7. I contacted eight different housecleaning services in Marin County to ask what wage I might be able earn if I went to work for them. One refused to cite a range, while the remaining seven indicated that they pay between eight and eleven dollars per hour. I had someone else call each agency back in order to find out what they charge per hour for services. All eight charge from twelve to nineteen dollars per hour.

8. For instance, marital tax structures will not prove economically beneficial to lesbigay families. Given the tax bias in favor of single-earner families, and the economic reality that most lesbigay families must be dual-earners, most lesbigay families who filed jointly would face an increased tax burden, not a reduced burden (McCaffery 1997).

9. One of the families I studied jointly owned and operated a bed and breakfast. Each year they both had to pay a $300 license fee to the city to operate. If married,

they would only be required to pay a joint fee of $300. This is a good example of the kind of economic benefit of marriage that would accrue to those who own businesses, but certainly not to those who work for such businesses.

10. In the main, only quite wealthy lesbigay families can afford the costs of adoption. Moreover, due to the absence of a national healthcare system in the United States, only wealthy lesbigay families can pursue new reproductive technologies. Patterson (1995) reports that 58 percent of the lesbian baby-boom families she studied had annual household incomes exceeding $60,000.

11. Exceptions to this general pattern of marriage benefiting affluent lesbigay families might include marriage-related rights that entitle one to remain in a rent-controlled apartment upon the death of one's spouse if all family members failed to include their names on the original lease. This would have economic relevance to residents of San Francisco and New York City, which have rent-control laws, but to very few others.

12. I suspect that gay men tending to domestic work and caregiving partially contributes to the significant pay gap that prevails between gay men and straight men (Badgett 1995).

13. The use of "happiness" as a criteria for determining the worthiness of social and political institutions, including family formations, permeates this chapter. Such an emphasis reflects my indebtedness to the Enlightenment thinkers, notably Thomas Jefferson. I believe, as did Jefferson, that the pursuit of happiness is both a private and a public concern. The contemporary consensus concerning the meaning of the pursuit of happiness emphasizes the individual pursuit of private happiness. Such an interpretation slights Jefferson's more inclusive concern that political institutions facilitate a wider, public happiness. My concern that legal marriage as it currently exists will bring greater happiness to an affluent elite, often at the expense of others, detracts from the wider pursuit of public happiness. See Willis (1978, chap. 10) for a more thorough discussion of Jefferson's understanding of the pursuit of happiness.

14. See *Work and Family: Policies for a Changing Work Force*, a report compiled by the National Research Council (1991) under the auspices of the National Academy of Sciences, for a variety of specific proposals that would behoove American families.

15. See Romero (1992, chap. 7) for concrete and fair suggestions as to how to conceive of and provide payment for domestic work.

references

Aaker, J. L., and J. Dean. 1993. The non-target market effect: Associated feelings of acceptance, alienation, or apathy. Paper presented at the annual meeting of Association for Consumer Research, Nashville, Tennessee.

Abel, E., and M. Nelson. 1990. *Circles of Care: Work and Identity in Women's Lives*. Albany: SUNY Press.

Acock, A., and D. Demo. 1994. *Family Diversity and Well Being*. Thousand Oaks, Calif.: Sage.

Amott, T., and J. Matthaei. 1996. *Race, Gender and Work: A Multi-Cultural Economic History of Women in the United States*. Boston: South End Press.

Aquilino, W. S. 1993. Effects of spouse presence during the interview on survey responses concerning marriage. *Public Opinion Quarterly* 55 (3): 358–76.

Atkinson, P., and M. Hammersley. 1993. *Ethnography: Principles in Practice, Second Edition*. London: Routledge.

Badgett, L. 1995. The wage effects of sexual orientation discrimination. *Industrial and Labor Relations Review* 48 (4): 726–39.

Badgett, L., and M. King. 1997. Lesbian and gay occupational strategies. In A. Gluckman and B. Reed, eds., *Homo Economics: Capitalism, Community And Lesbian And Gay Life*. New York: Routledge.

Bailey, J. M. 1995. Biological perspectives on homosexuality. In A. D'Augelli and C. Patterson, eds., *Lesbian, Gay, and Bisexual Identities Over the Lifespan: Psychological Perspectives*. New York: Oxford University Press.

Barrett, M., and M. McIntosh. 1982. *The Anti-Social Family*. London: Verso.

Bieber, I., et al. 1965. *Homosexuality: A Psychoanalytic Study*. New York: Basic Books.

Bell, A., and M. Weinberg. 1978. *Homosexualities: A Study of Diversity Among Men and Women*. New York: Simon and Schuster.

Berk, S. Fenstermacher. 1985. *The Gender Factory: The Apportionment of Work in American Households*. New York: Plenum Press.

Berk, S., and R. Berk. 1978. A simultaneous equation model for the division of household labor. *Sociological Methods and Research* 6: 431–68.

Bernard, J. 1982. *The Future of Marriage*. New York: Bantam Books.

Bieber, I., et al. 1965. *Homosexuality: A Psychoanalytic Study*. New York: Basic Books.

Blood, R., and D. Wolf. 1960. *Husbands and Wives*. Glencoe, Ill.: Free Press.

Blumer, H. 1954. What is wrong with social theory? *American Sociological Review* 19: 3–10.

Blumstein, P., and P. Schwartz. 1983. *American Couples*. New York: Morrow.

Bourdieu, P. 1984. *Distinction: A Social Critique of the Judgment of Taste*. Cambridge, Mass.: Harvard University Press.

Brines, J. 1994. Economic dependency, gender, and the division of labor at home. *American Journal of Sociology* 100: 652–88.

Cahill, S. 1989. Fashioning males and females: Appearance management and the social reproduction of gender. *Symbolic Interaction* 12 (2): 281–98.

Caldwell, M., and L. Peplau. 1984. The balance of power in lesbian relationships. *Sex Roles* 10: 587–600.

Chan, C. 1989. Issues of sexual identity in an ethnic minority: The case of Chinese-American lesbians, gay men, and bisexual people. In A. D'Augelli and C. Patterson, eds., *Lesbian, Gay, and Bisexual Identities Over the Lifespan*. New York: Oxford.

Chauncey, G. 1994. *Gay New York: Gender, Urban Culture, and the Making of the Gay Male World, 1890–1940*. New York: Basic Books.

Chodorow, N. 1978. *The Reproduction of Mothering: Psychoanalysis and the Sociology of Gender*. Berkeley: University of California Press.

Clark, D. 1991. Commodity lesbianism. *Camera Obscura* 25/26: 180–201.

Collins, R. 1992. Women and the production of status cultures. In M. Lamont and M. Fournier, eds., *Cultivating Differences: Symbolic Boundaries and the Making of Inequality*. Chicago: University of Chicago Press.

Collins, J., and M. Gimenez. 1990. *Work without Wages: Domestic Labor and Self-Employment within Capitalism*. Albany, N.Y.: SUNY Press.

Coltrane, S. 1989. Household labor and the routine production of gender. *Social Problems* 36 (5): 473–90.

———. 1998. *Gender and Families*. Thousand Oaks, Calif.: Pine Forge Press.

Connell, R. 1987. *Gender and Power*. Palo Alto, Calif.: Stanford University Press.

———. 1992. A very straight gay: Masculinity, homosexual experience, and the dynamics of gender. *American Sociological Review* 75 (6): 735–51.

Coontz, S. 1992. *The Way We Never Were: American Families and the Nostalgia Trap*. New York: Basic Books.

———. 1997. *The Way We Really Are: Coming to Terms with America's Changing Families*. New York: Basic Books.

Coverman, S. 1985. Explaining husband's contribution in domestic labor. *Sociological Quarterly* 26: 81–97.

Cowan, R. 1983. *More Work for Mother: The Ironies of Household Technology from the Open Hearth to the Microwave*. New York: Basic Books.

———. 1987. Women's work, housework, and history: The historical roots of inequality in work-force participation. In N. Gerstel and H. Gross, eds., *Families and Work*. Philadelphia: Temple University Press.

Curtis, R., and E. Jackson. 1977. *Inequality in American Communities*. New York: Academic Press.

Cutright, P. 1971. Income and family events: Marital stability. *Journal of Marriage and the Family* 33 (May): 291–306.

Daniels, A. 1988. *Invisible Careers: Women Civic Leaders from the Volunteer World*. Chicago: University of Chicago Press.

Davidoff, L., and C. Hall. 1987. *Family Fortunes: Men and Women of the English Middle Class 1780–1850*. London: Hutchinson.

D'Emilio, J. 1983. Capitalism and gay identity. In Ann Snitow, ed., *Powers of Desire: The Politics of Sexuality*. New York: Monthly Press Review.

Denmark, F., J. Shaw, S. Ciali. 1985. The relationship among sex roles, living arrangments, and the division of household responsibiilities. *Sex Roles* 12: 617–25.

DeVault, M. 1987. Doing housework: Feeding and family life. In N. Gerstel and H. Gross, eds., *Families and Work*. Philadelphia: Temple University Press.

———. 1991. *Feeding the Family: The Social Organization of Caring as Gendered Work*. Chicago: University of Chicago Press.

Diamond, T. 1992. *Making Gray Gold: Narratives of Nursing Home Care*. Chicago: University of Chicago Press.

Diaz, A. M. 1875. *A Domestic Problem: Work and Culture in the Household*. Boston: Osgood.

Dilallo, K., and J. Krumholtz. 1994. *The Unofficial Gay Manual: Living the Lifestyle.* New York: Doubleday.

Di Leonardo, M. 1987. The female world of cards and holidays: Women, families, and the work of kinship. *Signs* 12 (Summer): 440–52.

Dizard, J., and H. Gadlin. 1990. *The Minimal Family.* Amherst: University of Massachusetts Press.

Douglas, M. 1979. *The World of Goods.* New York: Basic Books.

Duggan, K. 1997. I earned this divorce. *New York Times,* 25 July. In A. Sullivan, ed., *Same-Sex Marriage: Pro and Con.* New York: Vintage.

DuGay, P. 1996 *Consumption and Identity at Work.* London: Sage.

Duncan, B., and D. Duncan. 1978. *Sex Typing and Social Roles: A Research Report.* New York: Academic Press.

Ellis, A. 1965. *Homosexuality: Its Causes and Cure.* New York: Lyle Stuart Inc.

England, P. 1992. *Comparable Worth.* New York: Aldine de Gruyter.

Epstein, C. 1988. *Deceptive Distinctions: Sex, Gender, and the Social Order.* New Haven, Conn.: Yale University Press.

Eskridge, W. 1996. *The Case for Same-Sex Marriage: From Sexual Liberty to Civilized Commitment.* New York: Free Press.

Ettelbrick, P. 1989. Since when is marriage a path to liberation? *OUT/LOOK, National Lesbian and Gay Quarterly* 6: 9.

Etzioni, A. 1969. *The Semi-Professions and Their Organizations.* New York: Free Press.

Faderman, L. 1991. *Odd Girls and Twilight Lovers: A History of Lesbian Life in Twentieth-Century America.* New York: Columbia University Press.

———. 1992. The return of butch and femme: A phenomenon in lesbian sexuality of the 1980s and 1990s. *Journal of the History of Sexuality* 2 (4): 578–96.

Ferree, M. 1976. Working-class jobs: Housework and paid work as sources of satisfaction. *Social Problems* 23: 431–41.

———. 1980. Satisfaction with housework: The social context. In S. F. Berk, ed., *Women and Household Labor.* Beverly Hills, Calif.: Sage.

———. 1990. Beyond separate spheres: Feminism and family research. *Journal of Marriage and the Family* 52: 866–84.

Fischer, E., and S. Arnold. 1990. More than a labor of love: Gender roles and Christmas gift shopping. *Journal of Consumer Research* 17 (Dec.): 333–45.

Folbre, N. 1994. *Who Pays for the Kids: Gender and the Structures of Constraint.* New York: Routledge.

Fowlkes, M. 1980. *Behind Every Successful Man: Wives of Medicine and Academe.* New York: Columbia University Press.

———. 1987. The myth of merit and male professional careers: The roles of wives. In N. Gerstel and H. Gross, eds., *Families and Work.* Philadelphia: Temple University Press.

Freitas, A., S. Kaiser, and T. Hammidi. 1996. Communities, commodities, cultural space, and style. *Journal of Homosexuality* 31 (1–2): 83–107.

Friskopp, A., and S. Silverstein. 1995. *Straight Jobs, Gay Lives: Gay and Lesbian Professionals, the Harvard Business School, and the American Work Place*. New York: Scribners.

Garfinkle, H. 1967. *Studies in Ethnomethodology*. Englewood Cliffs, N.J.: Prentice Hall.

Garnets, L., G. Herek, and B. Levy. 1990. Violence and victimization of lesbians and gay men: Mental health consequences. *Journal of Interpersonal Violence* 5 (3): 366–83.

Geerken, M., and W. Gove. 1983. *At Home and at Work: The Family's Allocation of Labor*. Beverly Hills, Calif.: Sage.

Gerson, K. 1985. *Hard Choices*. Berkeley: University of California Press.

———. 1993. *No Man's Land: Men's Changing Commitments to Family and Work*. New York: Basic Books.

Gerstel, N., and H. Gross, eds. 1984. *Commuter Marriage*. New York: Guilford Press.

———. 1987. *Families and Work*. Philadelphia: Temple University Press.

Gerstel, N., and S. Gallagher. 1993. Kinkeeping and distress: Gender, recipients of care, and work-family conflict. *Journal of Marriage and Family* 55 (Aug.): 598–607.

———. 1994. Caring for kith and kin: Gender, employment, and privatization of care. *Social Problems* 41 (4): 519–39.

Gilbert, D., and J. Kahl. 1993. *The American Class Structure: A New Synthesis*. 4th ed. Belmont, Calif.: Wadsworth Press.

Gilligan, C. 1982. *In a Different Voice: Psychological Theory and Women's Development*. Cambridge, Mass.: Harvard University Press.

Gimenez, M. 1990. The dialectics of waged and unwaged work: Waged work, domestic labor, and household survival in the United States. In J. Collins and M. Gimenez, eds., *Work without Wages*. Albany, N.Y.: SUNY Press.

Glazer, N. 1987. Servants to capital: Unpaid domestic labor and paid work. In N. Gerstel and H. Gross, eds., *Families and Work*. Philadelphia: Temple University Press.

———. 1991. Between a rock and a hard place: Women's professional organizations in nursing and class, racial, and ethnic inequalities. *Gender and Society* 5 (3): 351–72.

———. 1993. *Women's Paid and Unpaid Labor: The Work Transfer in Health Care and Retailing*. Philadelphia: Temple University Press.

Gluckman, A., and B. Reed. 1997. The gay marketing moment. In A. Gluckman and B. Reed, eds., *Homoeconomics: Capitalism, Community, and Lesbian and Gay Life*. New York: Routledge.

Goffman, E. 1959. *The Presentation of Self in Everyday Life.* New York: Anchor Books.

———. 1977. The arrangement between the sexes. *Theory and Society* 4 (Fall): 301–31.

Graycar, R., and J. Morgan. 1990. *The Hidden Gender of Law.* Annandale, N.J.: Federation Press.

Green, R. 1987. *The "Sissy Boy Syndrome" and the Development of Homosexuality.* New Haven, Conn.: Yale University Press.

Haist, M., and J. Hewitt. 1974. The butch-femme dichotomy in male homosexual behavior. *Journal of Sex Research* 10 (Feb.): 68–75.

Hammersley, M., and P. Atkinson. 1983. *Ethnography: Principles in Practice.* London: Tavistock.

Harry, J. 1984. *Gay Couples.* New York: Praeger.

———. 1988. Decision making and age differences among gay male couples. In J. De Cecco, ed., *Gay Relationships.* New York: Haworth.

Harry, J., and W. DeVall. 1978. *The Social Organization of Gay Males.* New York: Praeger.

Hartmann, H. 1976. Capitalism, patriarchy, and job segregation by sex. *Signs* 1 (3): 137–69.

———. 1981. The family as the locus of gender, class, and political struggle: The example of housework. *Signs* 6 (3): 366–94.

Herdt, G. 1991. *Gay Culture in America.* Boston: Beacon Press.

Hertz, R. 1986. *More Equal than Others.* Berkeley: University of California Press.

Hiller, D. 1984. Power dependence and division of family work. *Sex Roles* 10: 1003–19.

Hiller, D., and W. Philliber. 1986. The division of labor in contemporary marriage: Expectations, perceptions, and performance. *Social Problems* 33: 191–201.

Hochschild, A. 1972. Communal living in old age. In L. K. Howe, ed., *The Future of the Family.* New York: Simon and Schuster.

———. 1983. *The Managed Heart: Commercialization of Human Feeling.* Berkeley: University of California Press.

———. 1997. *The Time Bind: When Work Becomes Home and Home Becomes Work.* New York: Metropolitan Books.

Hochschild, A., and A. Machung. 1989. *The Second Shift: Working Parents and the Revolution at Home.* New York: Viking.

Hodges, H. 1964. *Social Stratification: Class in America.* Cambridge, Mass.: Schenkman.

Hughes, E. C. 1971 *The Sociological Eye: Selected Papers.* Chicago: Aldine-Atherton.

Humphreys, L. 1971. New styles in homosexual manliness. *Transaction* (Mar.-Apr.): 38–66.

Hunter, N. 1991. Marriage, law and gender: A feminist inquiry. *Law and Sexuality* 1 (1): 9–30.

Jaggar, A. 1983. *Feminist Politics and Human Nature*. Totowa, N.J.: Rowman and Allanheld Publishers.

Jensen, M. S. 1974. Role differentiation in female homosexual quasi-marital unions. *Journal of Marriage and the Family* 36 (2): 360–67.

Jones, D. 1996. Discrimination against same-sex couples in hotel reservation policies. *Journal of Homosexuality* 31 (1–2): 153–59.

Jones, J. 1985. *Labor of Love, Labor of Sorrow: Black Women, Work, and the Family, from Slavery to the Present*. New York: Vintage Books.

Kemp, A. A. 1994. *Women's Work: Degraded and Devalued*. Englewood Cliffs, N.J.: Prentice Hall.

Kennedy, E. L., and M. D. Davis. 1993. *Boots of Leather, Slippers of Gold: The History of a Lesbian Community*. New York: Routledge.

Kessler, S., and W. McKenna. 1978. *Gender: An Ethnomethodological Approach*. Chicago: University of Chicago Press.

Kessler-Harris, A. 1990. *A Woman's Wage: Historical Meanings and Social Consequences*. Lexington: University of Kentucky Press.

Kleinberg, S. 1992. The new masculinity of gay men, and beyond. In M. Kimmel and M. Messner, eds., *Men's Lives*. 2d ed. New York: MacMillian.

Komarovsky, M. 1953. *Women in the Modern World: Their Education and Their Dilemmas*. Boston: Little, Brown.

———. 1962. *Blue-Collar Marriage*. New York: Random House

Kurdek, L. 1988a. Perceived social support in gays and lesbians in cohabiting relationships. *Journal of Personality and Social Psychology* 54 (3): 504–9.

———. 1988b. Relationship quality of gay and lesbian cohabiting couples. *Journal of Homosexuality* 15 (3–4): 93–118.

———. 1992. Relationship stability and relationship satisfaction in cohabiting gay and lesbian couples: A prospective longitudinal test of the contextual and interdependence models. *Journal of Social and Personal Relationships* 9: 125–42.

———. 1993. The allocation of household labor in gay, lesbian, and heterosexual married couples. *Journal of Social Issues* 49 (3): 127–39.

Kurdek, L., and J. P. Schmidt. 1986. Relationship quality of gay men in closed or open relationships. *Journal of Homosexuality* 12 (2): 85–99.

Lewin, E. 1993. *Lesbian Mothers: Accounts of Gender in American Culture*. Ithaca, N.Y.: Cornell University Press.

———. 1998. *Recognizing Ourselves: Ceremonies of Lesbian and Gay Commitment*. New York: Columbia University Press.

Lopata, H. 1971. *Occupation: Housewife*. New York: Oxford University Press.

Lorber, J. 1994. *Paradoxes of Gender*. New Haven, Conn.: Yale University Press.

Lukenbill, G. 1995. *Untold Millions: Positioning Your Business for the Gay and Lesbian Consumer Revolution.* New York: Harper Business.

Lynch, F. 1992. Non-ghetto gays: An ethnography of suburban homosexuals. In G. Herdt, ed., *Gay Culture in America: Essays from the Field.* Boston: Beacon.

Lynch, J., and M. Reilly. 1985. Role relationships: Lesbian perspectives. *Journal of Homosexuality* 12 (Winter): 53–69.

Matthews, G. 1987. *Just a Housewife: The Rise and Fall of Domesticity in America.* New York: Oxford.

McCaffery, E. 1997. *Taxing Women.* Chicago: University of Chicago Press.

McWhirter, D., and A. Mattison. 1984. *The Male Couple: How Relationships Develop.* Englewood Cliffs, N.J.: Prentice Hall.

Mederer, H. 1993. Division of labor in two-earner homes: Task accomplishment versus household management as critical variables in perceptions about family work. *Journal of Marriage and the Family* 55 (Feb.): 133–45.

Mohr, R. 1994. *A More Perfect Union: Why Straight America Must Stand Up for Gay Rights.* Boston: Beacon.

Oakley, A. 1974. *The Sociology of Housework.* New York: Pantheon.

Ostrander, S. 1984. *Women of the Upper Class.* Philadelphia: Temple University Press.

Nardi, P. 1992. That's what friends are for: Friends as family in the gay and lesbian community. In K. Plummer, ed., *Modern Homosexualities.* London: Routledge.

Nardi, P., and D. Sherrod. 1994. Friendship in the lives of gay men and lesbians. *Journal of Social and Personal Relationships* 11: 185–99.

National Research Council. 1991. *Work and Family: Policies for a Changing Work Force.* M. Ferber and B. O'Farrell, eds.. Washington, D.C.: National Academy Press.

Newton, E. 1993. *Cherry Grove, Fire Island: Sixty Years in America's First Gay and Lesbian Town.* Boston: Beacon.

Nickolson, L. 1986. *Gender and History: The Limits of Social Theory in the Age of the Family.* New York: Columbia Press.

Oakley, A. 1974. *The Sociology of Housework.* New York: Pantheon.

Okin, S. M. 1997. Sexual orientation and gender: Dichotomizing differences. In D. Estlund and M. Nussbaum, eds., *Sex, Preference, and Family: Essays on Law and Nature.* New York: Oxford University Press.

Parsons, T., and R. Bales. 1955. The American family: Its relations to personality and to the social structure. In T. Parsons and R. Bales, eds., *Family, Socialization, and Interaction Process.* New York: MacMillan.

Patterson, C. 1995. Families of the lesbian baby boom: Parents' division of labor and children's adjustment. *Developmental Psychology* 31 (1): 115–23.

Peplau, L., and S. Cochran. 1988. Value orientations in the relationships of gay men. In J. De Cecco, ed., *Gay Relationships*. New York: Harrington Park Press.

———. 1990. A relationship perspective on homosexuality. In D. McWhirter, S. Sanders, and J. M. Reinisch, eds., *Homosexuality/Heterosexuality: Concepts of Sexual Orientation*. New York: Oxford University Press.

Peplau, L., and H. Amaro. 1982. Understanding lesbian relationships. In W. Paul et al., eds., *Homosexuality: Social, Psychological And Biological Issues*. Beverly Hills, Calif.: Sage.

Petuchek, J. L. 1992. Employed wives' orientation to breadwinning: A gender theory analysis. *Journal of Marriage and the Family* 54: 548–58.

Polikoff, N. 1993. We will get what we ask for: Why legalizing gay and lesbian marriage will not "dismantle the legal structure of gender in every marriage." *Virginia Law Review* 79: 1549–50.

Portrait of U.S. fertility shows average number of births, family-size differences are shrinking. 1985. *Family Planning Perspectives* 17 (Jan.-Feb.): 37–38.

Preston, J. 1995. Gender and the formation of a woman's profession. In J. Jacobs, ed., *Gender Inequality at Work*. Mountain View, Calif.: Sage Publication.

Rapp, R. 1982. Family and class in contemporary America: Notes toward an understanding of ideology. In B. Thorne and M. Yalom, eds., *Rethinking the Family*. New York: Longman.

Reich, R. 1998 My dinner with Bill. *The American Prospect* 38 (May-June): 6–9.

Reilly, M., and J. Lynch. 1990. Power sharing in lesbian partnerships. *Journal of Homosexuality* 19 (3): 1–30.

Robson, R. 1992. Resisting the family: Repositioning lesbians in legal theory. *Signs* 19 (4): 975–95.

Rollins, B., and K. Cannon. 1974. Marital satisfaction over the family life cycle: A re-evaluation. *Journal of Marriage and the Family* 32: 271–282.

Romero, M. 1992. *Maid in the USA*. New York: Routledge.

Rorty, R. 1989. *Irony, Contingency, and Solidarity*. Cambridge: Cambridge University Press.

Rosenthal, C. 1985. Kinkeeping in the family division of labor. *Journal of Marriage and the Family* 47 (4): 965–74.

Rubin, L. 1994. *Families on the Faultline*. New York: Basic Books.

Rudd, N. 1996. Appearance and self-presentation research in gay consumer cultures: Issues and impact. *Journal of Homosexuality* 31 (1–2): 109–34.

Ruggiero, G. 1985. *The Boundaries of Eros: Sex, Crime, and Sexuality in Renaissance Venice*. New York: Oxford University Press.

Saghir, M., and E. Robins. 1973. *Male and Female Homosexuality: A Comprehensive Investigation*. Baltimore: Williams and Wilkens.

Schneider, D. 1984. *A Critique of the Study of Kinship*. Ann Arbor: University of Michigan Press.

Schneider, D., and R. Smith. 1973. *Class Differences and Sex Roles in American Kinship and Family Structure*. Englewood Cliffs, N.J.: Prentice Hall.

Schor, J. 1992. *The Overworked American: The Unexpected Decline Of Leisure*. New York: Basic Books.

Schwartz, P. 1994. *Peer Marriage: How Love Between Equals Really Works*. New York: Free Press.

Shelton, B., and D. John. 1993. Does marital status make a difference? *Journal of Family Issues* 14: 401–20.

Sherry, J., and M. A. McGrath. 1989. Unpacking the holiday presence: A comparative ethnography of the gift store. In E. Hirschman, ed., *Interpretive Consumer Research*. Provo, Utah: Association for Consumer Research.

Singer, J. 1997. Husbands, wives, and human capital: Why the shoe won't fit. *Family Law Quarterly* 31 (Spring): 119–32.

Skolnick, A. 1991. *Embattled Paradise: The American Family in an Age of Uncertainty*. New York: Basic Books.

Smith, D. 1987. *The Everyday World as Problematic: A Feminist Sociology*. Boston: Northeastern University Press.

South S., and G. Spitze. 1994. Housework in marital and nonmarital households. *American Sociological Review* 59: 327–47.

Spanier, G., and P. Glick. 1981. Marital instability in the United States: Some correlates and recent changes. *Family Relations* 30 (3): 329–38.

Stacey, J. 1990. *Brave New Families: Stories of Upheaval in the Late Twentieth Century*. New York: Basic Books.

———. 1996. *In the Name of the Family: Rethinking Family Values in the PostModern Age*. Boston: Beacon.

Stack, C. 1974. *All Our Kin: Strategies for Survival in a Black Community*. New York: Harper and Row.

Steinberg, Stephen. 1989. *The Ethnic Myth: Race, Ethnicity, and Class in America*. Boston: Beacon.

Stoddard, T. 1989. Why gay people should seek the right to marry. In S. Sherman, ed., *Lesbian and Gay Marriage*. Philadelphia: Temple University Press.

Sullivan, A. 1993. The politics of homosexuality. *The New Republic* 208 (19 May): 24–26.

———. 1995. *Virtually Normal: An Argument about Homosexuality*. New York: Knopf.

Tilly, L., and J. Scott. 1978. *Women, Work and Family*. New York: Holt, Rinehart, and Winston.

Tripp, C. A. 1975. *The Homosexual Matrix*. New York: McGraw-Hill.

Troiden, R., and E. Goode. 1980. Variables related to the acquisition of a gay identity. *Journal of Homosexuality* 4: 143–56.

Tronto, J. 1987. Beyond gender difference to a theory of care. *Signs* 12 (4): 644–63.

Trumbach, R. 1977. London's sodomites: Homosexual behavior and Western culture in the eighteenth century. *Journal of Social History* 11 (1): 1–33.

Tuller, N. 1978. Couples: The hidden segment of the gay world. *Journal of Homosexuality* 3 (4): 331–43.

U.S. Bureau of the Census. 1991. *Money Income of Households, Families, and Persons in the United States: 1990.* Series P–60, no. 174. Washington, D.C.

Urry, J. 1990 Work, production and social relations. *Work, Employment and Society* 4 (2): 271–80.

Vanek, J. 1983. Household work, wage work, and sexual equality. In A. Skolnick and J. Skolnick, eds., *Family in Transition.* 4th ed. Boston: Little, Brown.

Voydanoff, P. 1992. Economic distress and family relations: A review of the eighties. *Journal of Marriage and the Family* 52:1099–1115.

Walters, A., and M. C. Curran. 1996. Excuse me, sir? May I help you and your boyfriend? Salespersons' differential treatment of homosexual and straight customers. *Journal of Homosexuality* 31 (1–2): 135–52.

Warren, C. 1974. *Identity and Community in the Gay World.* New York: John Wiley.

Weinbaum, B., and A. Bridges. 1976. The other side of the paycheck: Monopoly capital and the structure of consumption. *Monthly Review* 28 (3) (July-Aug.): 88–103.

Weinberg, T. S., and C. Williams. 1974. *Male Homosexuals: Their Problems and Adaptations.* New York: Oxford University Press.

West, C., and D. Zimmerman. 1987. Doing gender. *Gender and Society* 1 (2): 125–51.

Westkott, M. 1986. *The Feminist Legacy of Karen Horney.* New Haven, Conn.: Yale University Press.

Weston, K. 1990. *Families We Choose: Lesbians, Gays, Kinship.* New York: Columbia University Press.

Whyte, W. F. 1956. *The Organization Man.* New York: Simon and Schuster.

Wilensky, H. 1960. Work, careers, and social intergration. *International Social Science Journal* 12 (Fall): 543–60.

Williams, C. 1989. *Gender Differences at Work: Women and Men in Nontraditional Occupations.* Berkeley: University of California Press.

Willis, G. 1978 *Inventing America: Jefferson's Declaration of Independence.* Garden City, N.Y.: Doubleday.

Woods, J. 1993. *The Corporate Closet.* New York: Free Press.

Zaretsky, E. 1973. *Capitalism, the Family, and Personal Life.*

index

Abel, Emily, 6, 9

Adjustment: of family life to paid work, 189, 194–97; of paid work to family life, 193–94. *See also* Domesticity; Egalitarian pattern; Gravitating toward domesticity; Gravitating toward paid work; Specialization pattern; Work; Work schedule

African-Americans: conceptions of family among, 139, 214; extensive kin ties among, 138; media portrayals of, 178; middle-class lesbigay families and, 138; multiadult household pattern, 84, 95–97; number of participants in study, 25, 245–46, 248–49; opportunities for jobs and wages, 97; proportion of participants who grew up in California, 26, 139; service economy jobs and, 185; working-class lesbi-

gay families and, 214. *See also* Riggs

Asian-Americans: conceptions of family among, 138; conceptions of sexual identity as private and, 215; Hula group, 62; multiadult household pattern, 84, 95–97; number of participants in study, 25, 245–46, 248–49; proportion of participants who grew up in California, 26; shopping patterns and, 42; symbolic meanings of food, 42, 63; working-class lesbigay families and, 214

Badgett, Lee, 127, 171, 185, 252, 254

Bell, Alan, 12

Berk, Sarah Fenstermaker, 10, 50, 51, 69, 71, 77, 134, 178

Black-Americans. *See* African-Americans

Blumer, Herbert, 10

and envisioning, 77–83; meeting delivery and repair people, 74–75; occupation and, 97–101; paperwork, 74; pets and, 72–74; repair work, 75–76; variations among lesbigay families, 83–106
Hughes, C. Everett, 7
Hunter, Nan, 217

Income: consumption patterns and, 165; differences among family members, 12; differences between heterosexual and lesbigay earners, 127; differences between lesbian and gay male families, 130, 244–45; division of domesticity within lesbigay families and, 201; earning estimates of participants, 24; friendship patterns and, 134; household cleaning services and, 185; laundry services and, 185
Instrumental role, 11
Invisible work, 10; consumption work as, 145; dinner parties and, 57; divorce and, 220; domesticity as, 218–20; egalitarian myth and, 180–84; housework as, 71; kin work as, 116; making laundry invisible, 203; research on, 10; romanticizing domesticity and, 64. *See also* Consumption work; Emotion work; Feeding work; Housework; Kin work; Laundry; Meal planning; Monitoring

Kin keeper: defined, 114; within lesbigay families, 113–16
Kinship: conceptions of, 130, 252; created via kin work, 115; economic claims and, 132; structures among lesbigay people, 113
Kin work, 10; character of, 109–10; children and, 132–33; class and, 116–21; creating family via, 140–41; ethnic/racial identities and, 138–40; gender and, 133–35; length of relationship and, 135–38; occupation and, 122–29; urban/suburban comparisons, 129–32; variations among lesbigay families, 116–40
Kith: as chosen family, 110–11; and kin compared, 110–13
Knowledge: consumption work and, 144; about domesticity, 8; about food, 31; about food costs, 46; about food preferences, 33;

about food supplies, 38; about housework, 82; as integral to domesticity, 17; as invisible, 180; of product performance, 157; of social etiquette, 115
Kurdek, Lawrence, 12, 15, 77, 78, 138, 214, 216, 251, 253

Labors of love, 6
Latina/Latino-Americans: conceptions of family among, 139–40, 214; maintaining ethnic identity through food, 63; multiadult household pattern, 84, 95–97; number of participants in study, 25, 245–46, 248–49; proportion of participants who grew up in California, 139; service economy jobs and, 185; shopping patterns, 42; working-class lesbigay families and, 214
Laundry: class and, 85; conflicting views of who does it, 94; defined, 72; doing laundry together as symbolic of relationship, 187; keeping "dirty laundry" hidden, 175; laundry services among the wealthy, 185; monitoring the pace of, 80; participants making it invisible, 203; real and metaphorical use of the term, 175; standards of cleanliness and neatness, 82; underreporting of, 85; working at home for wages and doing, 193
Leisure, 91, 147; housework and, 81; monitoring of leisure activities, 80; perceptions of consumption as, 143; perceptions of domesticity as, 115; perceptions of yard work/gardening as, 74; significance to family life, 111
Lesbigay, defined, 5
Lewin, Ellen, 113, 132
Lopata, Helen, 10, 82, 161
Lorber, Judith, 9
Lukenbill, Grant, 26, 210, 211, 252

Marriage, 3, 4, 12; rejecting widely held models of marriage, 16, 220–26
Masculinity, gay men and, 15. *See also* Gender
Material resources: kin work and, 122; maintaining family life and, 121, 124, 210–14
Mattison, Andrew, 12, 13, 20, 22
McWhirter, David, 12, 13, 20, 22
Meal planners, 31

Stacey, Judith, 4, 110, 170
Stack, Carol, 10, 26, 119, 215, 252
Steinberg, Stephen, 24, 130, 138
Sullivan, Andrew, 4, 224

Tronto, Joan, 9

Warren, Carol, 59
Weinbaum, Batya, 10, 70, 145
Weinberg, Martin, 12, 129
West, Candace, 50, 134, 178
Westkott, Marcia, 17, 134
Weston, Kath, 27, 110, 111, 210
Woods, James, 99, 204

Work, 10; definitions of, 6. *See also* Consumption work; Emotion work; Feeding work; Housework; Kin work; Occupations; Provisioning work; Work, paid
Work, paid: affecting family life, 19–20, 124, 187–202
Work schedule: altering to pursue domesticity, 189; domesticity and, 115, 124; flexible schedules among the affluent, 193, 200; minimal family and, 213

Zimmerman, Don, 50, 134, 178
Zussman, Robert, 128